The Archaeology
of
Northamptonshire

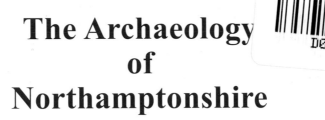

The Archaeology
of
Northamptonshire

Edited by

Martin Tingle

Northamptonshire Archaeological Society
2004

Published by The Northamptonshire Archaeological Society 2004
www.northants-archaeology.org.uk

ISBN 0 9507151 2 3

Cover picture:
The Roman 'Gladiator' claspknife from Piddington. An iron blade folded back into a bronze handle which depicts a secutor, *a gladiator equipped with a visored helmet, a sword and a square shield, It was found in the south east corner of the walled courtyard in a layer dated to the period 200-250 AD.*
(photograph: Simon Tully, British Museum)

Produced for the Society by Past Historic, Kings Stanley, Gloucestershire
Printed in Great Britain

Contents

List of Illustrations

Acknowledgements

This book began its gestation almost five years ago, at a meeting to inaugurate the English Heritage sponsored regional research agendas for archaeology. As such each of the chapters should be regarded as a view of archaeology for the new millennium, although some additions have been made to the texts over the last four years. I would like to thank Glenn Foard, in the first instance, for proposing the idea of this book and the various authors who contributed to it. They in turn have expressed gratitude to Christine Addison, Jenny Ballinger, Ann Bond, Jenny Burt, Graham Cadman, Myk Flitcroft, David Hall, Glenn Foard, Brian Giggins, John Humble, Michel Kerrou, Paul Martin, Andy Myers, Phillip Riden and Paul Woodfield for help in the preparation of the text.

Charlotte Walker copied many of the photographs from the Sites and Monuments Record while Andy Chapman supplied still more from the Northamptonshire Archaeology archive. I am also indebted to Tracy Britnell and Greg Phillips who produced the maps and Myk Flitcroft for providing data from the SMR. Several individuals have been very helpful in securing permissions to reproduce material and I would particularly like to thank Angela Boyle, Dr. Frances Healy, Dennis Jackson, Lindsay Jones, James Pickering, Roy Friendship Taylor, Prof. Steve Upex and Paul Woodfield. Thanks also to Drew Grey and Dr. Steven Hollowell for their advice on book selling.

1
Archaeology in Northamptonshire

MARTIN TINGLE

COUNTY ARCHAEOLOGY

It has often been observed that the boundaries of an English county are peculiarly inappropriate to serve as the basis of an archaeological study and in this, Northamptonshire is no exception. The modern county is a modified medieval administrative unit that would previously have occupied a space on the periphery of the Anglo-Saxon kingdom of Mercia. In the late Iron Age and Roman periods, it would have fallen somewhere between the tribal boundaries of the Catuvalauni, the Dobunni and the Coreiltauvi, prior to which, the evidence for landscape division is fragmentary.

The county occupies part of the Jurassic deposits of the Midlands, which have been uplifted in the north west, where a landscape of undulating clay predominates. In contrast, to the south and east, erosion by the river Nene and its various tributaries has exposed a range of clays, sands limestones and marls. In addition there are flat limestone plateaux in the south west and north east. Although the county is not a distinct geographical entity, the variety of soils and topography found in Northamptonshire represents a reasonable sample of the physical geography that makes up the East Midlands (Taylor & Fowler 1980, v-vi)

THE MYTH OF THE MIDLANDS JUNGLE

One of the most influential and misleading orthodoxies of British archaeology in the early twentieth century, was that throughout prehistory, central England was covered in a dense, impenetrable forest. This implied that, with a few notable exceptions, almost the entire centre of the country contained no archaeological remains that pre-dated the Roman period and that widespread clearance of the landscape was the work of Anglo-Saxon settlers. It was an accepted truth for almost a century and even today makes occasional appearances within otherwise well informed texts.

The idea of a densely forested interior for Briton appears to derive from a single reference in Tacitus that states *'Most of the Island is flat and thickly wooded'*, (Ireland 1986,19-20). With no other evidence at their disposal, this was adopted by antiquarian writers of the seventeenth century who at the same time saw a parallel between the likely appearance of prehistoric Britain and contemporary accounts of the newly discovered lands of America.

In 1659, John Aubrey characterised the prehistoric landscape of north Wiltshire as *'a shady dismal wood'* whose inhabitants were *'two or three degrees, I suppose, less savage than the Americans'* (Piggott, 1989, 62). In 1712 John Morton affirmed in his Natural History of Northamptonshire that…

'Before the Romans came amongst us, tis probable that a Great part of the Island, especially the Midland and Northern parts, were overrun with Woods, as we find the countries inhabited by savages usually are, in other parts of the world' (Morton 1712, 549)

Such speculation continued into the second half of the nineteenth century but by then, the model for prehistoric Britain was no longer the woods of New England but the jungles of equatorial Africa, which by then had become the focus of both exploration and territorial division by the European powers.

In 1914, J.P. Williams wrote a guide to field archaeology in which he characterised the landscape of prehistoric lowland Britain thus...

'Two points must be thoroughly grasped. The impenetrable character of natural forest and the swampy impassable state of the river valleys. There were bare downs with patches of beech wood but nowhere could one escape altogether from the proximity of the forest.... This jungle was so thick that only along tracks made by wild beasts could it be pierced by man. It was the haunt of bear and wolf and savages who hunted one another in its gloomy depths when pastoral man first began to feed his herds on the downs.' (Williams 1914, 5)

The more extreme character of this imagined

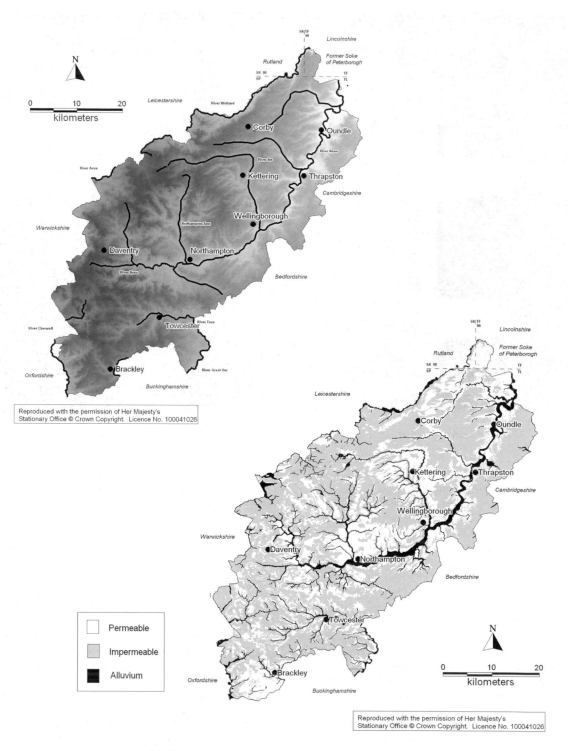

1.1 Northamptonshire: Topography and simplified geology

1.2 A model for the prehistoric landscape of the Midlands from 'In Darkest Africa' by H. M Stanley

landscape probably derived from the impact of Darwinian theory upon some of the more influential figures in late nineteenth century archaeology. Augustus Pitt Rivers was not alone in believing there to be an almost universal application for the notions of evolution and natural selection (Bowden 1991, 54). Not only animals, but also people, their behaviour, their artefacts and the landscapes that they inhabited, were all seen as being subject to evolutionary development. Written accounts of the interior of Africa seemed to confirm that 'primitive' people with rudimentary technology would inhabit wild and undeveloped places. That Prehistoric Britain had once resembled modern Africa could also have seemed evident from finds of lion, rhino and hyena bones in excavations such as those of Kent's Cavern in the 1860s (Todd 1987, 44).

In 1933, Cyril Fox's description of Early Iron Age Britain retained the impenetrable character of the forests although their physical description

had become more measured. Rioting jungle was replaced by a forest of damp oakwood through which a squirrel could cross the country from end to end without once having to emerge from the canopy. There remains however, an emphasis on the hostility of the woodlands, the dangerous wild animals that lived within them, and the reluctance of early Man to encroach upon them (Fox 1933, 82). In 1943, Jacquetta and Christopher Hawkes described prehistoric East Anglia and the Vale of York as *'Swampy and hard to traverse'* while the Midlands was *'impossible for human settlement and all but impenetrable'*. (Hawkes & Hawkes 1943, 12). The apparent concentration of monuments in the south of England was seen as a genuine reflection of prehistoric population distribution as late as 1949 when it was stated that...

'The British Midlands are, over a large area a virtual blank in the archaeological record, not from imperfect archaeological investigation, but because no effective

penetration of their heavy forest was made until the early historic period' (Piggott 1949, 64).

This view of the Midlands continued to appear in the works of influential landscape historians such as W.G. Hoskins but was increasingly at odds with a growing body of evidence derived from aerial survey, which revealed cropmarks in areas that had previously been thought uninhabitable. This was further confirmed as evidence from fieldwalking became systematised and the excavation of pre-historic sites began to include the reconstruction of past landscapes based on empirical data from preserved flora and molluscan remains.

The Midlands could well have been extensively forested throughout prehistory, however it was never credible to view all such woodland as either unproductive, impenetrable or uninhabitable. The prolonged acceptance of the jungles of prehistoric Britain were a significant factor in underestimating the archaeological potential of central England, a trend that has only recently been reversed

THE ANTIQUARIANS OF NORTHAMPTONSHIRE

The earliest record of an archaeological find from the county of Northamptonshire is thought to be the Roman coins from Towcester and Borough Hill which William Camden mentioned in his record of the antiquities of Britain, published in 1586. In a fashion that was to typify Romano-British studies thereafter, he devoted most attention to discovering the modern location of sites that appeared in the texts of classical writers. He concluded erroneously that two settlements mentioned in the Antonine Itinerary, Bannaventa and Tripontium were located at Weedon and Towcester and that hill forts at Borough Hill and Guilsborough were likely to be Roman fortresses constructed in 47 AD by governor Ostorius Scapula (Moore 1998). It was not until the eighteenth century that studies of the county alone were published by John Morton and John Bridges.

In 1712, Morton, the rector of Oxendon, wrote

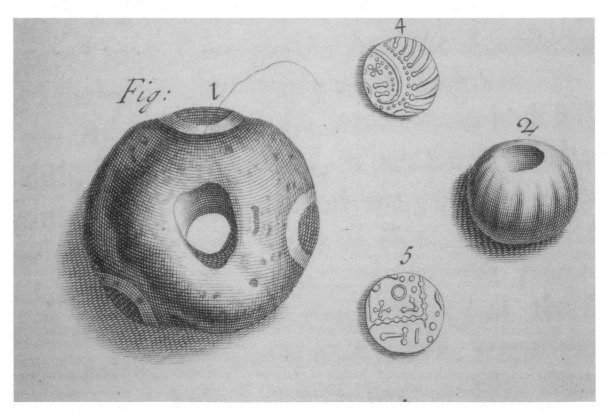

1.3 Finds illustrated in The Natural History of Northamptonshire by John Morton. Reproduced by permission of Northampton Libraries and Museum Service

The Natural History of Northamptonshire, in which a single chapter was given over to the consideration of pre-Norman antiquities. Morton includes a single page of illustrations depicting two beads and a single coin together with the plan of a mosaic. Of the beads, the larger is from *'near Rowel in an old woad ground that has been ploughed'* while the smaller (Fig 1.3) was from the woad ground at Dingley. The coin is unprovenanced although Morton compared it to one that appears in William Camden's *Brittannia* It is in fact an Anglo-Saxon *sceat*; a rare find in Northamptonshire (M Cuteis pers comm). He also illustrates a mosaic that had been found in 1699 during the earliest known excavation in the county; that of a Roman villa at Nether Heyford which was uncovered by a local clergyman, the Reverent and Worthy Mr H Gray. Unlike later authors, his explanation of the apparent paucity of prehistoric remains in the county did not attest to the excessive afforestation, but rather the character of the prehistoric peoples themselves:

'Tis scarce to be expected that at this Distance of Time we should meet with any Remains.. of the Older Britains, and particularly of those that inhabited our Inland Parts; the Inland Britains, as we learn from J. Caesar's Account of them, being in a particular manner Rude and Artless' (Morton 1712, 529).

John Bridges remains today a seminal figures in local studies because of his *History and Antiquities of the County of Northamptonshire*, a remarkable achievement considering he neither wrote nor illustrated the work (Brown & Foard 1994, 170). What distinguished Bridges from other county historians was the way in which he set about collecting material for his study, employing an archivist, a team of copyists, a map maker, an engraver and several artists (Brown & Foard 1994, 171). Following his death in 1724, thirty volumes of manuscripts passed to his brother William who appointed editors to produce a parish by parish account of the county, that finally appeared in 1791. Although there are some archaeological observations particularly in relation to the earthworks of deserted medieval villages and a series of maps showing archaeological features that have subsequently disappeared, most of the published text is concerned with architectural descriptions of churches and the lineage of various landed families. This may result from the particular interests of Bridges editors since in his original notebooks there are sometimes more detailed

records of archaeological remains than appears in the text of the *History*. At Borough Hill, the Roman barrow group is mentioned in the *History*, while in the relevant notebook, there is a sketch plan with measurements of their dimensions and spacing (Brown & Foard 1994, 178).

In 1815, George Baker proposed a series of volumes with the same title as Bridges work, to rectify, as he claimed, some of the latter's deficiencies regarding family pedigrees and the description of country houses (Brown & Foard 1994, 173). Only five volumes were published covering the western half of the county when ill health and financial problems forced the abandonment of further work and in 1842 his collection of books, prints and antiquities was sold to a fellow antiquarian, Sir Henry Dryden of Cannons Ashby. Dryden spent much of his life in antiquarian studies including the excavation of a pagan Anglo-Saxon cemetery at Marston St Lawrence (Fig 1.4). A contemporary of Dryden, but living at the opposite end of the county was Edmund Artis, the house steward of Earl Fitzwilliam at Milton. Between 1821 and 1827 he conducted extensive excavations of the Roman town at Castor which he published in a volume of plates entitled *The Durobrivae of Antoninus*.

Sir Henry Dryden helped to found the Architectural Society of the Archdeaconry of Northampton in 1844 and was active on the committee, which on 6 August 1866 brought about the opening of Northampton Museum (Moore 1998). The Museum's first honorary curators of antiquities were Dryden and Samual Sharp, an antiquarian and collector who is perhaps best remembered for his reports on Northampton Castle and of the Roman finds from Duston (Sharp 1871, 1882). They assembled a large and varied display, mostly of objects on loan from their own collections or from those of gentlemen sympathetic to their cause. However within a few years, lacking an adequate budget or full time staff, the museum began to loose its loaned display items which were replaced by assorted curiosities such as an unusually shaped carrot, a double coconut, a piece of the Rock of Gibraltar and a hot cross bun (Moore 1998).

By 1884 the Museum had moved into larger premises on Guildhall Road and for the first time a Keeper was appointed in the person of Thomas George who held the post until his death in 1920. By this time an impressive display of Iron Age material from Hunsbury, Romano-British finds from

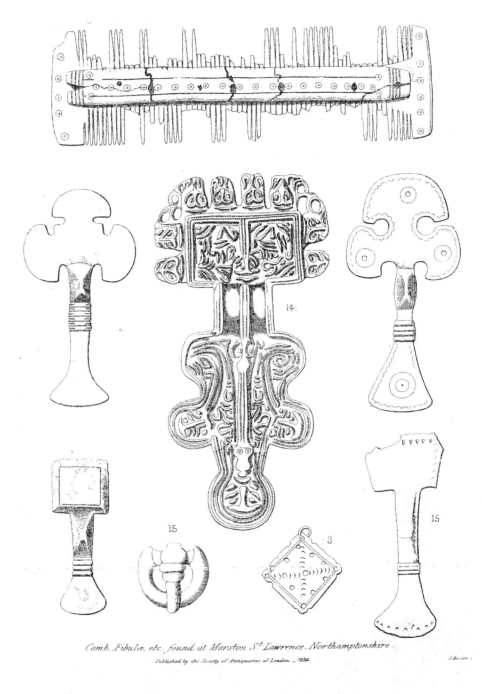

Comb, Fibulæ, etc, found at Marston S.ᵗ Lawrence, Northamptonshire.
Published by the Society of Antiquaries of London. _ 1884.

1.4 Finds from Dryden's excavation of an Anglo-Saxon cemetery at Marston St Lawrence reproduced from Archaeologia

Irchester and Duston and grave goods from Anglo-Saxon cemeteries formed the nucleus of the modern archaeological collection (Moore 1998).

THE GROWTH OF ARCHAEOLOGY

The formation of the archaeological record can be seen as a process in which accumulations of artefacts are at first preserved from the natural processes of decay and then, after an indeterminate passage of time, released either by natural erosion or the effects of human agency, whereupon some of these are recognised and reported to the wider archaeological community. For much of the country, including Northamptonshire, the period following the industrial revolution saw an unprecedented exposure of archaeological remains. Intensification of arable agriculture together with the limited introduction of mechanised ploughing revealed some new sites but more important factors were the expansion of towns, the construction of roads and railways, and the increased extraction of minerals for industry and construction. In the latter case the commercial exploitation of ironstone and latterly gravel has produced some of the most spectacular finds from within the county and probably destroyed many more.

One of the earliest attempts to record the threatened archaeology of Northamptonshire came about in 1879 when work began to enlarge Northampton's railway station, thus removing most of the remains of Northampton Castle. This prompted the Diocesan Architectural Society to plan and photograph the site as well as produce section drawing of areas with preserved stratigraphy (Law 1880). In addition there was a study made of the artefacts that were revealed, illustrating any complete vessels and listing finds of metalwork, coins, bone and even the masons marks on architectural fragments (Sharp 1882).

It has been estimated that during 50 years of

1.5 Part of Northampton Castle before its demolition. Reproduced by permission of the Historic Environment Team © Northamptonshire County Council

ironstone quarrying in the county, approximately 10 Early Bronze Age burials, 15 Roman villas or farms, 20 pagan Anglo-Saxon cemeteries, as well as major multi-period sites at Duston, Desborough and Kings Sutton, and a Roman settlement at Kettering were exposed, although virtually no record of them survives (Moore 1998). The number and types of sites that may have been destroyed without any recognition can only be guessed at. Occasionally a particularly striking object such as the Desborough Mirror (see Colour Plate 1) would be brought to public attention but there was rarely any attempt to record the context of such finds. One partial exception to this occurred during the period between 1880 and 1886 when ironstone quarrying began within the hill fort at Hunsbury. An attempt was made to have the hillfort protected under the new Ancient Monuments Act of 1882, but this failed because of the likely cost of compensating the landowner and therefore quarrying proceeded (Ryland, Adkins & Serjeantson 1902). Removal of the topsoil revealed as many as 300 pits measuring between 5 and 10 feet (1.5-3 metres) in diameter and up 7 feet (1.8 metres) in depth (Dryden 1885, 55). As Thomas George observed:

'They were full of black mould and in them were found the numerous artefacts that now comprise one of the finest collections, I believe, of Pre-historic antiquities in England' (George 1887, 339).

An attempt was made by the chairman of the quarry company to recover as much of the material as possible and an illustrated catalogue of the finds was published (Dryden, 1885). This included a vast array of bronze brooches, pottery, glass, iron weapons and tools as well as approximately 150 querns, all of which were deposited in Northampton Museum (Fig 1.6).

Sadly, the belated attempts to record the finds from Hunsbury proved to be an exception rather than the rule. In the mid 1920s, Ironstone quarrying between Brixworth and Scaldwell revealed large numbers of Roman pottery kilns together with quantities of allegedly medieval jewellery and coins. These were apparently bought up by a private collector from London and thus no record of them survives beyond a story in the local newspaper (Moore 1998).

DEVELOPING ARCHAEOLOGY

In 1942, professional archaeology came to North-amptonshire in the form of W.F. Grimes, excavating a small Iron Age site at Draughton for the Ministry of Works and R. J. C. Atkinson conducting the rescue excavation of an Anglo-Saxon cemetery in Nassing-ton (Moore 1998). Other large scale excavations included John Alexander's work at Northampton Castle between 1961 and 1964 and D.J. Smith's investigation of a villa, threatened by ironstone quarrying at Great Weldon, which took place over 26 weeks between 1953 and 1956 (Smith, Hird & Dix 1988-9). Atkinson returned in 1952 to cut a section through the rampart of the Hunsbury hill fort which he characteristically failed to publish, although the drawings from this excavation eventually appeared in print over forty year later through the work of Dennis Jackson (Jackson 1993/4, 11).

Increasing urban development and mineral extraction during the late 1960s and early 1970s led to the appointment of professional archaeologists by the Ministry of Works, the Northampton Development Corporation and the County Council. In the case of the former, this led to the remarkable career of Dennis Jackson, who in 1967 gave up his job as a brickwork contractor and spent the next thirty years excavating and publishing some of the most important sites in the county (Jackson 1998/9). The posts within the Development Corporation and the County Council formed the nucleus around which permanent teams of archaeologists were established. One major excavation from this period was that of the causewayed enclosure at Briar Hill. In 1972, air photography revealed a substantial segmented enclosure, made up of two concentric circuits covering approximately three hectares, in an area that had been designated for housing development (Bamford 1985, 2). The subsequent excavation took four years to complete during which period 150 weeks were spent on site. At the time, Briar Hill was the first causewayed enclosure north of the Thames valley to be fully excavated (Bamford 1985, 2).

Although the Soke of Peterborough was formally detached from Northamptonshire by the 1974 re-organisation of county boundaries, the archaeological links between the two continued. The Nene Valley Research Committee conducted excavations in both areas, notably at Ashton near Oundle, and distributed the first report of the nationally important excavation at Fengate near Peterborough (Pryor 1974).

The 1960s and 1970s were also a period of growth for amateur archaeology within the county. Throughout the nineteenth century, archaeology had been discussed and published within groups such

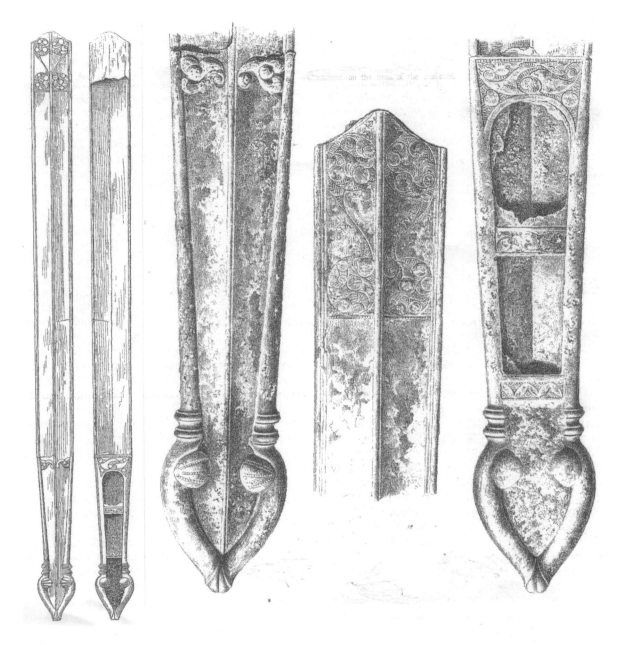

1.6 An Iron Age Scabbard recovered during Ironstone quarrying at the Hunsbury Hillfort reproduced from Archaeologia

as The Architectural Society of the Archdeaconary of Northampton and the Northamptonshire Natural History Society, however even within these, it was clearly a minority interest. In 1962 however, Richard Hollowell, an amateur field archaeologist and aerial photographer, set up the Upper Nene Archaeological Society (Brown 1998/9). UNAS continues today as a thriving organisation based around the long-term

1.7 The Piddington Proto-Villa Excavation. Photo by Roy Friendship-Taylor

excavation of a Roman villa at Piddington (Friendship-Taylor & Friendship-Taylor 1997).

Other local archaeological societies appeared at Wellingborough (1964), Oundle (1970) and Towcester (1972) together with, in 1965, the Northamptonshire Federation of Archaeological Societies (Moore 1998). The Federation published seven editions of its Bulletin containing notes of recent archaeological discoveries and a cumulative bibliography for the county. The Bulletin for 1971 was given over entirely to a summary of the fieldwork and air photographs of Richard Hollowell, while in 1973 it changed its title to Northamptonshire Archaeology and published a full excavation report by Dennis Jackson. In 1974 the Federation became known as the Northamptonshire Archaeological Society and its journal Northamptonshire Archaeology adopted the format that it retains to the present day.

LANDSCAPE ARCHAEOLOGY

From the 1960s onwards, aerial surveying revolutionised perceptions of the archaeological record of Britain, particularly in the Midlands. A combination of RAF cartographical surveys, the work of archaeological surveys based in Cambridge and the remarkable contribution of individuals such as Jim Pickering and Dick Hollowell revealed a profusion of cropmarks in areas thought previously to be archaeological voids. This work has continued to the present day, expanding the database of the County Sites and Monuments Record.

Although some earthwork sites were discovered in this way and many known sites were better understood from an elevated perspective, aerial survey was predominantly directed at arable land-scapes. The specific soil conditions that interact with archaeological remains to produce cropmarks, parchmarks or soilmarks are not evenly distributed throughout the county. By their very nature crop-marks and soilmarks are only seen in arable land, which it has been estimated, makes up only about 30% of the total area of the county (Taylor & Fowler 1980, v). Even if the amount of arable land has increased since this estimate was made, the potential for aerial survey may actually have declined. Lately there has been an increasing trend away from the cultivation of cereals to oil seed plants whose growth characteristics do not so readily facilitate the production of cropmarks.

The gravel terraces and the adjacent limestone soils of the Nene valley and its associated tributaries are both suitably for arable agriculture and tend, by virtue of their free draining character to produce most of the known crop mark sites in the county. Heavier clay soils, have in the past been predominantly pasture, and even when ploughed, do not allow the free passage of soil moisture that encourages cropmark formation. It is possible for archaeological sites appear in grassland either as very slight earthworks or as parchmarks. The former can be obliterated when medieval cultivation resulted in the creation of extensive (if now declining) areas of ridge and furrow while the latter is dependant on the complex localised interaction of soil, vegetation and weather conditions.

Areas of surviving medieval formal woodland are also obviously devoid of cropmarks but sometimes, by virtue of never having been ploughed, they have preserved prehistoric sites in a remarkable condition. One of the most striking examples of this was at Brigstock, where the creation of a medieval deer park excluded arable agriculture and even after disparking, the area became permanent pasture with only limited ploughing in recent times (Foster 1998-9, 133). As a result, when a circular earthwork within the park was excavated, it revealed an exceptionally well preserved late Iron Age round house (see Fig 1.8) with numerous internal features which were approached through an upstanding bank and ditch by a stone-surfaced causeway (Jackson 1983, 12).

Between 1985 and 1993 the most ambitious and far reaching multi-period landscape surveys undertaken to date was initiated in Northamptonshire, attempting to link systematic field survey over large areas with extensive excavations, documentary research and environmental studies. The Raunds Area Survey covered an area of 40 square kilometres made up of the parishes of Raunds (including the medieval parish of Stanwick), Ringstead, Hargrave with parts of Irthlingborough, Denford and Shelton. It examined a transect of the Nene Valley from the flood plain, through the gravel terraces and onto the boulder clay plateau, in an area that was both of great archaeological potential and under considerable threat from gravel extraction, road building and the construction of houses.

Initially the main focus for prehistoric invest-igation was to be at Irthlingborough where the river Nene divides into two channels to form a 70 hectare 'island'. Here there was both the potential for waterlogged environmental deposits and a group of cropmark ring ditches as well as upstanding round barrows protruding through the alluvium. All but one of these barrows were excavated together with a group of hitherto unknown monuments that were revealed during the excavation of a deserted Saxon and medieval hamlet at West Cotton. A range of Neolithic and Bronze Age monuments were located including a Long Mound and a Long Enclosure, both over 100 metres in length and orientated on a single point. Excavations of later sites within the survey area also revealed unexpected prehistoric features such as the Neolithic causewayed ring ditch, that was found during the excavation of the Redlands Farm villa.

The late Iron Age and Roman periods were to be investigated through the excavation of an entire nucleated rural settlement at Stanwick. The settlement at Stanwick covered approximately 10 hectares and included not only a villa but also a group of substantial and separate stone buildings laid out in a regular fashion along a series of radiating trackways. In its final phase (constructed unusually late in the fourth century) the Stanwick villa had a symmetrical frontage of corridor and wing rooms, a new bath suite, mosaic floors and a room with under floor heating. The hypocaust channels were constructed of re-used stone which included funerary monuments featuring scenes from classical mythology. Two kilometres south west of Stanwick, the Redlands Farm villa was found to have originated from a second century mill. The building developed with wing rooms, mosaic floors and under floor heating, however by the later fourth century it was partially demolished. This lead to the remarkable discovery that an entire rear gable wall of one of the wings had collapsed outwards and was almost completely intact (Crosby pers comm).

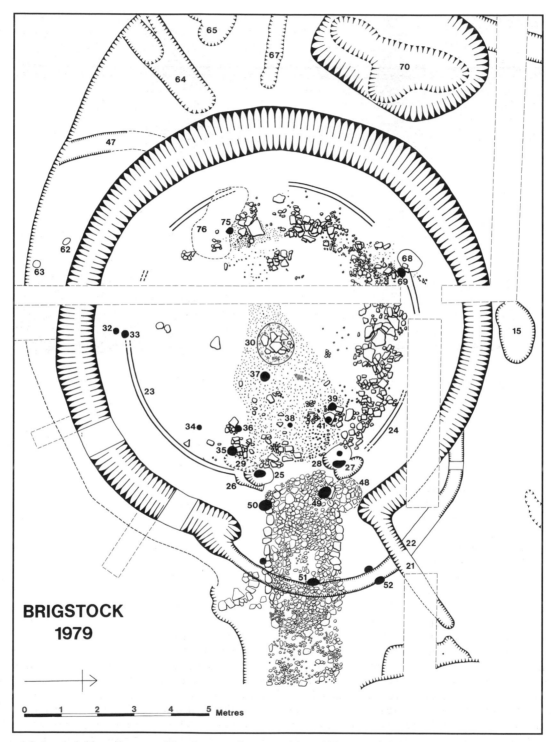

**BRIGSTOCK
1979**

0 1 2 3 4 5 Metres

1.8 A remarkably well preserved Iron Age roundhouse surviving within a medieval deer park at Brigstock. Plan by
Dennis Jackson

1.9 A medieval tenement at West Cotton, Raunds fronting onto the village green and with a central kitchen range.
Reproduced by permission of the Northamptonshire Archaeology © Northamptonshire County Council

The excavations at Stanwick produced a vast amount of material, most of which is Romano-British in date. There are 2.8 tonnes of pottery and over 200 boxes of animal bone as well as 1600 soil samples for environmental analysis. The 11,000 individually recorded finds included over 3500 Roman coins and 1000 pieces of personal adornment (e.g. brooches, bracelets and hairpins). The excavation records include over 2000 A1 size sheets of site plans and more than 2700 photographs (V. Crosby pers comm).

The core of the project was an examination of the transition of settlement in the late Roman period into the Anglo-Saxon and then medieval period. At North Raunds, three separate excavations at Furnells Manor, Langham Road and Burystead examined the growth of the manor and its immediate hinterland, while at West Cotton a late Saxon Manor and medieval tenements were investigated. In addition to large scale area excavation, a 6 year programme of fieldwalking was planned that would eventually be the largest and most intensive systematic fieldwalking survey in Britain. It is a

matter of some regret that although the fieldwork for the Raunds project is finished and some of the final reports, notably that of the fieldwalking, were completed several years ago, to date (spring 2004) only the excavation of the Anglo-Saxon church and churchyard at Raunds Furnells has actually been published, although other volumes are expected shortly (Boddington 1996).

In recent years there has been an expansion both in the number of excavations within the county and the number of organisations that have been carrying them out. The Northamptonshire Archaeology Unit has continued to conduct major excavations of medieval Northampton, which they have published in an exemplary manner. Amongst many notable discoveries, it has recently located the most complete sequence of the town's defences that include a revetted bank and substantial ditch dating from the early 10th century (Chapman 1998-9, 25). The unit has also acquired an international reputation for Garden Archaeology following its restoration of part of the Gardens at Hampton Court. In addition, they have made notable discoveries such as that of the first Roman vineyard in England, closely followed by an Anglo-Saxon royal burial in which there were a range of fine grave goods including, only the fourth helmet to have been found in this country (Meadows 1996/7). Today, there is without doubt more archaeological work being carried out, as a result of recent planning legislation, than at any time previously. This has begun to produce a far more balanced picture of Northamptonshire's past, and illustrates its rich potential for future research.

2
Palaeolithic and Mesolithic

THE PALAEOLITHIC

GREG PHILLIPS AND ALEXANDER (SANDY) KIDD

INTRODUCTION

The earliest evidence for human occupation in Britain is currently dated to *circa* 500,000 BP, and is attributed to the warm period known as the Cromerian complex, which predates the Anglian glaciation (Roebroeks and Kolfschoten 1994). From *circa* 500,000 BP until 13000 BP Britain lay at, and sometimes beyond, the northern limit of human occupation.

The latter part of the Quaternary is characterised by successive warm and cold phases, recorded most completely within deep-sea marine sediments. However the correlation with terrestrial geological strata remains tentative and unfortunately, despite some useful studies, the Quaternary geological record of Northamptonshire is far from being completely understood.

Northamptonshire lies beyond the southern and eastern core of counties that are rich in Lower and Middle Palaeolithic finds (Roe 1968, vii; Roe 1981, 132-133). While there has been no history of systematic Palaeolithic research in the county, some 80 Lower and Middle Palaeolithic stone artefacts (mostly Acheulian hand-axes) have been recorded from a total of 32 locations. These finds comprise less than 0.5% of the 'complex' level records on the Northamptonshire Sites and Monuments Record.

The only certain Upper Palaeolithic artefact from the county, a reindeer antler 'Lyngby' axe, has been dated to 10,320 ± 150 BP (OxA-803) (Cook & Jacobi 1994, 75). This was found during gravel extraction at Grendon in 1982 and represents the only such find to be made in this country (Fig. 2.2). However, a sizeable unstratified flint blade with triangular cross section from Northampton has been tentatively identified as Upper Palaeolithic.

2.1 A hand-axe from the Nene valley.
Reproduced by permission of the Historic Environment Team
© Northamptonshire County Council

THE NATURE OF THE PALAEOLITHIC RECORD

In discussing the nature of the evidence for this period the English Rivers Palaeolithic Project has drawn a distinction between *primary context sites* and sites where artefacts are found in *secondary contexts*, meaning those which have been disturbed and redeposited by natural agencies.

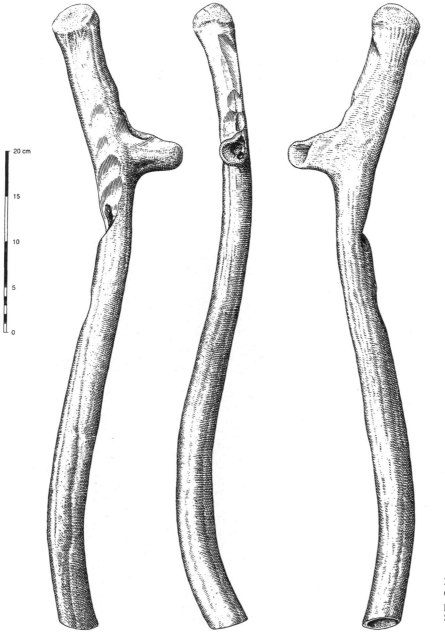

20 cm

15

10

5

0

2.2 The 'Lyngby' Axe from Grendon. Reproduced by permission of the Prehistoric Society

Northamptonshire has no examples of primary context sites, although the Wollaston assemblage of artefacts and waste are thought to be largely collected from a single primary context, which has unfortunately been lost to gravel quarrying.

There are a few 'surface' findspots from the county, from fields or superficial construction works, which consist of one or two artefacts in 'fresh' condition. The extreme rarity of Palaeolithic finds from field walking surveys (for example none were recovered during the Raunds Area Project) suggests that these surface sites are very rare and perhaps comprise few diagnostic artefacts. Indeed some of these finds could be more recent introductions, as has been suggested for a hand-axe from Borough Hill Hillfort, which was found in association with apparently deliberately deposited late Bronze Age metalwork (Jackson 1996-97).

The majority of Lower and Middle Palaeolithic finds have been made during gravel quarrying in the Nene valley where individual pits have produced small assemblages of up to 10 artefacts. Most of these quarry finds are in a 'rolled' condition but a few appear 'fresh'.

In principle, Palaeolithic artefacts may be found in any geological deposits of Cromerian or later date. Primary context sites are most likely to survive in fine-grained sediments, deposited during warmer climatic stages and in relatively low energy environments. As seen at the Middle Palaeolithic site at Glaston, Leicestershire, there is the potential for the survival of primary context lithic and bone material at locations which share the specific combination of geological and topographic relationships that have combined to preserve this rare open air site (Collcutt 2000).

The material from Glaston survived in an open air hilltop location, with bone material (of hyena, woolly rhino and horse) being preserved by the chemical properties of the junction of the Lower Estuarine Series sands and the overlying Lincolnshire Limestones. This geological junction is fairly widespread in the east of Northamptonshire, and there is potential for the discovery of further remains in similar hilltop locations within this part the county. Further research is proposed targeting these higher potential locations.

Low energy environments may also be preserved within the alluvial deposits of the Nene valley. The potential survival of such locations within the Nene valley has been demonstrated by the discovery of a pre-Ipswichian waterhole and animal pathway, with associated mammal fossils beneath the river gravels in a quarry at Little Houghton, Northampton (Smith 1995). Similarly well

preserved sites may well survive on the margins of the glacial lake deposits that underlie the Nene valley at Northampton, and may contain the remains hominid activity.

The unpublished collection of material from Wollaston gravel pit (Patenall and Richardson) appears to be a relatively fresh, cohesive assemblage comprising a hand axe, core, scrapers and flake debitage (some 20 pieces in total). Collected from a disturbed context during quarrying, it is likely that the majority of this collection originates from one deposit (now lost) and is therefore perhaps the most significant assemblage of Palaeolithic material from the county.

2.3 Hand axe from gravel workings at Wollaston

THE MESOLITHIC

GREG PHILLIPS

A HISTORY OF FIELDWORK IN THE COUNTY

There are currently 57 geographically separate find spots of Mesolithic date recorded on the Northamptonshire Sites and Monuments Record (SMR). These records range from single cores or tranchet axes to large field walking collections such as Duston and Honey Hill (Saville 1981b), as well as a few excavated examples such as Chalk Lane, Northampton (Williams and Shaw 1981) and Brixworth (Wymer 1977; Martin and Hall 1980; Ford 1994, 1995).

Of the individual Mesolithic sites in Northamptonshire, only the larger sites of Honey Hill and Duston are well-known in the national literature. The private field collection from Honey Hill has been published (Saville, 1981b), while the extensive Duston field walking assemblage (collected from reinstated topsoil following iron stone quarrying and held in Northampton Museum) exists only as a reference from the CBA Gazetteer of Mesolithic Sites in England and Wales (Wymer 1977).

Martin and Hall (1980) published results from their fieldwork in Brixworth parish, identifying two sites, one of which (Site 24) is possibly a refined grid reference for the Brixworth site listed in the 1977 CBA Gazetteer. These may also be coincident with the excavations that identified a diagnostic Mesolithic component in the lithic assemblages of the evaluations carried out by Jackson (1990) and Thames Valley Archaeological Services (Ford 1994, 1995), all their National Grid References falling within the same field.

Evaluation trenching at Towcester Meadow (Walker 1992) notable for the discovery of an Iron Age temple enclosure, also identified a lithic bearing horizon buried by 0.5m of alluvium and agricultural soils. The small amount of Mesolithic material was unfortunately heavily worm-sorted and unstratified, but does provide us with an indication of the potential for site survival buried within the alluviated deposits of lower energy stream beds and river valleys within the county.

The excavations at Chalk Lane, Northampton (Williams and Shaw 1981) identified a series of stratified features comprising several pits, and a series of intersecting gullies which were cut into the gravel terrace surface. These were possibly geo-logical, but did contain Early Mesolithic material that could have been derived from the surrounding area. This site is significant in contributing some of the only stratified Mesolithic features yet found within the county. The site also appears to be part of a wider scatter of Mesolithic activity covering the Ironstone outcrop and terrace gravels in the area of the later Saxon *Burh* in Northampton, close to the confluence of the two arms of the River Nene.

Other Mesolithic stratified deposits were excavated at Thrapston Quarry, Aldwincle (Jackson 1976, 1977). A very lengthy period of human occupation, coupled with later ritual use of the landscape started in the Mesolithic period. A few of the pits and hollows across the site are attributed to early prehistoric phases of activity on the site dating to this period. The site also included a multi-phase Neolithic mortuary enclosure with evidence of early Neolithic occupation that predated the ritual structures, however the site has since been largely quarried.

West Cotton Long Mound, excavated as part of the Raunds Area Project, produced an extensive collection of unstratified Mesolithic finds from the mound material. This was probably incorporated into the mound from the contemporary land surface (Parry forthcoming).

The lithic assemblage excavated at Briar Hill Neolithic Causewayed Enclosure also contained a Mesolithic component which deserves further attention, although it is thought to be early in date and therefore unfortunately may have little to contribute in terms of Mesolithic/Neolithic transition studies within the region (Chapman, pers. comm.).

A small amount of Mesolithic material was recovered from excavations of a later Neolithic occupation horizon at Ecton (Moore 1975), while a recent excavation at Burton Latimer has produced ephemeral evidence of possible anthropomorphic forest clearance with a single C^{14} date of 5910 ± 40 BP (4904 - 4714 cal BC). Neolithic agricultural features overly this in a second phase, but unfortunately no cultural material for either the Late Mesolithic or Early Neolithic has been recovered from the earlier phase.

Evidence for the latest Mesolithic/earliest Neolithic transition appears to date, to be sadly lacking in excavated sites within the county. As this ill defined

2.4 Two Mesolithic tranchet axes from the Nene valley

crossover phase is of crucial importance to national research frameworks it is entirely appropriate that further effort is focused on attempting to identify which (if any) of the recently discovered Mesolithic find spots exhibit Late Mesolithic typological characteristics in association with Early Neolithic material (English Heritage 1997, PC1 page 44; Prehistoric Society 1999).

Hall and Martin provide us with the bulk of new Mesolithic material for the county with the results of their reconnaissance field walking survey, which extends the rapid collection methodology adopted for the Fenland Project to cover the whole of Northamptonshire. Their interim report on prehistoric settlement patterns listed some 36 new sites in the county, with a further 24 new sites added so far by fieldwork following that publication (Hall 1985 & pers comm)

This new data doubles the SMR total records for Mesolithic sites from 57 to 117, so that there are now more than 4 times the known Mesolithic find spots than listed in the CBA Gazetteer (See 2.4). This equates to the discovery of nearly 4 sites per annum since the publication of the CBA gazetteer in 1977.

As analysis of the material collected by Hall and Martin continues, key new sites are emerging which do require urgent attention and cataloguing. One such site appears to be a lithic scatter identified in Preston Capes parish, on a band of Marlestone Rock Bed on the valley sides of a tributary at the headwaters of the River Cherwell.

The site has been defined by one field walking transect (approximate site area 6.7 hectares), and compares in dimensions to just over two thirds of the area of the lithic scatter at Honey Hill (which is roughly 10 hectares). The new site appears to be extremely prolific, with a reconnaissance collection of 800 flints from one 300m x 5m transect. As an approximate 2% sample of the entire plough soil assemblage and assuming an even distribution of lithics across the whole site, this would equate to around 2,000,000 pieces of worked flint in the plough soil alone.

Following the Mesolithic resource assessment (Phillips 2000), opportunities for additional field-work on Mesolithic sites have been sought through agri-environment initiatives. Surface collection was carried out in a field to the north of Elkington parish, lying 1.25 kilometres to the west of the large Mesolithic settlement scatter at Honey Hill.

The field is situated on a flat hilltop overlooking the Avon valley and is partially bisected by a steep combe that forms an isolated promontory of Middle Lias Silts and Clays. Surface collection began in the south-east corner of the field and initially no finds of worked flint were recovered. However, around the edge of the combe and at the tip of the promontory a small but dense concentration of worked flint was located. The assemblage comprised 108 pieces of

worked flint together with 11 burnt but apparently unworked pieces. The assemblage included eight broken and intact blades, a blade core and two microliths. Both of the microliths were broken, but one appears to be a plain obliquely blunted point. The remaining retouched pieces were two scrapers; one has been made from a core fragment while the other is almost perfectly round with complete peripheral retouch. All of these pieces have parallels with the assemblage recovered from Honey Hill, which itself lies on Northamptonshire Sand and Ironstone (Tingle pers comm).

THE POST-GLACIAL ENVIRONMENT OF NORTHAMPTONSHIRE

Currently the closest pollen assemblages for the period are to be found in the Cambridgeshire Fens and at Narborough Bog in the Soar Valley, Leicestershire. At Narborough, the pollen record indicates that the Mesolithic floodplain comprised an alder-hazel woodland surrounded by mixed oak woodland with up to 27% pine composition (Brown 1999).

2.5 Blades and microliths from Elkington

Throughout the Holocene, the Nene valley appears to have gone through a process of gradual change. From a shifting and unstable braided river system, with many channels separated by shifting sandbars, fewer, more stable channels formed and were separated by gravel islands, leading towards a more stable, channelled flow regime (Castleden 1976; Brown 1999; Macklin 1999; Parry forthcoming).

As seen in the Seine Valley (Mordant and Mordant 1992) it is within the smaller rapidly changing channels that transient Mesolithic groups could have exploited regular fishing opportunities, setting wicker fish traps and targeting the relatively well drained gravel islands within the floodplain as short term processing sites (Brown 1999).

Environmental data from the county for the period is very scarce, although there is certainly potential for its recovery through the implementation of recent planning legislation. The floodplain of the Nene appears to offer the greatest potential for the recovery of waterlogged environmental data, due to the pressure on the valley for gravel extraction. It is also likely that the floodplains of the Welland and the other rivers within the county will contain these early remnant riverine deposits, however these areas are under less pressure from aggregate extraction.

Several small pockets of peat have been identified on British Geological Survey maps at Silverstone and in several locations by Hall and Martin during their survey, but potentially the most important site lies in Greens Norton. Here a deposit of peat some 5m x 15m surrounds a spring, is still wet and is certain to hold extensive environmental data (D. Hall pers comm). The sampling of this peat deposit to provide a local environmental control for the county could provide important information for all periods.

The Raunds Area Project sampled and dated a total of five palaeochannels from the Nene valley, one of which spans the Late-Devensian and early Holocene (Parry forthcoming; Brown 1999). A radiocarbon date of 9370 ± 170 BP (HAR-9243) was obtained from organic sediments from the lower levels of this channel (Parry forthcoming). This demonstrates the potential for other surviving palaeochannels of Pre-boreal (Pollen Zone IV) and Boreal (Pollen Zone V/VI) date to survive within the floodplain, some of which may contain cultural material, but which in any case can potentially contribute significantly to our knowledge of the Post-Glacial environment in the county.

Higher valley tributaries also have potential for preserving environmental deposits as illustrated by the transect of cores analysed from Apethorpe (Sparks and Lambert 1961). This contained fragmentary surviving lacustrine deposits from the Late-Glacial, dating from late in the Younger Dryas (Pollen Zone III) to the Atlantic (Pollen Zone VIIa), in relatively close proximity (1.5 km) to a prolific find spot, albeit in a neighbouring tributary valley in Woodnewton parish (G. Johnston pers comm).

Other areas of high potential for the prospection of Mesolithic cultural material not buried or eroded by later fluvial action may include the various tributary fans located above the level of Holocene river activity (Macklin, 1999) identified on the British Geological Survey maps of the county as Alluvial Fan. These relatively long lived valley bottom features may preserve evidence of activity from the early Post-glacial period, and would presumably be characterised by long term reuse by Neolithic, Bronze Age and later populations.

MESOLITHIC SETTLEMENT PATTERNS

Hall and Martin provide some compelling evidence for the targeting of light, well-drained soils by Mesolithic groups as settlement sites. In their 1985 paper all of the sites listed lay on well-drained soils on a sub-strate of limestone, ironstone, gravel or sand. The new sites added since that publication indicate that this pattern is true for the county in general, adding the Marlestone Rock Beds, Great Oolite Limestone, Glacial Sand and Gravel and the Lower Estuarine series to the list of permeable geologies exploited. In addition, as their collection extends geographically across nearly the whole county exclusive of geology, this pattern can be accepted as a coarse representative distribution, rather than one influenced by highly selective survey work.

Recent detailed landscape survey across the Millfield Basin in Northumberland on a 1km to 3km wide transect, included close transect field walking and test pitting, bears out this selective site-targeting hypothesis (Waddington 2000).

By grouping geology and soil types into *ecozones*, Waddington demonstrated that Mesolithic groups were *generally* targeting settlement on well drained gravels and sandstones, preferably adjacent to the wetland habitats important for economic exploitation, and avoiding wetland and clay habitats for *habitation*. It should be noted however that smaller (and there-

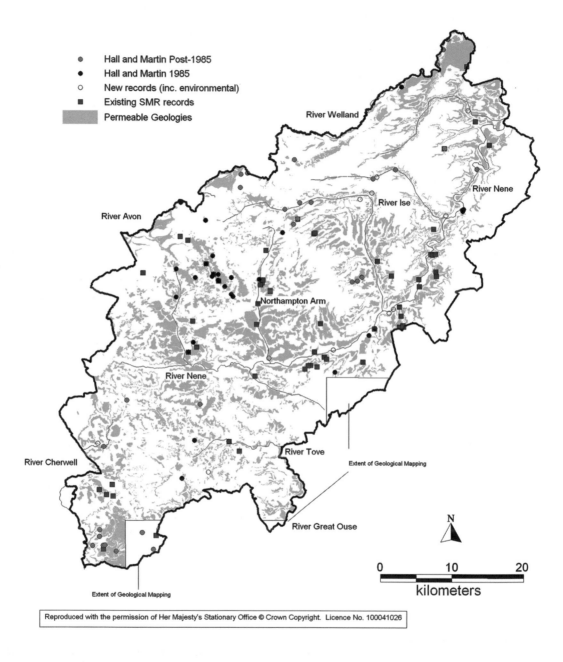

2.6 The distribution of Mesolithic sites in Northamptonshire

fore more difficult to detect via field walking) sites indicative of brief periods of activity are found on these geologies, probably due to short episode hunting activities (note the Elkington site and its scale compared to the nearby Honey Hill site).

It is possible to define a riverine distribution for a large portion of the Mesolithic finds from the county. These tend to cluster on the gravel islands of the floodplain and permeable geologies exposed on the valley sides by the down cutting of the Rivers Nene, Welland, Ise, and Cherwell.

Although the environmental evidence is lacking, it is likely that during the Mesolithic, the clay land areas of the county were covered in dense Oak and Pine woodland, offering limited visibility and low calorific yields for foraging or hunting groups.

Generally Mesolithic site location appears to be influenced by three major considerations: Light soils for settlement sites, the topographic prominence commanding reasonable views of the landscapes and the proximity to water (Hall 1985; Jacobi 1978a)

The distribution map (2.6) shows two major patterns. Firstly, a large set of find spots corresponds with the exposed permeable geologies on the flanks of the Nene Valley with views over the floodplain. This distribution is mirrored by finds in the Welland Valley on the Northamptonshire/ Leicestershire border, where the Medbourne Project has demonstrated a preference for Mesolithic communities to target prominent topographical locations on the northern bank, and Hall and Martin's fieldwork has added definition to the southern bank (Knox pers. comm.).

There are hints that this riverine distribution pattern was mirrored within the Ise Valley, which extends north from the Nene in a major tributary valley and cuts through similar geologies. However, large scale development and quarrying in this area has had a severe impact on archaeological fieldwork and destroyed large areas of the valley landscape. Fourteen sites are recorded on the SMR in the upper reaches of the tributaries of the Ise, and near the headwaters of the Ise itself (see below), and a small amount of additional field walking material collected prior to extensive quarrying has been identified (Burl Bellamy pers comm). This has recently been examined, adding three new sites within the upper Ise valley around Geddington.

Secondly, a cluster of find spots can be seen in the north-west uplands. If this distribution is examined more closely it can be seen that the sites are exclusively located upon Northamptonshire Sand and Ironstone, Glacial Sand and Gravel, or Marlestone Rock Bed. These are the best-drained geologies within a largely Upper Lias Clay and Boulder Clay environment.

Obviously, if the distribution is correct the north west 'uplands' appear to have attracted a higher Mesolithic population over time than the other 'upland' areas between the river valleys within the county. One hypothesis for this anomalous distribution could be that the area, situated at the heads of the Ise, Welland, Warwickshire Avon, and the Brampton Arm of the Nene acted as a 'crossroads' zone between river systems for the groups that were exploiting them.

If this is the case, it would be one example of a general trend in site concentration between the heads of river valley systems that could be tested across the region. Indeed within Northamptonshire, a second smaller but less well defined concentration can be seen to the south of the county, between the headwaters of the River Cherwell, Tove and Great Ouse, again mostly on permeable geologies such as Great Oolite Limestone, Marlestone Rock Bed, and Northamptonshire Sand and Ironstone.

CHRONOLOGIES

Chronological studies within the county have hardly begun. The analysis of the Honey Hill assemblage by Alan Saville tentatively assigned a large component of the microlithic assemblage to a bridging phase of the Mesolithic on purely typological grounds, after Jacobi's (1978b) reassessment of the Horsham material. The assemblage is characterised by obliquely blunted points and other points with inverse basal retouch (Saville 1981b). Lithics from other sites need to be reassessed in the light of recent typological advances, while material from Duston and Preston Capes requires a thorough analysis followed by some form of publication.

CONCLUSIONS

The general trend towards selective use of permeable geologies, coupled with the possibility of landscape zones used as common routes between river valleys is also an intriguing phenomena. It deserves closer scrutiny within the region, and poses significant research questions about the use of river valleys as common route ways in what was a highly mobile economy. For example, is the lack of sites within the Watford gap glacial gravels a distribution influenced by natural barriers further downstream?

The results of landscape survey within the county are impressive, despite the fact that some survey methodology is likely to be too coarse to reveal some of the smaller, single episode Mesolithic sites. However as the Northamptonshire results show, other counties lacking a similar survey resource probably have significant numbers of Mesolithic sites awaiting discovery and elucidation.

3

The Monument Builders:
The Neolithic and Bronze Ages
(4500 BC-1000 BC)

ANDY CHAPMAN

PREHISTORIC LANDSCAPES

In some parts of Britain evidence of the lives of our prehistoric ancestors is still visible above ground. There are the grassy banks and ditches of large earthwork enclosures, the long and circular mounds where they buried their dead, or the impressive standing stones and stone circles that can still attract gatherings of people in the present day.

Up to forty years ago, few prehistoric sites had been found in Northamptonshire, or in the Midlands in general, and it was believed that this was because these areas had been sparsely populated backwaters. The accidental finds of flint or stone artefacts were seen as coming from the casual loss of tools by people probably merely passing through. The occasional burials that were uncovered came from the later part of the period, in the Bronze Age, perhaps as part of the very first wave of true settlement.

What this view did not take into account was that the Midlands have been dominated by arable farming for hundreds of years. So it was not that prehistoric people had ignored these areas, but that hundreds of years of ploughing had flattened the earthworks, leaving the evidence of their presence hidden beneath the modern fields. Clues as to the quantity of these hidden sites began to emerge with the more widespread use of aerial photographic reconnaissance, and by 1960 the cropmarks of ploughed out prehistoric sites in the arable fields of the Nene valley were being found in unexpected numbers (RCHME 1960). Ironically, just as this unknown archaeological wealth was being discovered its destruction was also occurring at an ever-faster rate. In the Nene valley gravel extraction was a major threat, and excavation in advance of gravel digging over the past 30 years has provided archaeologists with opportunities to explore and

uncover the detailed stories of several important sites Beyond the Nene valley there is still much to learn, but programmes of fieldwalking have recovered prehistoric worked flints scattered across the fields in every part of the county, showing that they were also exploiting the higher and often clay covered and wooded land (Hall & Hutchings 1972, Martin & Hall 1980). So, as a result of the past forty years of work we can now see how our prehistoric ancestors created monuments in earth and stone over a period of some 3500 years, that would have rivalled some of the most famous sites in the country.

At the beginning of the Neolithic the landscape of the county would not have been recognisable to us. It had been thought that no one had lived here because most of the land was covered with dense, impenetrable oak forest, but the study of preserved pollen, seeds and charcoal has shown that it was actually a much more varied landscape. It was dominated by less dense woodland containing most of the trees and shrubs that occur in our present deciduous woods and hedgerows, and these provided food, as nuts and berries, and a range of timber for building and making tools and equipment. Signs of people would have been slight, but you might have seen some smoke drifting up through the trees from a small fire as a band of hunters cooked the meat of a wild deer they had just killed. In the valleys the dams of beavers would have been more evident than any influence of humans.

By the end of the period the valley and hillsides were largely cleared of woodland and on the open grassland there were herds of cattle and flocks of sheep and small fields of wheat and barley. Stone tools had been replaced by bronze, and the landscape was scattered with numerous grassed-over, but still known and visited, earthworks and mounds.

One thing was still largely missing; substantially

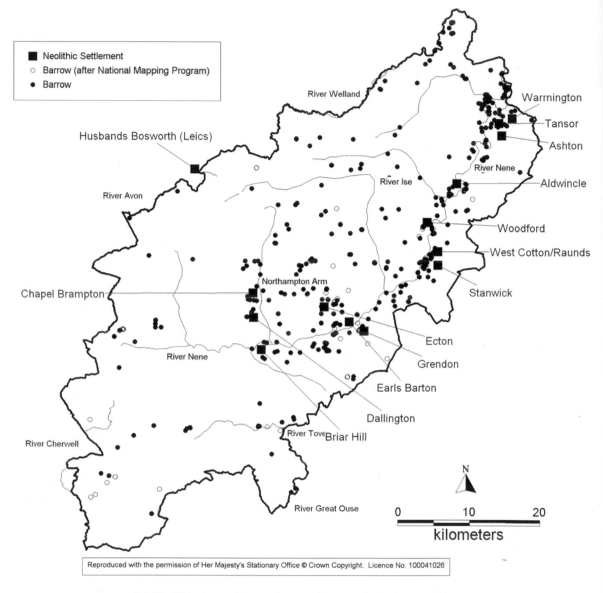

3.1 Neolithic sites and Bronze Age round barrows in Northamptonshire

built permanent houses. Even though these people were the first farmers, they were not like later farmers, with permanent fields and living in a farm house or a village. In the Neolithic period people were still semi-nomadic, as their ancestors had been. Initially, they probably did not herd their animals but controlled them indirectly by burning areas of woodland to create better pasture where the animals would stay. Gradually, over many centuries this changed to full domestication, and by the later Bronze Age we see the first appearance of boundaries running across the countryside to define territories. Similarly, they did not cultivate large fields of wheat and barley. They cleared and planted small plots that could be tended by a handful of people. There were also still extensive areas of woodland providing a seasonal harvest, and the river valleys would have been rich in waterfowl and fish.

26

So, for much of the year each community or tribe was probably split into smaller family groups, living in tent-like houses that could be transported across country from valley to woodland to pasture to field so they could exploit all opportunities for food gathering. It was only in the middle and late Bronze Age that larger fields were marked out with ditches, banks and hedges, and we also occasionally find the remains of timber-built roundhouses, probably a transformation of a circular tent into a more durable form.

It is because of the absence of permanent houses and settlements that so much of the story of Neolithic and Bronze Age life that follows is really a story of death, as so often it is only the burial sites that have survived to tell their story.

THE NEOLITHIC (4500-2200 BC)

THE FIRST FARMERS MARKETS: CAUSEWAYED ENCLOSURES

In the late 1970s a team from the Northampton Development Corporation Archaeology Unit excavated for four winters on a bleak hillside overlooking the Nene valley at Briar Hill, Northampton, prior to the building of a new housing estate (Bamford 1985). To the casual observer little could be seen on the shattered ironstone that lay beneath the topsoil, but careful cleaning revealed a pattern of elongated pits that marked out a large enclosure, which had first been recognised on aerial photographs. Many such sites have been known in southern England since the 1930s, but their discovery in the Midland river valleys was much more recent, and Briar Hill was the first to be extensively excavated (Figs 3.2 and 3.3).

At Briar Hill two parallel lines of pits formed a near circular enclosure up to 162m in diameter, while on the eastern side further pits marked out a more regular, elliptical inner enclosure, measuring 92m north-south. These sites are known as *causewayed enclosures* because the ditch circuits are made up of numerous pits with gaps, or causeways, between them, rather than having continuous ditches broken only at a few gateways. The soil and stone from the pits would have been dumped alongside in heaps to form a bank, but these had been ploughed away long ago. The pottery and flint found at these sites, as well as radiocarbon dating of charcoal from the ditches, shows them to be the first large-scale earthworks to be constructed in this country; the earliest appearing soon after the establishment of the first farming communities between 4500 and 4000 BC.

There has been much disagreement about how these enclosures were used. It has been argued that they were settlements, but with all evidence of the houses ploughed away, however, this argument fails as remains of Bronze Age and Iron Age houses have been found on similar sites. At many excavated sites it has also been shown that animal and, sometimes, human bone, and pottery, flints and stone objects found in the ditches had not been merely casually dumped as rubbish, but had been carefully placed in groups. This burial of used and broken objects, and of animal and human bone, is believed to be the ritual offering of these things to the mother, or earth goddess who had brought the people into being and gave them life and food. As the survival of these people depended on their animals, crops and the wild harvest, all of which were subject to the vagaries of the weather and disease, the making of such ritual deposits was part of everyday life as their only means of protection against such misfortune. At Briar Hill very little of this evidence survived as the acid soil had eaten away the bone, but a chain of small pits on the north-western side of the inner enclosure did contain pottery, worked flints, fragments of polished stone axes and broken querns and rubbing stones.

Most archaeologists now agree that these sites functioned as central meeting places: prehistoric markets. As their lives were spent following their animals, sowing their small arable plots and exploiting natural food sources, there was a need for people to gather at intervals, probably at fixed times like midsummer or midwinter perhaps, to confirm their common allegiance as members of the same community, or tribe. They could also exchange news, food, tools and arrange marriages to ensure their longer-term survival.

The excavations at Briar Hill illustrated some very important aspects of these sites. Radiocarbon dating showed that the site was used as a meeting place for about 2000 years. This is astonishing when you consider that our oldest respected sites

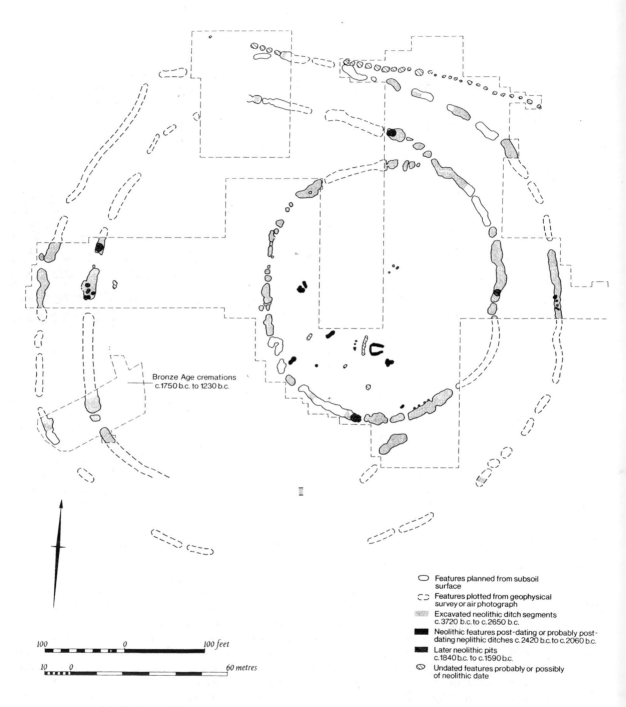

Bronze Age cremations
c.1750 b.c. to 1230 b.c.

100   0   100 feet

10   0   60 metres

◯   Features planned from subsoil surface

⊂⊃   Features plotted from geophysical survey or air photograph

▨   Excavated neolithic ditch segments c. 3720 b.c. to c. 2650 b.c.

■   Neolithic features post-dating or probably post-dating neolithic ditches c. 2420 b.c. to c. 2060 b.c.

▮   Later neolithic pits c. 1840 b.c. to c. 1590 b.c.

◐   Undated features probably or possibly of neolithic date

3.2 The Briar Hill causewayed enclosure. Reproduced by permission of RCHME/English Heritage

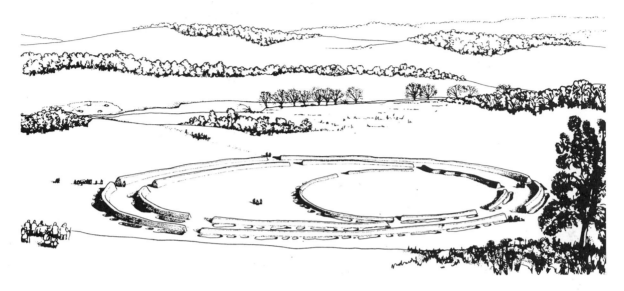

3.3 A reconstruction of the Briar Hill causewayed enclosure. Reproduced by permission of Northamptonshire Archaeology
© Northamptonshire County Council

are our churches, and these have been standing for little more than a thousand years, half the time that the Briar Hill enclosure was in use. The story does not even end there, as we will see later that a final use of the site for burial in the middle Bronze Age adds another five hundred years to its lifetime. The way these site were maintained over this time is also interesting. The ditches were made up of elongated pits, like a string of sausages, but it was shown that each 'sausage' was itself made up of several shorter, near circular or oval pits 3.0-4.0m in diameter and 1.0-2.0m deep. These had often been dug when the neighbouring pit had silted up, and would have been visible only as a shallow hollow. So, for most of its 2000 years of use, the enclosure would have consisted of little more than a faint ring of grassed over shallow hollows and low banks or mounds, perhaps set within a forest clearing. New pits would have been excavated only at intervals of many decades, perhaps only once in every generation. This shows how little the way of life of these people changed for nearly 2000 years.

At least two more causewayed enclosures are known to exist in the county. One is also in Northampton, only 4 km to the north of Briar Hill

at Dallington (RCHME 1985, fig 2). The other is at the other end of the county at Southwick, between Oundle and Peterborough. Like Briar Hill, they lie on the valley sides or higher ground quite near to the River Nene. Only small-scale excavations have been carried out at these two sites, but we can imagine that they were used in a similar way and for a similar period of time.

DEATH AND BURIAL:
OVAL AND LONG BARROWS

While the causewayed enclosures were the meeting places of the living, the earliest burial monuments across most of lowland Britain were the *long barrows*; elongated mounds of soil or stones retained by timber or stone walls and usually flanked by deep ditches on either side. Under the higher eastern end there would be timber or stone-built chambers to hold the bones of the dead; these may have been either free-standing or set within a small mound. They often contained heaps of mixed bones from several people, rather than intact skeletons, indicating that the chambers were frequently reopened, with earlier burials being disturbed and

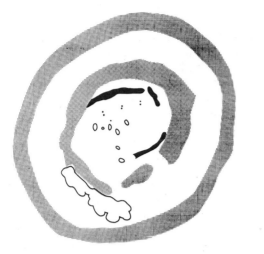

Aldwincle , the Mortuary Enclosure

Grendon Quarry, Ring Ditch V

0   50m

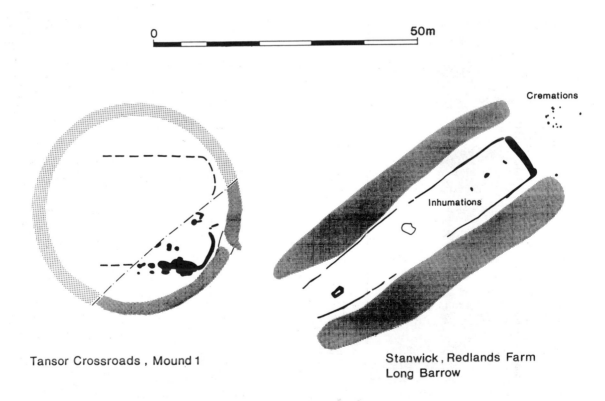

Tansor Crossroads , Mound 1

Cremations

Inhumations

Stanwick , Redlands Farm
Long Barrow

3.4 Neolithic oval and long barrows in Northamptonshire. Reproduced by permission of Northamptonshire Archaeology
© Northamptonshire County Council

rearranged when later burials were made. Some bones may even have been brought in from bodies left to decay elsewhere. While the final form of these monuments was as a mound, the building of the mound often occurred only as the final act at the end of many hundreds of years of use. The earliest were built soon after 4000BC, while the final mounding over may have occurred as late as around 2200BC, when the first round barrows were appearing.

In Northamptonshire there are several possible long barrows, particularly in the south-west near to Oxfordshire, but none of these has been confirmed by excavation. Along the Nene valley there were no known examples until 1989 with the discovery and excavation by Oxford Archaeology of the Stanwick long barrow (Colour Plate 2). It lay towards the southern end of the Raunds/Stanwick complex of prehistoric monuments, which are discussed below (Healy and Harding forthcoming). At the broader, north-eastern end of the mound there was a deep trench that had held massive timber posts forming an imposing facade, while smaller posts supported the long sides of the mound. No original burials survived at the eastern end, but there was a small stone cist to the west containing a few human bones. Three later Neolithic burials inserted into the mound showed that its use continued into later centuries, and a group of shallow pits to the east of the mound contained cremation burials of middle Bronze Age date.

The reason for the rarity of long barrows within the county is that Northamptonshire also had its own unique style of Neolithic burial monument, the oval mortuary enclosure and barrow. These cannot be easily found because of the coincidence in shape with the circular burial mounds of the early Bronze Age, and the excavation of all the known examples has started out by examining what were thought to be large round barrows.

The first was discovered in 1968 by Dennis Jackson while investigating a group of round barrows at Aldwincle that were about to be destroyed by gravel

3.5 The burials in the mortuary house at Aldwincle. Reproduced by permission of Dennis Jackson

extraction (Jackson 1976). It had a long history of construction and use. Initially, a timber structure had stood within a rectangular enclosure marked by a shallow gully. Later, a deeper ditch was dug to enclose an oval area. Within this enclosure there was a pair of deep post-pits that may have held the end posts of a tent-shaped mortuary house 2.0m long. Between the posts two people had been buried. One lay tightly crouched, with the legs drawn up to the chest, as if trussed in this position. The other consisted of a heap of disarticulated bone, perhaps from an earlier burial that had been moved aside when the second person was buried (Fig 3.5). They were both adult males, but the bones were too poorly preserved to say much more about them, although signs of arthritis on both shows that they were not young. The two posts were D-shaped, and 0.7m in diameter, indicating that they were probably the two halves of a single split trunk. These end posts may have stood well above the top of the mortuary house, perhaps being decorated with carved or painted spiral patterns, as is seen on stone-built tombs in other parts of the country. There was also a second pair of similar post-pits, but no traces of any burials had survived. At the end of the lifetime of the mortuary enclosure a new outer ditch was excavated, and the soil was used to create a central mound that covered and sealed from further disturbance all the earlier burials.

A further two monuments of similar size have been found in the Nene valley. At Grendon there was a near square enclosure, excavated in 1974 in advance of gravel working (Gibson & McCormick 1985). There was a ditch on three sides, but along the north-eastern side there was a gully or slot. Within this gully there were pockets of darker soil and charcoal from a series of oak posts 0.2-0.5m in diameter that had either rotted or been burnt in-situ. These would have formed an impressive timber facade 22m long with a narrow, 1.5m wide opening giving access to the central area. These posts too may have been decorated. It is likely that there were once burials within this enclosure, but all traces had been lost. The enclosure was surrounded by a pair of ditches, suggesting that there were two periods of mound construction perhaps associated with later burials (Fig 3.4).

At Tansor crossroads, on the line of a new road, part of a further oval barrow was excavated by Northamptonshire Archaeology in 1995 (Chapman 1996-97). Here the mortuary enclosure was rect-angular, with a line of pits along the southern side

that had been recut, suggesting that a line of large timber posts had been replaced more than once. To the east there was a shallower slot that may have held a timber facade, as at Grendon. Within the enclosure there was a deep pit that may have held an end post of a timber mortuary house, as at Aldwincle, but the remainder lay outside the excavated area and in the acid soil no bone had survived. Later a circular ditch was dug and the clay was used to form a substantial central mound. A further similar site has also been found lower down the Nene valley, on the outskirts of Peterborough. In this case the central mound still survived, and in the top of the mound were the remains of several early Bronze Age cremation burials, showing that these monuments continued in use for over a 1000 years. Similar evidence had probably been lost to ploughing at the Northamptonshire sites, but at Tansor we know that the prehistoric mound was still visible 3000 years after it was built as the remains of two Anglo-Saxon burials were found there.

While these Northamptonshire burial mounds are oval, the post-pits of mortuary houses and the presence of intact and disturbed burials is typical of the practices found at long barrows, showing that they all belong to a common tradition. It is also interesting that the four oval barrows and the single long barrow lie along the Nene valley at evenly spaced intervals of between 10.5 and 12.5 km. There may be other examples waiting to be discovered that would break this apparent pattern, but it is possible that each of the known sites served a single community, or tribe, each of which occupied a territory extending roughly 11.5 km along the Nene valley.

MONUMENTAL LANDSCAPES: THE RAUNDS/ STANWICK MONUMENT COMPLEX

So far we have looked at single monuments, but it is likely that at least some of these had nearby contemporary sites that have not been found due to the limited areas that have been examined in detail. In one place it has been possible to examine an extensive area of the Nene valley floodplain, and this work has revealed a landscape containing numerous prehistoric monuments spanning some 3000 years of use and respect. At Raunds and Stanwick a major programme of fieldwork and excavation, the Raunds Area Project, was carried out in advance of road building and gravel extraction through the second half of the 1980s as a joint venture

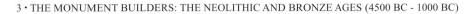

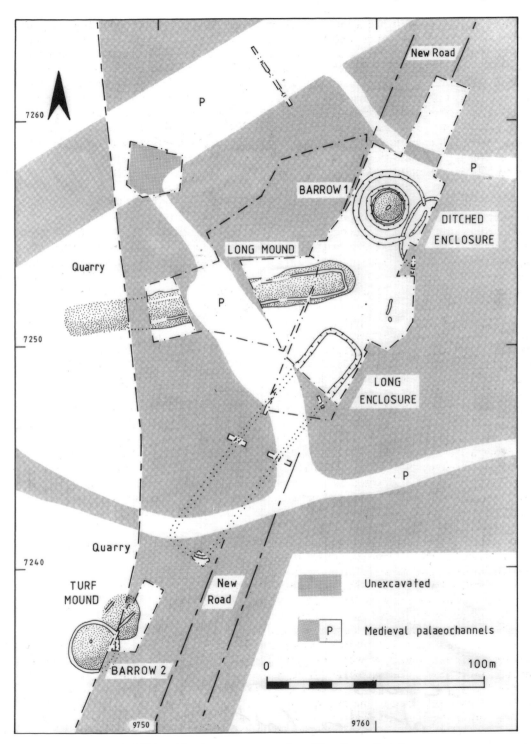

3.6 The prehistoric monument complex at West Cotton, Raunds.
Reproduced by permission of Northamptonshire Archaeology © Northamptonshire County Council

between the County Council Archaeology Unit and English Heritage. The main part of the excavation programme was to examine Iron Age and Roman settlement at Stanwick and the deserted medieval village of West Cotton, and the prehistoric part of the project initially only involved the excavation of four round barrows threatened with destruction.

Over the next few years understanding of the prehistoric use of the valley was transformed as a series of previously unknown monuments were discovered beneath the medieval village, a Roman temple, and under the alluvial clays deposited by floods. What emerged was a landscape of ritual monuments that is of national importance, and which illustrates just how much has lain hidden along the river valleys of the Midlands (Healy & Harding forthcoming).

A concentration of monuments lay at the northern end of the area, partly hidden under the deserted medieval village of West Cotton. The monuments included an oval mound, a long enclosure and a long mound in use between 4000 and 3000BC, and, after several centuries with no monument building, a large multi-ditched round barrow was constructed at about 2000BC and continued in use well into the early Bronze Age.

The long enclosure was 117m in length, but the only artefacts recovered from the ditch were two cattle tibia, a red deer antler and a few flints. We do not know what such sites were used for, although one idea is that they may have been places in which bodies were exposed to decay. The oval mound to its south was probably constructed of turf, and while there was nothing underneath it, two gullies on the top held timber fences on the same alignment as the long enclosure, as if it may have formed a viewing platform. The long mound was a more complex monument. Numerous lines of stake holes were

3.7 A reconstruction of the long mound at West Cotton, Raunds.
Reproduced by permission of Northamptonshire Archaeology © Northamptonshire County Council

found beneath the mound showing that the turf and soil had been heaped up in a series of rectangular compartments. At the eastern end there was a more complex arrangement of stake holes that may have held wattle panels forming a forecourt and facade set in front of a small chamber, as in the reconstruction, but no burial remains were found. Later this area was itself covered by extending the mound. A shallow gully cut into the top of the enlarged mound may have held a timber fence.

Other Neolithic monuments in the area had similarly complex histories, and numerous radio-carbon dates have been obtained so that a detailed chronology of their development and use can be con-structed, making it one of the most fully explored and understood prehistoric landscapes in the country.

When the Neolithic mounds at West Cotton had fallen out of use, at about 2500 BC, a timber platform was constructed at the edge of the nearby river channel. A layer of brushwood and smaller branches was consolidated with dumps of gravel and two alder trunks, on which axe marks were still visible. The clay above this platform contained much animal bone, and one or two pieces of human bone, and it may have been a ritual platform for the dumping of feasting debris and other remains into the river channel. This change from ritual dumping in pits to deposits placed in water is seen elsewhere at this time and later, most dramatically in deposits of broken bronze weapons and tools found at Flag Fen near Peterborough (Pryor 2002).

LATER ENCLOSURES

While the causewayed enclosures formed the meeting places of the first farmers in the earlier Neolithic, over much of the country they fell out of use when a new type of enclosure appeared: the *henge* monument. These were usually circular in plan, with substantial ditches and only one or two entrances, and the bank was constructed outside, rather than inside the ditch, showing that they were not defensive. Like the earlier enclosures, they marked a plot of land used as a meeting place and ritual centre. While these sites are widely scattered across the country, there are only a handful of possible examples in Northamptonshire. There may be one on the hillside above the monument complex at West Cotton, Raunds (Humble 1994). Another appears to sit within the causewayed enclosure at Dallington, Northampton, as if directly replacing

the earlier monument. Something similar happened at Briar Hill, but here it involved a remarking of the earlier enclosure by the cutting of pits, possibly post-pits, into the silted enclosure ditches. A series of pits and a small horseshoe-shaped timber building in the interior also belong to this time, and were associated with the use of a distinctive type of highly decorated pottery, known as grooved ware, that is often found at henge monuments. The timber building was formed from three pairs of large posts, and might have been quite high, perhaps serving as either a watchtower or a platform for the exposure of bodies. So, at Briar Hill the old enclosure was refurbished and reused, instead of constructing a new style henge monument.

MOMUMENT ALIGNMENTS

In Neolithic monuments the entrances, the location of burials or the alignments of enclosures and mounds are often to the east or north-east. There is no doubt that this preference is genuine, but the question of what it means is more difficult to answer. At its simplest, it may relate to the direction of the rising sun, with north-easterly alignments pointing to the midsummer sunrise, the most important time of the year to prehistoric people. Their lives were built around the annual cycle of the seasons, and the death and rebirth of plants and animals that happens as part of that cycle. The changing pattern of the sun's movements were therefore part of that same cycle, while the monthly pattern of the moon's phases provided their only ready means of measuring the passage of time week to week. They therefore followed and understood these patterns and constructed their monuments to respect these celestial events. Having done this, these same monuments could then be used as practical calendars to mark the passage of the year. Just how far their understanding of the movements of the sun and moon extended has been, and will continue to be, a subject of much debate.

Another aspect is the possible use of simple geo-metry. Some monuments are only roughly circular, as if the line of the ditch was only roughly paced out before digging began. Others are quite closely circular as if an arc was actually scribed out on the ground, perhaps using a length of rope swinging around a central post. Other enclosures are clearly non-circular with a distinct axis of symmetry, such as the inner ditch at the Briar Hill causewayed enclosure. This has an elliptical plan that appears to be a deliberate and accurate shape with the axes aligned on the cardinal compass points. It has also been suggested that some of these more complex shapes were drawn out as circular arcs centred on the points of right-angled triangles with sides in the ratio of 3:4:5. Other archaeologists still find it difficult to believe that our prehistoric ancestors had the technical ability to combine the construction of geometric shapes with astronomical alignments based on the rising and setting points of the sun and moon.

HABITATION SITES

Even though we do not find substantial houses or villages, there is a little evidence that shows us something of the way people lived in the later Neolithic. They must have lived in light-weight structures, presumably with a timber frame and a covering of animal skins, that have left no below ground traces for us to find. The conical tepee of the north American Indians or the circular near flat-roofed, yurt of the Mongolian herdsman of the steppes of central Asia may be the best comparisons from recent times.

Whenever people live anywhere for a length of time they inevitably leave something behind. The best evidence is from a site at Ecton, near Northampton discovered by Richard Hollowell close to the River Nene in 1971 during gravel extraction (Moore and Williams 1975). The central feature was a shallow, rectangular hollow some 4.4m long by 3.6m wide. Within this there were three smaller hollows filled with burnt clay and charcoal rich soils, one of which contained a hearth formed from several river-worn cobbles. This would appear to have been a house site, but whether it was a small timber building or a hollow formed under or beside a movable tent-like structure is uncertain. Nearby there was a scatter of further shallow hollows containing dumped hearth debris. Across the area, but particularly within the rectangular hollow, there was a scatter of some 800 pieces of flint and fragments from at least 18 different pottery vessels, representing the domestic debris but, unfortunately, the soils were too acid for animal bone to have survived. The pots were highly decorated bowls of later Neolithic date, known as Mortlake ware.

On large scale excavations of later sites, part-icularly on the gravel on the Nene valley, other individual or small clusters of pits containing Neolithic or Bronze Age pottery and flints have been found, and these too presumably mark temporary house sites. In the 1990s large scale excavations on Iron Age and Roman sites at Wollaston by Northamptonshire Archaeology found several pits of Neolithic date containing pottery, flints and polished stone axes, and three pits excavated by Dennis Jackson in a gravel quarry at Gretton in 1979 contained Beaker pottery. Two of these lay within a ring of shallow postholes that may have formed a house 6.0m in diameter.

In addition, extensive programmes of fieldwalking carried out in various parts of the county have recovered scatters, and some more localised concentrations, of worked flint which must mark the locations of temporary camp sites. This work has shown the presence of prehistoric people right across the county, even on the clay-covered uplands where we have found little evidence for the building of monuments.

FLINT, POTS AND STONE

Prehistoric people made use of a whole range of materials to make their tools, clothes and houses. Unfortunately for archaeologists most of these were organic, such as wood, plant fibres and leather. Much evidence has therefore been lost, or is only rarely found, and what we are left with are the items that do not decay, the tools in flint or stone, the fired clay pots, and bone objects.

Today, in the affluent west, where few need worry about where their next meal is coming from, fashions change from year to year, if not more rapidly. In the Neolithic and Bronze Ages, where survival depended on the annual repetition of the cycle of life, death and rebirth for plants, crops, animals and people, fashions were more conservative. Changes only appear to have happened at intervals of several hundred years, each marking a major change in their way of life.

Hundreds or even thousands of flints may be found on a single site made from small nodules of gravel flint, either dug out of riverbanks or from the ditches of the monuments. The majority of the flints found are waste flakes, the unwanted debris left over from the knapping of a nodule, but a small proportion are tools fashioned by careful shaping of the struck flakes. Large flakes were fashioned into knives, and some had serrated edges for cutting

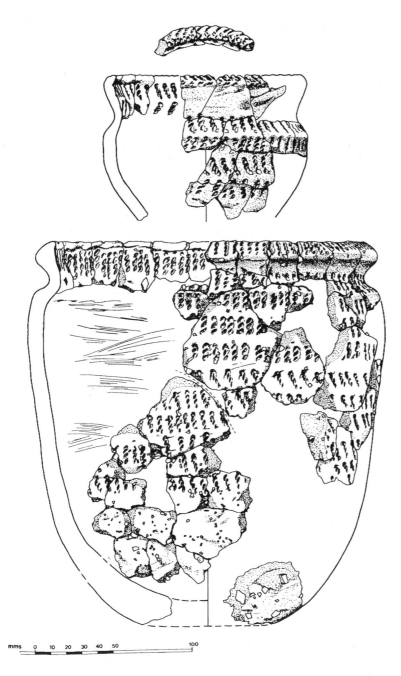

3.8 Neolithic pottery, Peterborough-type wares: An Ebsfleetbowl and a Mortlake jar from Ecton Reproduced by permission of Dennis Jackson

mms 0 10 20 30 40 50   100

tougher materials. Scrapers with blunt, circular ends were used for cleaning animal skins. Other flakes were notched or pointed, and were used for working wood, bone or leather. For hunting they had flint arrowheads, leaf-shaped in the Neolithic and barbed-and-tanged in the Bronze Age (Fig 3.13), and these are often the most finely made items.

Small numbers of larger flint and stone implements are also found, and many of these were probably obtained by trading with neighbouring tribes. In

3.9 Prehistoric Flint: A flint dagger from West Cotton round barrow.
Reproduced by permission of Northamptonshire Archaeology © Northamptonshire County Council

particular, there are the polished flint and stone axes that were used to fell the trees. From the types of stone used it can be shown that these came from as far away as the Lake District, Cornwall and Wales, showing that valuable objects were traded right across the country in the early Neolithic. Other fine pieces include the large flint daggers that may have been specially made to accompany the dead in their round barrows (Fig 3.9).

Neolithic and Bronze Age pots were typically handmade and thick-walled. They were fired in bonfires, so when they are found they are usually very soft and fragile. Each period had a distinctive style of pottery. In the early Neolithic they used plain, round-bottomed pots or bowls. Later, decoration was added with fingertip incisions on the rim or neck. In the later Neolithic there was a mixture of round and flat-bottomed pots, often with thick and elaborate rim shapes and typically

decorated all over in a range of techniques including incisions, cord impressions and finger-pinching. These styles included Peterborough wares, often found at burial sites, and barrel or bucket-shaped grooved ware pots, often found at henges.

With the appearance of round barrow burial a high point was reached with the smaller, more finely-made Beaker vessels, typically orange or red in colour and with the decoration forming bands of geometric patterns. Most of the early Bronze Age pots that are found are urns, often quite large and used to contain cremation burials. The early examples were often decorated all over but on the later, collared urns only the thick collars were decorated. The middle Bronze Age urns were often decorated with thick applied strips, and by the end of the Bronze Age there was a decline in decoration to simple finger-tip impressions on the rim or around the body

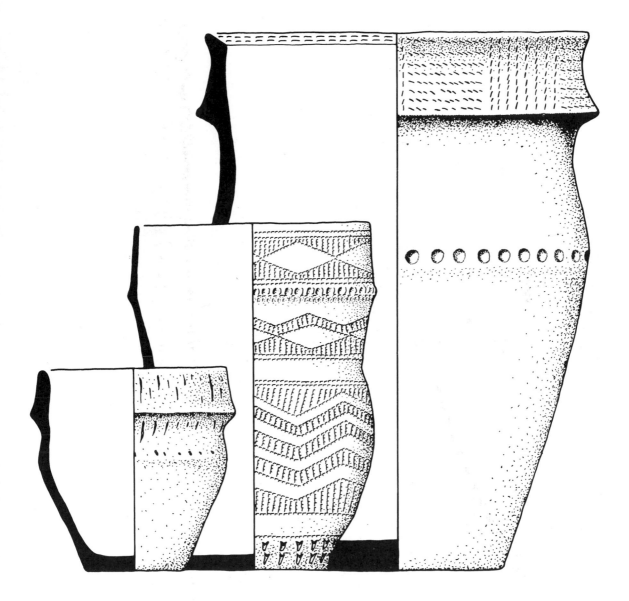

3.10 Bronze Age pottery: a small urn, a long-necked Beaker and a collared urn from the Beaker period round barrow at West Cotton, Raunds. Scale 2:5. Reproduced by permission of Northamptonshire Archaeology
© Northamptonshire County Council

THE BRONZE AGE (2200-1500 BC)

BEAKERS AND BARROWS

Dramatic changes occurred at the end of the Neolithic with the appearance of the round barrow as the new form of burial monument, and the final mounding over of the Neolithic mortuary sites. This change, from communal monuments to the burial of individuals, reflected broader changes in society, as for the first time we can clearly see the presence of individual people who had the wealth to command the building of a mound to mark their passing. At this time metals first appear in the form of bronze tools and weapons, and the use of gold.

A completely new form of pottery also appeared, the well made and highly decorated Beaker pots. It was once thought that these had been brought in by invaders from the continent, the so-called Beaker

People. The truth is more complex, and while some new settlers may have been arrived, all of the new practices and objects are now thought to be the result of the appearance of the new social divisions, of rich and poor. At least some of this new status may have been acquired by controlling the manufacture of the new bronze tools. The burial of quantities of cattle bone at some round barrows shows that ownership of cattle herds, and the land on which they grazed, was also a source of individual wealth and prestige. Society had evidently moved quite a long way from the lifestyle of the first farmers.

The numerous round barrows are the most common earlier prehistoric site, and from aerial photography a few hundred have been recorded in the county. Many of them lay along the Nene valley, but most of these have been ploughed flat. The line

3.11 The beaker burial at West Cotton, Raunds. Reproduced by permission of Northamptonshire Archaeology
© Northamptonshire County Council

of mounds visible on the skyline at Three Hills Barrows, Woodford are among the few that can still be seen and visited by the public.

Early barrows at Stanwick and West Cotton were excavated in the 1980s as part of the Raunds Area Project. These both lay on the margins of the floodplain of the River Nene near the earlier monuments, and their mounds were still partly intact. They represent the pinnacle of Beaker period round barrow construction. At the centre of each the primary burial of an adult man was accompanied by a Beaker pot, a large flint dagger, jet buttons and other objects (See Colour Plate 2). The burial at Stanwick was inside a plank built chamber within a deep grave, above which a stone cairn had been constructed. On top of the cairn nearly 200 cattle skulls had been heaped up as either funeral offerings or as the debris from funeral feasting. At both barrows there were two main ditches, showing that the mound was successively enlarged to reach some 35m in diameter, probably as further burials were made both on and around the mound (Colour Plate 3). The later burials were mainly deposits of cremated bone placed in large pottery urns. Although this was a period of change, respect for the past is still evident. At Stanwick the heap of cattle skulls included skulls of the auroch, the larger ancestor of the domesticated cattle, and these were several hundred years old when they were deposited, as was a boar tusk placed with the burial itself. These items appear to have been kept and looked after for several generations, perhaps as treasured heirlooms recording past family deeds. At West Cotton this was taken further, as the 1000-year old bones of two people were buried directly beneath the Beaker burial.

For a while both inhumation and cremation burials occurred at the same time, but soon cremation became the normal form of burial and remained so through to the end of the Bronze Age. There are no large barrow cemeteries in the county, but there are several smaller clusters of barrows. These were often grouped around earlier monuments, perhaps partly in respect for the earlier traditions but perhaps also as a demonstration of how new ways of life, and death, were taking over from the old ways. At Aldwincle there were four barrows near to the Neolithic oval barrow (Jackson 1976). Two of these contained Beaker-style burials of adult men, both of whom had been buried in coffins fashioned from hollowed-out tree trunks. At Grendon four of the five barrows to the south of the mortuary enclosure have been excavated, and remains of inhumation and cremation burials of adults and some children were found, despite extensive damage from ploughing (Gibson and McCormick 1985). There were also many ploughed out barrows around the Beaker barrows and Neolithic monuments at Raunds and Stanwick.

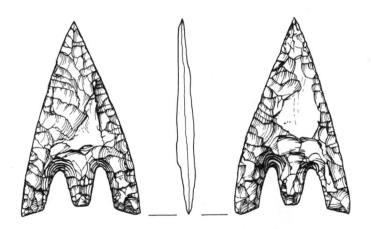

3.12 Prehistoric Flint: a finely made barbed and tanged arrowhead from a Beaker burial at
Warmington. Scale 1:1. Reproduced by permission of Northamptonshire Archaeology
© Northamptonshire County Council

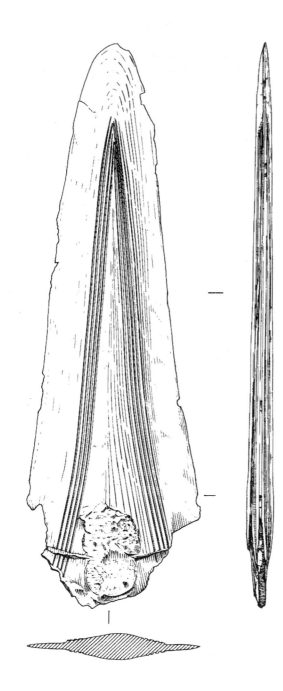

3.13 A bronze dagger from the Earls Barton barrow. Scale 5:6.
Reproduced by permission of Dennis Jackson

During excavations at the Roman town of Ashton, near Oundle in the early 1980s, two crouched Beaker burials were found without any encircling ditches, and another was found in 1995 only 3.8 km to the north at Warmington (Fig 3.12). This burial was accompanied by a fine collection of grave goods, including a Beaker pot, a broken flint knife, a worn flint rod used as a strike-a-light, and a finely-made but unused, barbed-and-tanged arrowhead. While ditches did not surround these burials, it is possible that they may have been under mounds constructed purely from the turf and topsoil stripped from an area over and around the burial sites.

Burial in round barrows continued for several centuries, until around 1500 BC, but the later barrows were usually much smaller, often at little as 15m in diameter. One of the first modern barrow excavations was that of a large barrow at Earls Barton belonging to this later period. Although the mound still survived, it was only recognised during stripping for gravel extraction in the winter of 1968, and was excavated by Dennis Jackson (1984). Little had survived of the primary burial apart from an area of burnt soil, a few scraps of cremated bone and a fine early bronze dagger The excavation of this site was also important as it provided the first radiocarbon dates from a Bronze Age site in the county.

THE END OF THE MONUMENTS
(1500-1000 BC)

By 1500 BC the last burials under round barrows had been made. Middle and late Bronze Age burial sites did not have any earthworks, or other visible marker. The cemeteries only consisted of small groups of pits each containing a heap of cremated bone, sometimes within or accompanied by a pottery urn. Lacking any evident markers, these cemeteries have only been found by accident.

After 3000 years one returns again to Briar Hill, where a cluster of 27 cremations were found inside the causewayed enclosure, and we must wonder whether the site was chosen by accident or if there was still a folk memory of its former importance (Bamford 1985). Four of the cremations were within large, undecorated urns, and the remainder may have been in leather or woollen bags. One cremation was accompanied by a tanged flint arrowhead that had been burnt on the funeral pyre. Other similar cremation cemeteries have been found at Chapel Brampton in 1970, near Kelmarsh during road construction in 1992 (Chapman 1999), and at the eastern end of the Stanwick long barrow. Others must still await discovery.

For most of this period evidence of permanent settlement is only rarely found. Under the Roman villa and Iron Age settlement at Stanwick, earlier ditches and remnants of a roundhouse probably belonged to a small farmstead surrounded by small fields where crops were grown and animals corralled. A similar, but better preserved site, has been excavated further down the Nene valley at Fengate, near Peterborough. Next to Fengate, at Flag Fen, bronze tools and weapons, often deliberately broken before they were thrown or placed in the shallow water has painted a vivid picture of the ritual deposition of valuable objects at this time (Pryor 2002). In Northamptonshire we have nothing so spectacular, but bronze axes, swords and daggers have occasionally been found, sometimes buried in pits along with scrap pieces. It is believed that these were hoards belonging to bronze smiths who never returned to recover their hidden stores of the precious metal.

CONCLUSION

In the thirty-five years since the excavation of the Earls Barton round barrow, archaeology has transformed our understanding of Neolithic and Bronze Age Northamptonshire. From a sparsely visited backwater, it has become a landscape alive with people who not only survived but prospered sufficiently to be able to devote much of their energy towards building and maintaining enclosures as meeting places and in marking the burial places of their dead with large earthwork monuments.

Through this time we see long periods of stability broken by episodes of sudden change in their way of life, and in the monuments they constructed and the tools that they used. From the semi-nomadic communities of the early Neolithic moving across a landscape without visible boundaries, they became communities marking out territories and respecting the power and wealth of certain successful individuals, who no doubt acted as tribal chieftains. The stage was therefore set for the next period of major change, the appearance of established farming communities using a new metal, iron.

4

Northamptonshire in the First Millennium BC

ALEXANDER (SANDY) KIDD

INTRODUCTION

As with much of lowland England, the first millennium BC in Northamptonshire is characterised by the introduction of iron working between 800 BC and 600 BC. There is also evidence for large-scale organisation of the landscape related to the expansion of agricultural production, the construction of hill forts and other defended sites and, at least from the Middle Iron Age onwards, numerous domestic settlements. There is a considerable increase in archaeological evidence from the Late Bronze Age/Early Iron Age to the Late Iron Age, which is suggestive of major population growth. Distinct formal ceremonial and burial sites are very rare but there are signs of ritual activity on 'domestic' settlements. Towards the end of the Iron Age, Northamptonshire stood on the periphery of a zone of rapid social change in South Eastern England, which was heavily influenced by continental contacts. However, the Roman conquest itself did not cause widespread upheavals with most Late Iron Age sites continuing to be occupied well into the Romano-British period.

The physical geography of Northamptonshire was a significant factor influencing patterns of Iron Age inhabitation. The river valley gravels with their swathes of light free-draining soils and easy access to water had been favoured locations since the Neolithic and occupation continued to intensify. Other sizeable areas of light soils were provided by the Northampton Sands, which outcrop over large areas around Northampton and Corby, and by Jurassic limestone found primarily in the extreme southwest and northeast of the county. In contrast, glacial deposits dominate the higher ground in the southern, western and central parts of Northamptonshire, principally boulder clay that would have been more difficult to cultivate. Substantial areas of the clay lands were wooded in the Middle Ages and would presumably have been amongst the last areas to face clearance in prehistory,

although the rate and extent of prehistoric woodland clearance is poorly understood. The presence of outcrops of iron-rich ores in the Rockingham Forest area will have been a new factor affecting local communities during the first millennium BC. To the north-east of the modern county lay the wetlands of the Fens, an area of considerable importance in the later Bronze Age as indicated by the extensive field systems found around the Fen edges and the impressive ritual centre at Flag Fen.

Climate is another external influence to be considered, although its significance is debatable. It is generally held that the British climate deteriorated at the beginning of the 1st millennium BC with the onset of colder and wetter conditions, which did not ameliorate until the middle of the millennium. In the Fens there is evidence of increasing wetness with marine transgression in the north and extensive freshwater wetland in the south. Although there is evidence from elsewhere in Britain for a retreat from uplands and wetlands at this time, the impacts of climate change on Northamptonshire are less easy to demonstrate. It seems possible that the increasing marginality of life in Britain's uplands and wetlands may have increased the attractiveness of, and pressure upon, the resources of Northamptonshire whilst it has been suggested that climate change may be a factor behind a major shift from pastoral to mixed farming in the Early Iron Age (Pryor 1998).

THE NATURE OF THE EVIDENCE

In order to understand the basis for archaeological interpretations it is necessary to briefly review the sources of evidence for this period along with their strengths and limitations. In 1999 the Northamptonshire Sites and Monuments Record contains details of 520 Iron Age sites which comprise 7.3% of all entries reflecting the county's strong tradition of Iron Age research from the 1960s up to the present day. Aerial survey, fieldwalking, geophysical survey, earthwork survey, metal-detecting and excavation have all

4.1 Iron Age sites in Northamptonshire

made significant and distinctive contributions to Northamptonshire's later prehistoric archaeological record but each has its own biases and limitations. Also, it must always be remembered that many sites have been destroyed without record whilst even more are as yet undiscovered – interpretations based on such incomplete knowledge must necessarily be somewhat tentative and provisional.

Few Iron Age sites survive as upstanding field monuments in Northamptonshire due to the destruction wrought primarily by medieval and modern ploughing. The Royal Commission for Historic Monuments has surveyed the surviving earthworks of Northamptonshire's major defended sites but sadly these are mostly heavily denuded. Other monuments survive only as isolated examples in woodland such as the undated Egg Rings enclosure in Salcey Forest, a short stretch of a triple ditch system at 'The Larches', Stowe-Nine-Churches and a slight earthwork ditch and bank in former heath land at Harlestone Firs which appears to be a continuation of an adjacent pit alignment cropmark. Taken in isolation, these few visible monuments gave previous generations of archaeologists a false picture of Iron Age Northamptonshire as being densely wooded and sparsely populated.

Aerial survey provides a means of detecting buried sites through patterns of differential crop growth – in dry weather a buried ditch or pit retains moisture enabling the crops above it to grow more vigorously thus appearing as a dark mark. A long-term programme of aerial survey undertaken by Glenn Foard has provided invaluable coverage of permeable geologies under arable cultivation but results are patchy on clay lands (where soils tend to retain moisture) and the technique is of little value in areas of permanent pasture and woodland. Combining information from many photographs

can allow extensive landscapes to be mapped thus placing more localised ground investigations into a wider context.

Structured fieldwalking to recover pottery from ploughed fields has been widely undertaken in North-amptonshire by both professionals and amateurs, although unfortunately few results have yet been fully published. The most notable examples are the Brigstock Survey (Foster, 1988 and 1998-9), the Raunds Area Survey (Parry, forthcoming) and the work of David Hall and Paul Martin. However, the technique has its limitations being restricted to arable land and affected by the friability of Iron Age pottery which tends to break down under prolonged ploughing making some sites effectively undetectable.

The limitations of fieldwalking mean that geo-physical survey is now usually the technique of first preference for large-scale developer-funded surveys. Magnetometer survey has proved particularly effect-ive at detecting the often substantial pits and ditches

4.2 The Iron Age hillfort at Crow Hill, Irthlingborough, as discovered by aerial photography in 1986. The hillfort ditch is revealed as a broad dark band. Reproduced by permission of the historic Environment Team © Northamptonshire County Council

of Middle and Late Iron Age settlements; although less substantial sites can be problematic targets.

Properly recorded amateur metal detecting has the potential to enhance our understanding of this period, particularly with respect to Late Iron Age coinage (e.g. Curteis, 1996a and 1997) and Late Bronze Age metalwork. However, ensuring proper recording and reporting presents a continuing challenge.

Many archaeological excavations have taken place in advance of development beginning in the 1960s but with a gathering of both pace and scale in the 1990s under the influence of recent planning legislation. Excavations provide a wealth of detailed data unobtainable by other methods such as detailed dateable site plans, stratified artefacts and a wide range of environmental evidence. Particular mention should be made of Dennis Jackson's invaluable excavation work, primarily on the ironstone quarries of northeast Northamptonshire, and his exemplary publication record (Jackson 1998/9). Recent major excavations at Wollaston, Crick and Courteenhall promise to transform our understanding of Northamptonshire's Iron Age settlement patterns and landscapes.

Having established that Iron Age remains are widespread across the Northamptonshire landscape, another rather different way of looking at the survival of this resource is to estimate the general state of preservation of Northamptonshire's pre-medieval landscape using computerised mapping techniques. 'Condition zones' can be defined to indicate areas where the land is thought to have remained unploughed during medieval and modern times (essentially historic woodland and former heath converted to woodland); land which has been ploughed (further sub-divided into sites where earlier remains may have been partially protected by alluvium or the surviving open field ridges and fields where the ridge and furrow has been ploughed flat) and finally land affected by quarrying and modern development. Only 2-3% of Northamptonshire's land surface falls within the first, unploughed, category whilst some 12% has been largely destroyed by modern development. The overwhelming majority of land (85%) has been, and in many cases continues to be, under the plough with consequent truncation and loss of buried deposits – within this area the best preservation is likely to be found under alluvium (6%) or extant ridge and furrow (5%). The fact that there are still no effective controls on plough damage and only ten monuments of Iron Age date are legally protected scheduled ancient monuments does not augur well for the long-term survival of our better preserved sites.

CHRONOLOGY

The first millennium BC is no exception to the general principle that a firm chronological framework is essential to understanding the development of

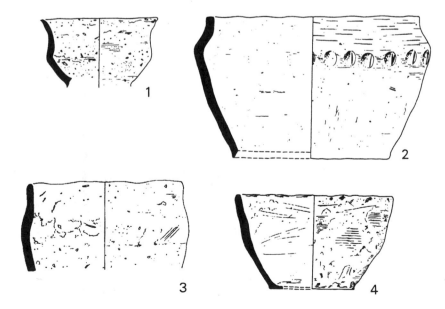

4.3 Early Iron Age pottery from Gretton. 1: carinated bowl; 2: round shouldered jar with finger-tip decoration; 3: ovoid jar; 4: open bowl. Reproduced by permission of the Dennis Jackson

society. Unfortunately, radiocarbon dating, which has proved so useful in earlier prehistory, is of less utility in the Iron Age because kinks in the calibration curves used to translate radiocarbon measurements into 'real' dates give date ranges of several hundred years which usually do little more than confirm dates attributable to artefacts on stylistic grounds. Although some metalwork can be closely dated it is rare and so the basic chronological framework for the Iron Age is provided by pottery. David Knight's research provides the ceramic chronology for the Iron Age of Northamptonshire (Knight, 1984 & 2002) supplemented for the Late Iron Age/Roman transition by the work of Roy Friendship-Taylor (Friendship-Taylor, 1998). Knight identifies four distinctive ceramic phases beginning with the supplanting of the Bronze Age Deverel-Rimbury tradition by Post Deverel-Rimbury 'plainwares' in the late 2nd millennium BC. These 'plainwares' were replaced before 800 BC by Late Bronze

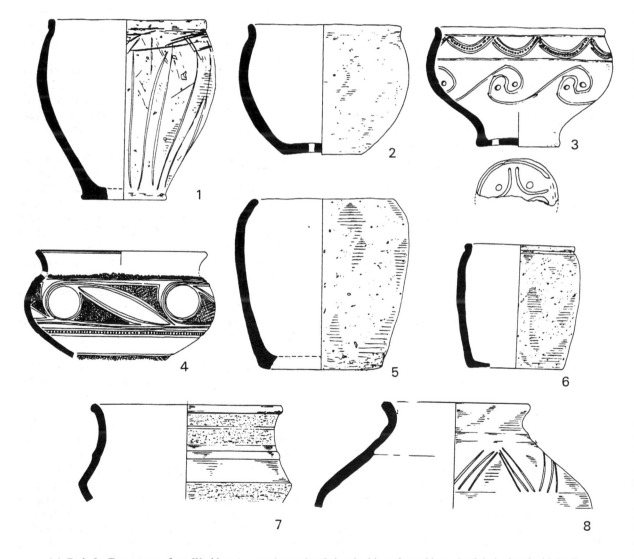

4.4 Early La Tene pottery from Weekley: 1: scored ware jar; 2: bowl with perforated base; 3: globular bowl with La Tene decoration; 4: Imported 'Glastonbury ware' bowl. Late La Tene pottery from Weekley: 5: slack-sided jar; 6: bead rim jar; 7: wheel-thrown carinated bowl; 8: round shouldered jar with everted rim. Reproduced by permission of Dennis Jackson

Age/Early Iron Age styles characterised by angular forms and geometric decoration (Fig 4.3). Late Bronze Age/Early Iron Age pottery continues until the 4th or 5th centuries BC when earlier La Tène wares appear with more rounded forms sometimes with scored or curvilinear decoration. Late La Tène style pottery develops from the mid/late-1st century BC incorporating a simplified version of the earlier tradition. It is typified locally by undecorated slack-profiled jars with channel or bead rims with more sophisticated wheel-thrown forms appearing in the 1st century AD (Fig 4.4).

Although a basic ceramic sequence has been established there remain serious problems with closely dating first millennium BC sites in Northamptonshire. Pottery fabrics are dominated by shell throughout the period and are rarely diagnostic of a particular style. Most ceramic forms are long-lived and examples of diagnostic forms and decoration are rare in most assemblages. There are also differing views over the date range of some diagnostic types, such as early La Tène curvilinear pottery, difficulties in recognising distinctive Late Bronze Age ceramics and concerns that differences in ceramic assemblages between some sites may reflect social or functional distinctions rather than chronology.

THE LANDSCAPE OF THE LATE BRONZE AGE/EARLY IRON AGE

Evidence for Late Bronze Age/Early Iron Age occupation in Northamptonshire is less common than that for the Middle and Late Iron Age. The distribution of sites is focussed on the permeable geologies along the Nene valley, although the majority of defended sites lie on the higher ground in the west of the county and a few are known on the clay lands. Recorded sites are generally fewer in the west and south of the county, probably due to the greater prevalence of permanent pasture and lower development pressures in these areas.

Hillforts and other defended sites are a distinctive feature of Late Bronze Age and Iron Age Britain. A total of eleven confirmed or probable examples are known in Northamptonshire whilst others surely remain undiscovered. The earliest defended sites are a 100m diameter circular enclosure at Thrapston (Hull 1998) and, probably, the 54 hectare contour hillfort on Borough Hill, Daventry (Jackson, 1993-4b and 1996-97; RCHME 1981, 63-65). Although the Thrapston enclosure has only been partially

excavated it appears comparable to the so-called 'Springfield-style ringforts' which are characteristic of high-status domestic settlement in Eastern England comprising a circular banked and ditched enclosure containing one or more large timber roundhouses. It seems likely that other ringforts of this type remain to be discovered, for example a 150m diameter roughly circular earthwork at Thenford is loosely associated with a Late Bronze Age metalwork hoard. Borough Hill represents an entirely different phenomenon - although the defensive ramparts are now much denuded and incompletely understood the entire hilltop seems to have been enclosed by multiple massive earthen ramparts and ditches which, although formally undated, bear comparison with large Late Bronze Age/Early Iron Age hill-top enclosures found in Wessex (Cunliffe 1991, 346-348 & 357). Late Bronze Age metalwork and a few small pits and postholes associated with Late Bronze Age/Early Iron Age ceramics have been found in the interior (Jackson 1996-7).

Northamptonshire hillforts typically comprise an earthwork bank and ditch enclosing an internal area of between one and three hectares sited in a commanding topographical location (Fig 4.1). Evidence for timber-strengthened ramparts have been found at a number of hillforts. This type of construction, which in Southern England is thought to be usually of Early Iron Age date, involves the retention of a rubble and earthen fill within a box-like timber structure normally secured by two rows of substantial earth-fast posts. Excavation has identified such structures within the ramparts at Hunsbury (Jackson, 1993-4a), Rainsborough (Avery et al, 1967), Guilsborough (Cadman 1989), Castle Yard, Farthingstone (Knight 1986-7) and possibly Crow Hill, Irthlingborough (Parry forthcoming, 361-386). The earliest ramparts at Hunsbury and Rainsborough hillforts have been dated to the Early Iron Age but the evidence from the other sites is equivocal. Hillforts would have appeared as ostentatious symbols of power as best exemplified at Rainsborough where the rampart was faced with stone and an elaborate entrance constructed comprising a causewayed approach between massive defensive ditches flanked by palisades and bastions to a gateway which was overlooked from a bridge and flanked by two guardhouses (Figs 4.5 and 4.6). The need for substantial defences is shown by the eventual destruction of the ramparts and gateway by fire, presumably following an attack as the remains

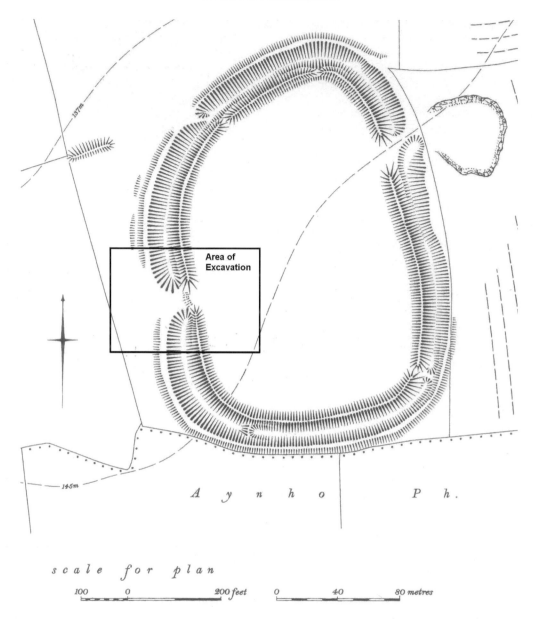

Area of
Excavation

scale for plan

100   0   200 feet   0   40   80 metres

4.5   The Rainsborough hillfort. Reproduced by permission RCHME/ English Heritage

of a wounded and burnt skeleton were found beneath charred roof timbers in the southern guardroom.

Undefended domestic settlements of the Late Bronze Age/Early Iron Age are not well represented, probably because they are difficult to detect being typically small, lacking an enclosing ditch, and comprising a handful of post-built structures and pits. Examples have been excavated at Gretton, Great Oakley and Weekley Wood (Jackson and Knight, 1985; Jackson, 1982; Jackson, 1976). Un-enclosed Late Bronze Age/Early Iron Age sites apparently also represent the earliest phases of the long-lived settlements at Crick (Hughes, 1998) and Wilby Way, Wellingborough (Enright and

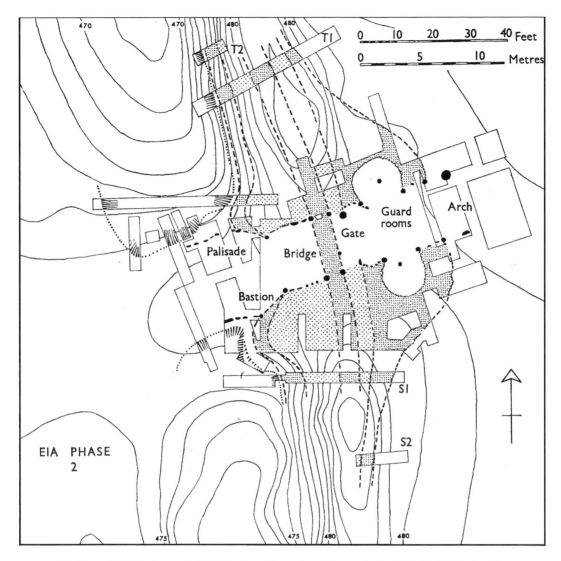

4.6 Plan of the Rainsborough hillfort gateway. Reproduced by permission of the Prehistoric Society

Thomas, forthcoming). In contrast, it is notable that the extensively investigated Iron Age landscape at Wollaston is seemingly devoid of Late Bronze Age/Early Iron Age settlement (Ian Meadows, 1995 & pers comm). It seems possible, albeit difficult to prove, that these small short-lived sites reflect a dispersed and mobile settlement pattern not dissimilar to that of the earlier Bronze Age.

The earliest evidence for extensive field systems in Britain is attributed to the Middle to Late Bronze Age with major systems covering many tens of square kilometres now recognised in such diverse areas as Dartmoor, the Thames Valley and the Fen margins. These are planned landscapes of ditched boundaries, enclosures and droveways often laid out on a common axis (described as 'co-axial') and apparently associated with intensive livestock farming. Despite the proximity of the Fengate field systems there is so far only one example of a comparable Middle Bronze Age field system in Northamptonshire – this underlay the Roman villa complex at Stanwick (Neal, 1989; Parry, forthcoming).

4.7 A pit alignment at Wollaston (A-B). Reproduced by permission of the Historic Environment Team
© Northamptonshire County Council

Elsewhere in the county the earliest identifiable land boundaries are the 136 pit alignments, which have been recorded by aerial survey and excavation. Pit alignments are easy to describe but hard to interpret functionally. In their simplest form they comprise a line of usually sub-rectangular pits, typically 2m x 1.5m x 1m deep, set 1-2m apart and running for some hundreds of meters. Although pit alignments

can appear as isolated features they also often occur in clusters as elements of complex long-lived landscapes. Most pit alignments lie on the permeable geologies of the Nene valley, although smaller numbers are known on the permeable geologies of the southwest and northeast of the county and a few have been recorded on clay geologies. Where excavated they are invariably found to be earlier

4.8 Excavation of a pit alignment at Upton. Reproduced by permission of Northamptonshire Archaeology © Northamptonshire County Council

than Middle Iron Age settlements and, where dating evidence is available, a Late Bronze Age/Early Iron Age date is usually indicated. The best understood example of such a complex landscape is found in the floodplain of the Nene at Wollaston where a pit alignment system of co-axial form covering an area of about 2.5km² was laid out during the Late Bronze Age/Early Iron Age. Preliminary results suggest that the pits at Wollaston mighty be the end product of the repeated cleaning of originally shallow features and that the alignments divided up blocks of pasture (Ian Meadows, pers comm). It seems that the pit alignments develop later than the co-axial field systems although it is uncertain whether they reflect different agricultural systems or specific social/cultural practices. Whatever their origin and purpose their laying out indicates the existence of much open ground at least on the

lighter free-draining soils. Pit alignments were not the only form of land boundary as both single and double linear ditches have been dated to the Late Bronze Age/Early Iron Age at Gretton (Jackson 1974; Jackson and Knight, 1985). Linear ditches are a common feature on aerial photographs but are not dateable on morphological grounds, although it is tempting to suggest that a distinctive series of triple ditches which cut off spurs of higher ground in the Brampton/Pitsford area to the northwest of Northampton might be related to the complex of pit alignments in the same area.

THE LANDSCAPE OF THE MIDDLE IRON AGE

Evidence for Middle Iron Age occupation is fairly common and widespread across Northamptonshire with the greatest concentration of sites along the

Nene and Ise valleys and some sites present on the clay lands. As for the Early Iron Age, western and southern Northamptonshire is noticeably under-represented.

New hillforts may have been built in the Middle Iron Age at Crow Hill (Parry forthcoming) and Castle Yard, Farthingstone (Knight 1986-7), although earlier origins are equally possible given the limited evidence available. On morphological grounds, the unexcavated smaller hillfort at north end of Borough Hill (RCHME 1981, 63-65) is also likely to have been built in the Middle Iron Age. The early timber strengthened ramparts were vulnerable to destruction or decay necessitating refurbishment at Hunsbury (Jackson 1993-4a), Rainsborough (Avery et al 1967) and, probably, Guilsborough (Cadman 1989) where the timber structures were replaced by a simple ditch and earthen bank, the latter presumably topped by a palisade. The elaboration of hillfort defences by multivallation (the constructing additional ramparts and ditches) evident at both Rainsborough and Borough Hill is generally regarded as a late phenomenon but an early date has been argued for both these sites (see above) and the matter must remain open pending further investigation. However, alternative arrangements seem to have been made at Hunsbury and Borough Hill where small defended enclosures appear to have been deliberately positioned to cover dead ground outside the main fort. Information about occupation inside Northamptonshire's hillforts is sparse. Nineteenth century antiquarian accounts of quarrying inside Hunsbury hillfort recorded large numbers of pits and recovered a wide range of artefacts indicating the sort of intensive occupation expected of a 'developed' hillfort (Baker 1891; Dryden 1885; Fell 1936; George 1917; RCHME 1985) but it is unclear whether the site was continuously occupied from the Early Iron Age. Survey and small-scale excavation at Crow Hill and Rainsborough have also demonstrated occupation in the Middle Iron Age. For the other sites there is simply insufficient information to indicate whether they were major centres, short-lived refuges or simply abandoned earthworks.

Non-hillfort settlements are found across the whole county and are especially common along the Nene and Ise valleys. They can be divided into three broad morphological categories; Open settlements, Enclosed settlements and Agglomerated settlements

Open settlements typically comprise a small group of timber roundhouses with ancillary structures, such as the 4-or 6- post arrangements often interpreted as raised granaries, and pits but lack substantial enclosing ditches. Small open settlements appear to be more characteristic of the Late Bronze Age/Early Iron Age than the Middle Iron Age but this may simply be because they are less easily discovered than enclosed sites and so under-represented in the archaeological record. The best example of an open settlement dating to the Middle to Late Iron Age is the fully excavated site at 'The Lodge', Crick (Chapman 1995).

Settlements comprising ditched enclosures, each usually less 0.5 than hectares in extent, containing at least one, more usually several, roundhouses with associated ancillary structures and pits are the most common Middle to Late Iron Age settlement type. Large numbers of this class of settlement have been recorded by aerial photography and field survey, most notably in the Upper Nene Valley. Excavations in Brigstock Park revealed a small settlement enclosure that had not been ploughed and was therefore in an unusually good state of preservation (see Chapter 1, this volume). Here a roughly circular bank and ditch enclosed an internal area about 20m in diameter containing a roundhouse defined by a wall trench, substantial entrance postholes and a drainage gully. A chalk path led up to the east facing entrance and continued into the interior to form a floor which had several burnt patches suggesting possible hearth sites. A distinctive sub-type of enclosed settlement are the so-called 'Wootton Hill style enclosures' which have been described as a localised mainly late Iron Age monument class consisting of 'small enclosures, each surrounded by an exceptionally deep ditch and additionally strengthened by banks, stockades and elaborate gateways' (Dix and Jackson 1989, 158) which normally lie on the sites of earlier settlements situated on higher ground and may be associated with hillforts and/or Roman villas. Sixteen confirmed or possible examples of this monument class can now be identified. Although Wootton Hill style enclosures have previously been described as being primarily of Late Iron Age date it is notable that many of the excavated examples (e.g. Aldwincle, Brigstock, Stanwell Spinney) are associated with early La Tène ceramics and so, in view of the uncertainties over chronology outlined above, it seems preferable to see them as a Middle to Late Iron Age phenomenon.

Agglomerated settlements are characterised by their much greater size which ranges from about 5 hectares at Wilby Way to at least 12 hectares at Crick (Plate 4) as well as by the presence of both

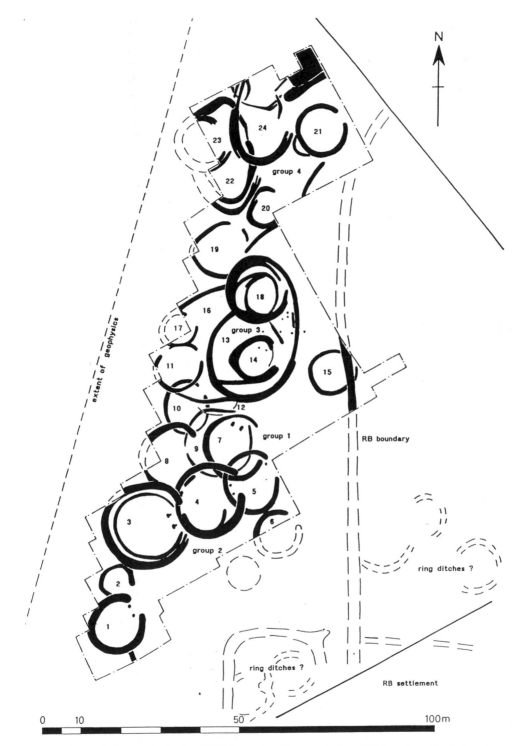

4.9 Iron Age settlement at The Lodge, Crick. Reproduced by permission of Northamptonshire Archaeology
© Northamptonshire County Council

enclosed and unenclosed elements and seemingly by greater longevity of occupation and perhaps diversity of function within the settlement. This type of settlement had not been widely recognised or understood in Northamptonshire (or indeed elsewhere) until recent development-led projects at Crick (Chapman 1995; Hughes 1998; Roy Kings pers comm) and Wilby Way, Wellingborough (Windell 1981; Enright and Thomas forthcoming). Agglomerated settlements are probably much more common than is currently appreciated because reliance on aerial survey and partial excavation may lead to their mis-classification as open or, more often, enclosed settlements. Other likely examples can be identified from survey at Kingsheath, Northampton (Shaw, Webster and O'Hara 1990), at the partially excavated site at Twywell (Jackson 1975) and perhaps beneath Stanwick villa where the current post-excavation programme is suggesting that the large Iron Age settlement was much longer-lived than had hitherto been recognised (V. Crosby pers comm). Whereas the smaller open and enclosed settlements represent farmsteads presumably belonging to a single family group these agglomerated sites probably had somewhat larger populations. Nevertheless it is doubtful whether any of these sites could properly be described as a 'village'. Stratigraphic evidence shows that only a small proportion of the roundhouses could have been occupied at any one time. At Crick evidence of flooding and frequent rebuilding suggests that the site was inhabited on a seasonal basis whilst elsewhere (e.g. at Wilby Way) we might be seeing the extended household of a higher-status family. Further research is needed to resolve these issues.

Many excavations have revealed evidence for field systems and trackways of Middle Iron Age date (e.g. Weekley: Jackson and Dix 1986-7) but only through aerial survey and recent large-scale investigation in the gravel quarries at Wollaston (Meadows 1995) has it been possible to begin to understand the extensive agricultural landscapes which existed in the Middle Iron Age and continued to operate into the Romano-British period. On the permeable geologies, linear ditch systems stretching for several kilometres with associated axial boundaries and settlements are a common feature. Good examples are known from Ecton/Sywell and the Bramptons in the Nene valley and near Rainsborough hillfort in the southwest of the county. Dating evidence for these systems is often limited but at Wollaston

the regular blocks of land defined by Early Iron Age pit alignments continued to be used, albeit apparently now defined by hedges, into the Middle Iron Age. Settlement and ancillary enclosures were inserted into this landscape at regular intervals and are associated with a changeover from pastoral to mixed agriculture (Meadows 1995 and pers comm). A rather different and less regular landscape is emerging from current work at Courteenhall on the south side of Northampton where a localised cluster of five Middle to Late Iron Age enclosures with associated field systems has been identified situated on outcrops of glacial sand overlooking a brook on the edge of the boulder clay plateau (Ovenden-Wilson 1997; Thomas 1998). The Middle Iron Age landscapes of the clay land plateaus are less well known but enclosures have been recorded and a linear system apparently similar to those on permeable geologies is known at Brigstock (Foster 1988 and 1998-9) providing the first evidence for intensive occupation of these previously unfavoured lands.

THE LANDSCAPE OF THE LATE IRON AGE

The Late Iron Age in South Eastern England is a period of rapid social change marked by the increasing influence of the Roman Empire, initially transmitted indirectly through the Celtic tribes of Northern France but applied more directly following the conquest of Gaul in the mid 1st century BC. It becomes possible to identify the tribes, and some of the rulers, of Southern and Midland England through their Roman-inspired coinage and to detect dramatic changes in settlement patterns, funerary practices and exchange networks. Individual rulers seem to have utilised access to prestigious imported goods, such as wine and fine tablewares, to build up their power base and adopt expansionist policies. The construction of *oppida* - large high status settlements often associated with extensive dyke systems – and distinctive cremation burials, sometimes rich in grave goods are characteristic of this period with the nearest major centre being at Verulamium (St.Albans).

Northamptonshire lay on the edge of this South Eastern cultural transformation but, by way of contrast, shows a considerable degree of continuity from the Middle Iron Age. Settlements such as those at Weekley, Wakerley and Crick ('The Lodge' site) which originated in the Middle Iron Age continued to be occupied into the Late Iron Age whilst newly founded settlement enclosures, such as that at Clay Lane, Ecton (Windell 1983), follow established Middle Iron Age traditions. Hill (1987) has suggested that the terms Middle and Late Iron Age should be used as cultural, rather than chronological, designations and that there is considerable overlap between these cultures in Eastern England – this view applies well to Northamptonshire which displays both late and partial adoption of the main facets of the South Eastern Late Iron Age. The problem is exemplified by Wollaston where enclosed farmsteads founded in the Middle Iron Age shifted to adjacent sites in the early Roman period but with little evidence for an intervening period characterised by Late La Tène ceramics (Meadows, 1995 & pers comm).

The general lack of Late Iron Age evidence from hillforts suggests they had been largely abandoned by this time, although Crow Hill may be an exception as it was apparently refortified by the insertion of a palisade (Parry forthcoming). The best candidate for an oppidum in Northamptonshire is at Duston (Friendship-Taylor 1998, 148-170; RCHME 1985, 252-257) but there are no dykes and unfortunately the site was largely destroyed in the 19th century so its status may never be properly understood. There is also evidence for Late Iron Age occupation on the sites of the Roman towns at Titchmarsh (Curteis, Jackson and Markham 1998-9), Towcester (Walker 1992) and Irchester (Hall and Nickerson 1967) hinting at pre-Roman origins for these places (Fig 4.1). Smaller sites such as Weekley (Dix and Jackson 1986-7) and Piddington (Friendship-Taylor 1989 & 1998, 225-247) appear to have been of high-status as indicated by the construction of Wootton Hill style enclosures at the former and presence of imported pottery at the latter. Villas were later constructed at both Weekley and Piddington following a general trend for villas to be constructed on sites that had been occupied during the Late Iron Age.

Considerable numbers of Iron Age coins have been found in Northamptonshire with the most significant groups coming from the Roman small towns at Duston, Oundle (Ashton) and Titchmarsh as well as the Late Iron Age settlements/Roman villas at Stanwick and Weekley and a probable Roman temple at Evenley. The earliest coins found in the county are Gallo-Belgic E staters, which are dated to the early/mid 1st century BC. Subsequent coinages suggest that by the late 1st century BC central and southern Northamptonshire had come within the orbit of the Catuvellauni, the most powerful tribe in Southern Britain based at Camulodunum (Colchester) and Verulamium (Colour Plate 5). A concentration of Corieltauvian coins in the northeast of the county suggests this part of Northamptonshire may have fallen within their territory whilst in the southwest the Cherwell may have marked the boundary with the Dobunni (Curteis 1996a and 1997 ; Cunliffe 1991, 110-118 & fig 7.9).

By the end of the Iron Age it is clear that most of the Northamptonshire landscape was densely populated and intensively utilised by a mixed agricultural economy. Considerable clearance and colonisation had taken place on the formerly wooded clay lands, especially to the south of the Nene and in the Rockingham Forest area, but the extent of residual woodland is uncertain. Most settlements and landscapes display evolutionary rather than radical change as an immediate consequence of the Roman conquest, although possible exceptions may be found at Brigstock (Foster, 1998-9) and Crick, where the breakdown of the agglomerated Middle Iron Age settlement pattern might relate to the construction of Watling Street.

THE AGRICULTURAL ECONOMY

The Iron Age was a time of major population growth as evidenced, for example by the more than doubling of the numbers of sites producing Middle or Late Iron Age ceramics compared to those with Late Bronze Age or Early Iron Age pottery. This increasing population will have generated a requirement for greater agricultural production. Other pressures on the agricultural economy will have been the climatic downturn of the early 1st millennium BC and perhaps an increase in non-food producing elite and craft specialists in the Middle to Late Iron Age.

There is much evidence from survey and excavation for fields and buildings presumably used for agriculture but it is to environmental evidence that we must turn for corroboration of these interpretations and a better understanding of food production and consumption. Unfortunately Northamptonshire lacks the wetlands and peat bogs which elsewhere have preserved rich organic deposits and the long pollen sequences needed for reconstructing vegetation change, although sampling of waterlogged deposits in old abandoned river channels has provided some promising results for earlier periods. Most Iron

Age sites in Northamptonshire are not permanently waterlogged and so preserve only a narrow range of environmental evidence, principally bone and carbonised plant remains. Unfortunately, published analyses of animal bone and carbonised plant assemblages are of limited value and at present it is only possible to give a broad indication of species represented. For example, spelt wheat and six-row hulled barley were found in Middle Iron Age pits at Twywell (Jackson 1975, 90-91). Spelt and emmer wheat and barley were present at Wilby Way where the assemblage was held to be representative of localised subsistence farming (Thomas and Enright forthcoming). The most common animal species are usually cattle and sheep/goat with pig, horse and dog of secondary importance and other species rare. The recent large-scale excavations should improve on these basic observations and it is to the results emerging from Wollaston that we must look for the most significant contribution to understanding the agricultural economy. The picture emerging primarily from the sampling of abandoned river channels and other waterlogged deposits at Wollaston is one of Middle Bronze Age woodland clearance creating an open pastoral landscape in the Late Bronze Age/Early Iron Age followed by the development of a mixed agricultural regime in the Middle to Late Iron Age (Brown and Meadows 1996-97; Meadows 1995). Mollusc assemblages provide further evidence for an open landscape on the higher ground overlooking the Nene valley in the Middle Iron Age from Blackthorn, Northampton (Williams 1974) and Wilby Way, Wellingborough (Enright and Thomas forthcoming). However, unlike river valleys such as the Ouse and Thames, there is as yet little evidence for pre-medieval alluviation in the Nene Valley which might be expected as a result of extensive arable cultivation (Robinson forthcoming, 42-45), although alluvial deposits recently found in the fills of a pit alignment at Grendon might be of later Iron Age date. Away from the Nene valley there is very little comparable environmental data and obtaining such information, especially from the clay plateaus, should be accorded a high priority to investigate patterns of local diversity. For example, a model of seasonal occupation can be suggested at Crick, which might indicate a more mobile settlement pattern in northwest Northamptonshire.

As we have seen, sufficient information is available to enable morphological analysis of the Iron Age/Romano-British landscape over wide areas of the Upper Nene valley. However, the great challenge to comprehending the changing nature of Iron Age agriculture lies in moving towards an understanding of processes of woodland clearance and the expansion of agricultural production. More attention needs to be paid to identifying the archaeological correlates of expansion related to demographic growth, agricultural extensification and intensification, changes in crops, cultivation and livestock management regimes and shifts towards more specialised production. This should be possible in a period that saw such major changes as the construction of the first extensive field systems and permanent settlements, a shift from an intensive pastoral regime to mixed agriculture and major demographic growth.

CRAFT PRODUCTION

Northamptonshire Iron Age sites have provided evidence for iron and bronze working, the spinning and weaving of wool, the preparation of skins and leatherworking and possibly the manufacture of objects of bone, antler, horn, lead, jet, glass, wood and basketry (Knight 1984). Pottery was also undoubtedly produced in the county throughout this period but possible evidence for bonfire kilns is limited to Weekley (Dix and Jackson 1986-7). By far the greatest range of evidence for craft production comes from Hunsbury hillfort suggesting that this was an important local manufacturing centre (Knight 1984, 187). Elsewhere, the small quantities of craft-related artefacts and materials recovered suggest that the only industry likely to be operating on a more than local level was the iron industry. Excavations at Great Oakley have shown that the nodular ores, which outcrop in ironstones of northeast Northamptonshire, were being extracted and smelted in the Early Iron Age (Jackson 1982). Possible Iron Age smelting furnaces have been recorded at Great Oakley, Wakerley (Jackson and Ambrose 1987) and Harringworth (Jackson 1981) whilst some of the slag scatters of the Rockingham, Salcey and Whittlewood Forest areas probably date to this period. Large quantities of iron-smelting slag have also been found at Castle Yard hillfort (Knight 1986-7), and smaller quantities of smelting or smithing slag are commonly found on settlements. A hoard of iron currency bars from Gretton (Jackson 1974) and a rare iron bloom from Crick (Hughes, 1998) may also be related to this industry (Fig 4.10).

4.10 Currency bar hoard from Gretton. Reproduced by permission of Dennis Jackson

RITUAL AND RELIGION

In contrast to the Neolithic and Bronze Age, distinctive ceremonial and burial sites are, with a few well-known exceptions, a rarity in the British Late Bronze Age and Iron Age. In the Late Bronze Age the deliberate deposition of fine metalwork into water as seen at Flag Fen formed a distinctive rite but is not exemplified within the modern county and seems to have come to an end in the Early Iron Age (Pryor, 1998). Elsewhere in Southern Britain both rectangular and circular structures within hillforts and underlying Romano-Celtic temples have been interpreted as shrines (Cunliffe 1991, 510-518) but no examples are yet known in Northamptonshire, most probably due to a lack of large-scale excavation in such locations. Recent Iron Age research has placed greater emphasis on evidence for ritual activities permeating everyday life typically seen in the orientation and layout of structures and the structured patterning of deposits of artefacts and human and animal bone on domestic settlements (e.g. Hill 1995). This is an area of considerable debate for one man's ritualised deposit of animal bones can be another's disposal of butchery or kitchen waste. However, although individual cases may appear unconvincing and open to mundane explanation, seen collectively some

more compelling patterns are beginning to emerge. Ritual structures have been tentatively identified within several settlements in Northamptonshire based on their orientation and associations - for example, at Weekley Early La Tène curvilinear decorated pottery was deposited in large quantities in association with a putative ritual enclosure from which three rare iron spearheads were also recovered (Adam Gwilt, pers comm) whilst placed deposits of antler, burnt pig bone and pottery have been observed in the ditch fills at the ringfort at Thrapston (Hull 1998). Most Middle Iron Age sites have some apparently structured deposits which are difficult to explain simply as rubbish disposal - examples include human and animal inhumations, the numerous querns placed in pits at Hunsbury and perhaps the frequent deposition animal skulls in the termini of enclosure ditches. The treatment of human remains is particularly enigmatic to modern eyes. There are no cemeteries and human bones appear as a minor element in many excavated bone assemblages. Small numbers of human burials occur in pits on settlement sites, although they often seem to have been accorded little ceremony and to have been treated little differently to other animals, such as dogs, which were also occasionally buried as whole carcasses. A particularly poignant example of a pit burial dated to the 4th or 5th century BC was excavated at Brackmills, Northampton in 1996 (Colour plate 6). A 30-40 year old woman had been bound and been thrown face-down into a pit but unlike most pit burials this one was accompanied by an artefact – a unique lead torc (neck ring). An adjacent pit contained a dog burial but it is not known if the two were contemporary. Pit burials have also been found at Twywell, Wilby Way and possibly Hunsbury hillfort – in the former case dog burials were also present (Jackson 1975). The full significance of this rite is not understood but it was clearly not 'normal' practice and invites comparison with the ritual execution found in the case of bog bodies such as Lindow Man.

The situation does not change dramatically in the Late Iron Age, although two small cemeteries are known situated just outside the Roman town defences at Irchester and Towcester respectively and a decorated mirror found at Desborough in the 19th century may have come from a high-status burial (Colour Plate 1). The Irchester cemetery contained at least four Aylesford-Swarling style urned cremation burials (Hall and Nickerson 1967) whilst at Towcester an apparently Late Iron Age inhumation cemetery appears to be situated within a ditched enclosure which has been compared to continental sacred sites called *Viereckshanzen* (Walker 1992). The considerable numbers of Late Iron Age coins recovered from the putative Roman temple site at Evenley may also be indicative of a Late Iron Age shrine, and may perhaps be related to coin hoards found in North Buckinghamshire.

IRON AGE SOCIETY

What can the evidence from Northamptonshire tell us about issues such as the scale and nature of social and political units and the relationships between

4.11 Pit burial excavated at Brackmills, Northampton in 1996. Note the tightly bound posture and lead torc around the woman's neck. Reproduced by permission of the Northamptonshire Archaeology
© Northamptonshire County Council

them? We should expect the archaeological record to be complex as it is structured by such diverse factors as religious belief, kinship, clientage and political alliances as well as more immediately practical needs such as effective land management and exchange of specialist products. Nevertheless, it seems reasonable to ask what progress has been made towards understanding the organisation of society in Iron Age Northamptonshire.

Northamptonshire's location in the centre of England resulted in its Iron Age societies absorbing influences from various different directions. In the Late Bronze Age the Thrapston ringfort forms part of an Eastern England tradition whilst the parallels for the contour hillfort on Borough Hill can be found to the south and west. The paucity of information for the Late Bronze Age/Early Iron Age restricts meaningful analysis but the collapse of the bronze exchange networks and lack of evidence for imported goods combined with the construction, and sometimes destruction, of hillforts in the Early Iron Age would perhaps be consistent with a more isolated, fragmented and unstable society.

The ubiquitous enclosed farmsteads of the Middle Iron Age suggest a more stable society based, at its lowest level, on discrete family units. Intermediate levels of social organisation, perhaps kin or clientage based, are suggested by the regular ordering of settlements within the co-axial system at Wollaston, by the clustering of some settlement enclosures into neighbourhood groups (e.g. Courteenhall) and by the grouping together of open and enclosed elements in the agglomerated settlements (e.g. Crick). By analogy with better-known hillforts in southern England, developed hillforts such as Hunsbury could have occupied the highest social level and performed specialised functions such as craft manufacturing, storage, defence and perhaps the regulation of external trade. The Upper Nene and Ise Valleys emerge as a distinctive cultural area, characterised by Hunsbury-style curvilinear decorated pottery and Wootton Hill style small defended enclosures. Within the early La Tene style curvilinear pottery there are localised sub-styles suggestive of distinct production and distribution areas (Jackson and Dix, 1986-7, 77-78).

Demonstrably imported artefacts are very rare in Middle Iron Age contexts in Northamptonshire but examples include querns found at Hunsbury from Derbyshire, Lincolnshire, Sussex and Kent (Ingle 1993-4), salt briquetage (fired clay containers) from Cheshire (Hughes 1998) and pottery from Leicestershire (Hughes, 1998; Knight, forthcoming) and the Lizard Peninsula (Jackson and Dix 1986-7). Although salt briquetage is present at Crick its absence from other sites may imply that the bulk of the county's salt was imported from the salterns in the Fens and/or along the Lincolnshire coast which did not use briquetage for transportation. The likely sources of these contacts covers a broad zone across Southern and Midland England which can be interpreted in terms of Northamptonshire's integration within the regional exchange networks of the Middle Iron Age (Cunliffe 1991, 444-497). Iron was probably Northamptonshire's main contribution to these networks but unfortunately this industry is poorly understood and its products cannot be traced to source.

In the Late Iron Age there is relatively little indication of the sort of major social changes which are such a distinctive feature of the South East and South Midlands, although a shift in the location of high status sites is indicated from hillforts to settlements which subsequently developed into Roman towns or major estate centres. This is a time when Northamptonshire appears to have become politically marginalised – perhaps a contested land between competing tribal groups, which was eventually absorbed into the expanding Catuvellaunian state.

CONCLUSIONS

Northamptonshire is fortunate in having a relative wealth of information for the Middle and Late Iron Age compared to most other counties such that is now possible to suggest an outline of developments in the period. The Earlier Bronze Age landscape of ceremonial monuments focussed on the Nene Valley gave way in the Late Bronze Age and Early Iron Age to the construction of the first field systems along with open and defended settlements; recent research both in Northamptonshire and elsewhere suggests that this phenomenon is linked to an intensification of livestock farming. By the Middle Iron Age there had been a shift to a mixed agricultural system accompanied by substantial population growth, longer-lived settlements and expansion into the previously little occupied (and presumably wooded) clay lands. By this time central Northamptonshire was probably occupied by a distinct cultural group, which was later absorbed by the Catuvellauni from whom aspects of the South Eastern Late Iron Age culture were adopted before the Roman conquest. Although the Catuvellauni initially resisted the Roman invasion of 43 AD they rapidly accepted and adapted to the new regime. The lack of evidence for a significant early Roman military presence in Northamptonshire suggests than the transition to Roman rule was not widely contested.

Despite the considerable progress made by archaeological research in recent years there are many inadequacies with the available data and unanswered questions - a challenge for the 21st century will be to not simply to reiterate old agendas and data collection techniques, but to apply more integrated theoretically driven approaches and to embrace new research techniques and questions. Another challenge will be to ensure the long-term preservation of a representative sample of the archaeological resource – something that has not so far been achieved even for all the few surviving earthworks let alone the extensive buried landscapes revealed by aerial photography which are under constant threat from plough erosion.

5
The Roman Period

JEREMY TAYLOR AND MYK FLITCROFT

INTRODUCTION

In broad terms, approximately a quarter of the records in the Northamptonshire Sites and Monuments Record relate to the Roman period, reflecting perhaps both the range and archaeological durability of the material record, and the long-standing antiquarian interest in the period. A large proportion of the undated cropmark sites in the SMR are, however, also likely to be Roman and/or Iron Age in date and should be added to this total. In Northamptonshire, the Roman period is characterized by intensively occupied and large scale rural landscapes. These are related to expanded agricultural production, regional scale craft and industrial production of pottery and iron, the construction and use of an extensive network of roads, and the foundation and development of many local market and religious centres. Discrete formal ceremonial sites are found in both small towns and rural sites, and detectable burial rites become far more common on both rural and small town sites with later Roman inhumation cemeteries common at larger settlements.

CHRONOLOGY

The basic framework for a ceramic chronology of the period is derived by combining information from a number of existing studies of particular wares, such as Howe & Perrin's guide to the pottery of the Nene Valley (1980). To this can be added the synthesis of larger excavated groups such as those from Towcester and immediately outside the county around Milton Keynes (Brown & Alexander 1982; Brown & Woodfield 1983; Marney 1989). An important area of former concern in dating Late Iron Age and first century coarse wares has recently been addressed by Friendship-Taylor (1998) but work of similar quality does not exist for the different fabric and form traditions found more commonly to the north and north west of the county. The recent publication of a number of backlog reports from the Nene and Welland research committee excavations near Peterborough, however, does now provide good basic data for a reappraisal in the former area.

For later periods, the Upper Nene valley grey-wares saw much early work through the excavation of kiln sites such as those at Ecton (Johnston 1969). The publication of excavations of shell tempered kilns at Harrold in Bedfordshire provides useful backgrounds for understanding these important regional coarse wares, but would benefit from synthetic study in the light of recent excavations (Brown 1972). Final publication of a number of outstanding major settlement excavations in North-amptonshire and at Odell in Bedfordshire should help improve the picture of common local coarse ware chronology. The Welland valley still remains something of a gap, which may only be improved with the publication of rural settlement excavations on the Leicestershire side of the valley (e.g. Empingham, Drayton and Ketton).

As with many areas there are special problems of constructing late 4th-5th century chronology in the absence of reliable late dated artefacts, and the possibilities for C-14 dating in this context, especially in relation to environmental data and continuing traditions of inhumation, need to be considered. Coinage also provides a good chronological source especially for urban and larger rural sites but low levels of coin loss (especially up to the 3rd century) on many rural sites and all first-second century settlements mean it is frequently of less value in this respect.

SETTLEMENT FORM

Evidence for the morphology and layout of settlements and the changing architectural traditions used within them are an important resource for studies of changing rural social organisation and status. This includes current evidence for settlement size and nucleation, especially in relation to the development and nature of non-villa rural

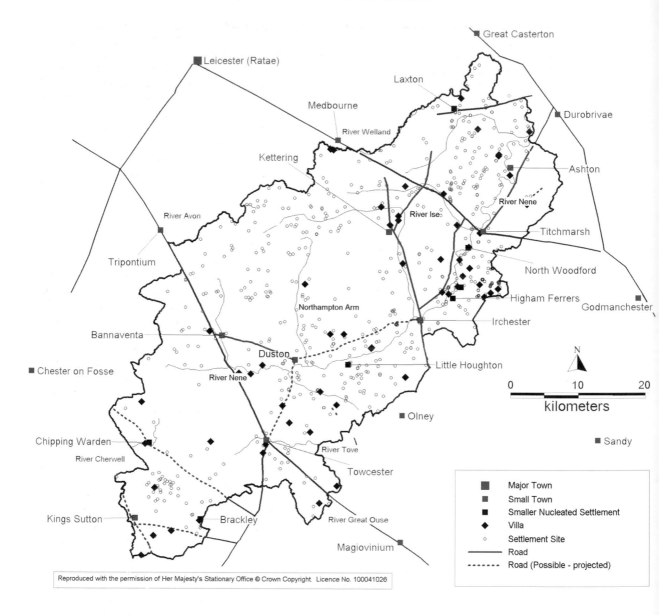

5.1 Roman Roads and sites in Northamptonshire

settlements and urban/roadside settlements during the mid-late Roman period.

The previous focusing of excavation on the architecture of villas and the conceptual separation of Iron Age from Roman has tended to fragment and bias our understanding of settlement architecture and morphology for the early part of the period. In particular, we have until recently, had a surprisingly poor understanding of the layout and morphology of entire early Roman farmsteads. It is clear, however, that small, enclosed settlements such as those found at Wootton Hill, Blackthorn, Wollaston, Earls Barton and Irchester, were transformed or abandoned during the Late Iron Age - early Roman transition (Jackson 1990, Williams & McCarthy 1974, Meadows 1996, Windell 1982, Atkins 2001,

Hall & Nickerson 1967). Where excavation has been sufficiently extensive, it is apparent that settlement was restructured around agglomerated groups of ditched enclosures and trackways predominantly of rectilinear form. These appear to be the norm for rural settlements in the early Roman period but excavated evidence suggests that these boundaries were ignored or altered to less archaeologically visible form (e.g. hedges) in the later Roman period. Some high status rural sites, such as Piddington, Stanwick and Cosgrove were enclosed in the later period, usually with walls that often followed earlier boundary divisions but now focused occupation around the main building range (Friendship-Taylor 1999, Neal 1989, Quinnell 1992).

Looking at domestic architecture on rural settlements, there appear to be distinctions between the traditions for central southern Northamptonshire and the northeast part of the county (as mentioned above, there is currently insufficient information to permit detailed comment on the northwest part of the county). In the central southern Northamptonshire, round houses are common and continue their gradual transformation from timber into stone. This development is paralleled by the foundation and gradual development, largely from the Flavian period, of row type villas such as Quinton, Piddington, Thorplands, Overstone, Brixworth and Redlands Farm (Friendship-Taylor & Friendship-Taylor 1997, Hunter & Mynard 1977, Williams 1976, Woods 1970, Keevill 1992).

In the north east of the county, the initial continuity of round houses was replaced from the 2nd century by aisled buildings and villas (e.g. Apethorpe: RCHME 1975; Great Oakley: Meadows 1993a; Wakerley: Jackson & Ambrose 1978). This seems to be part of a tradition extending through South Lincolnshire, North Cambridgeshire and Rutland of which Orton Longueville, Lynch Farm, Barnack, Empingham, Whitwell and West Deeping are part. Unfortunately, modern excavations of villas in the Lower Nene Valley are rare and so little can be said of this area with confidence.

Architecturally and decoratively, villas within the county range in scale from large sophisticated complexes of buildings which must have required substantial resources, to much simpler structures comprising little more than a single row of rooms. At the upper end of this scale the complexes at Cotterstock and Piddington may be cited as particularly lavish, long-lived examples.

The Cotterstock villa was first recorded in the mid eighteenth century but was only re-located by aerial photography in 1976. It has seen little modern excavation, but a recent synthesis of geophysical survey, fieldwalking, limited trenching and information from aerial photography presents a complex of unparalleled size within Northamptonshire (Upex 2001). The villa site includes four courtyards surrounded by ranges of buildings which cover an area approximately 70 metres across and up to 270 metres in length. It is by far the largest known structure of its kind in the lower Nene valley and thus comparable with courtyard villas such as Bignor (Sussex) and Chedworth (Glos).

The Piddington villa has been the subject of long-term excavation since 1979 by the Upper Nene Archaeological Society. Apart from a large collection of worked flints ranging in date from the Neolithic to the Bronze Ages, the main evidence for settlement at the site occurs in the late Iron Age with three post-built 'D-shaped' structures. Pottery from the post-holes of these structures suggest a date from c. 50BC. These structures were followed by at least three more round-houses of more conventional form of between 8 and 13 meters in diameter and were dated by pottery and metal-work from c. I AD - c. 40+ AD. This phase was followed by a Conquest period (43/44AD) military presence for a duration of between 10 to 15 years. From c. 70AD a timber proto-villa of at least 6 rooms emerged, to be followed some 30 years later on an adjacent site by a stone-built 'cottage type' villa (see Fig 1.7). A similar, but smaller detached building was added at an obtuse angle. Both of these buildings suggest occupation dating from approximately 90/100 to 120 AD. Both of these buildings were extended until they were linked in a single-winged ('L'-shaped) corridor building by a small bathhouse (colour plate 7). This building was extensively damaged by fire in the late Antonine period (c. 160's AD). Reconstruction followed with the addition of further rooms and a new detached bathhouse. By 280/290AD a further major refurbishment programme was in progress. However, this came to an abrupt end midway through the work, leaving unfinished structures, unpainted walls and quantities of building materials, including large piles of unused tesserae sited around the building. Only minimal activity is attested during this period with an unbroken but small sequence of coins from various locations throughout the

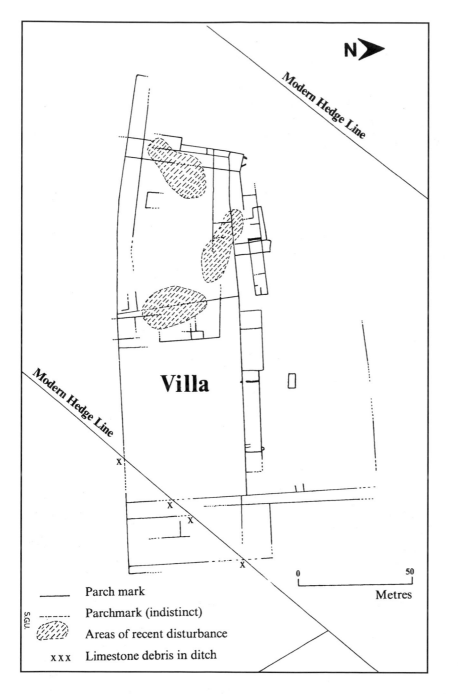

Parch mark

Parchmark (indistinct)

Areas of recent disturbance

x x x   Limestone debris in ditch

5.2 Plan of the courtyard villa at Cottestock. Reproduced by permission of the Nene Valley Research Committee

site covering the next decade. However, intensive occupation resumed around *c.* 330AD with at least 6 family units living within the area of the old villa. This type of occupation then continued in an unbroken sequence well into the 5th century,

followed by a small amount of Saxon occupation and a small cemetery (both groups may of course have been co-existing together).

Apart from being a detailed study of site morphology, the excavations at Piddington have

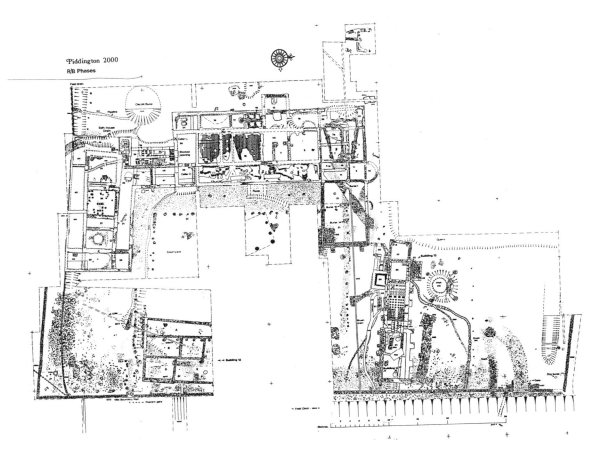

5.3 Ground plan of the Piddington Villa. Reproduced by permission of Roy Friendship-Taylor

been particularly significant for the information they have produced on the decorative schemes employed, showing that the villa's walls, colonnades, and roofs were all brightly coloured (See Colour Plate 8).

Although arguably of less architectural significance, in terms of sheer scale, the excavation of the villa at Stanwick is of national importance. The sites covered approximately 10 hectares and included not only a villa but also a group of substantial and separate stone buildings. Their excavation represents the first occasion that a villa has been fully excavated along with its estate buildings, including barns, a village and what appears to be a bailiffs residence. This not only reveals the morphology of the site but allows some attempt to be made to reconstruct its tenurial and social relationships

Substantial stone-built, or at least stone-founded,

circular buildings are a further element of the building repertoire seen on a number of rural sites. These are found throughout the country, but a review has been made of examples found in the Northamptonshire and Oxfordshire (Keevill and Booth 1997). While it might once have been assumed that they represented stone founded round houses and were as such a short lived fusion of Celtic design with Roman technology, the true picture is far more complex. They appear to have been constructed from the first to the third centuries and some appear to have been in use, well into the fourth. There is considerable variation in their size, the largest being up to 16 metres in diameter. Some, like those at Stanwick seem to be part of a villa estate, while others are found in association with temples and some seem to stand in isolation.

5.4 Carved head from the Stanwick villa. Reproduced by permission of the Historic Environment Team
© Northamptonshire County Council

Many appear to have been domestic habitations and in one example at Ringstead a timber roundhouse was rebuilt with stone footing and a tessellated floor. However, there is also evidence linking these structures with agricultural storage, agricultural processing, industrial, and religious functions. It is also clear that other important timber architectural traditions existed. These are poorly understood due, in the past, to the lack of any specific interest in their study and subsequently, because of their susceptibility to damage by cultivation.

At a larger scale, there are no major towns in the county but a pattern of smaller nucleated settlements linked in to the road network is reasonably well mapped. The archaeology of these settlements has recently been reviewed as part of the English Heritage funded 'Extensive Urban Survey' of North-amptonshire. Significant settlements are known to have existed at Whilton Lodge, Towcester, Duston, Irchester, Titchmarsh, Ashton, Kings Sutton and Kettering. With the exception of Towcester ('*Lactodurum*') and Whilton Lodge ('*Bannaventa*') the original names of the settlements are unknown.

The site named as Bannaventa in the Antonine Itinerary was known from finds recorded in the eighteenth century although its precise location, three kilometres north east of Daventry, was only determined in 1970 by aerial survey (Fig 5.5). This revealed a walled town enclosing an area approximately 220 metres across. Almost as soon as it was rediscovered, the site was threatened by gravel extraction necessitating a rescue excavation on approximately a quarter of the site. This revealed both extra-mural settlement and a round house beneath the tail of the rampart with other earlier features

At Towcester, excavations of the defences showed them to have been constructed around 170 AD and to be composed of a stone wall with a backing bank inside a ditch which was 23metres wide but only 1.5 metres deep (Brown & Alexander 1982). Some 400 metres south of the defences, three rescue excavations were along the line of the Alcester road revealed, not only how the road was constructed and maintained but that a series of ditched plots containing rectangular houses of timber and cob, were laid out on either side of the road. These appeared to be contemporary with the construction

5.5 The walled town of Bannaventa, visible to the north of the A5. Reproduced by permission of Mr J Pickering

of the defences and to have been part of a planned development of the area (Brown & Woodfield 1983).

Other large nucleated settlements have also been identified across the county at Stanwick, Higham Ferrers, Brackley and Laxton. These settlements, while larger than individual farmsteads do not appear to have the same roles or attributes as the 'small towns' above and may be more akin to medieval villages.

Where archaeological evidence is sufficiently detailed and comprehensive, many of these small towns seem to have had Late Iron Age predecessors such as Duston, Towcester, Irchester and possibly Ashton (RCHME 1985; Walker 1992; Hall & Nickerson 1967) Some, such as Titchmarsh and Brackley/Evenly were significant religious as well as economic foci.

The evidence currently available almost always suggests that growth was organic alongside major roads and dendritic patterns of track ways that linked the core of each settlement to their surrounding agricultural landscapes (e.g. Ashton, Titchmarsh, Irchester and Bannaventa). Enclosure within a defensive wall, when it happened, was a secondary event that cut across the existing grain of a town's layout and that only protected its core. Only three of the towns are believed to have ever developed such features: Bannaventa, Towcester and Irchester. The significance of this set is uncertain although two of the three settlements lie on Watling Street and other similarly sized settlements on this route, outside Northamptonshire (eg Water Eaton, Staffs), are similarly protected, this does not explain the enclosure of Irchester.

Little is known about the function, development

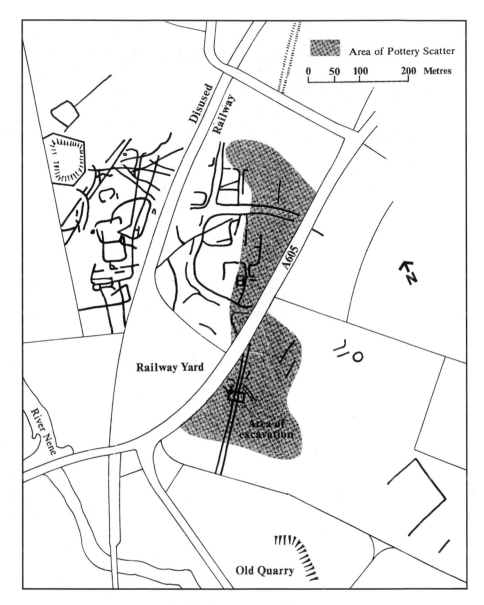

5.6 The Roman town at Ashton.
Reproduced by permission of the Nene Valley Research Committee

and emerging roles of these nucleated settlements during the Roman period. Few of the towns have had significant modern excavations in their core but those at Ashton constitute an extremely important dataset that requires publication. Excavation on the fringes or extramural areas of Towcester, Irchester and Bannaventa and rescue excavations at Titchmarsh help to fill out the picture, particularly with regard to artefactual and paleobiological evidence (Brown & Woodfield 1983; Windell 1984; Dix et. al 1991; 1994; Dix & Masters 1992; Masters 1997; Meadows 1997; Dix and Taylor 1988; NAU unpublished).

5.7 The Roman town at Irchester Reproduced by permission of the Historic Environment Team
© Northamptonshire County Council

COMMUNICATION NETWORKS ACROSS THE COUNTY

A composite picture of the major roads in the county has been available since the Royal Commission Survey volumes published between the late 1970s and mid 1980s and their mapping by Ivan Margary (1973). Map (5.1) shows the principal major roads in the county, i.e. those forming part of a regional or national communication network linking geographical locations, rather than the more local networks linking settlements to the surrounding agricultural landscape.

Perhaps the most significant Roman road (at least in terms of the wider national road network) is the part of the route known as 'Watling Street' running north-west across the country from London. Within Northamptonshire its course is generally followed by the modern A5 between Old Stratford and Lilbourne. The only other road line in the county of similar strategic importance is the 'Gartree Road', running from Leicester to link with Ermine Street at Godmanchester, which crosses from the Corby area to Clopton.

Other roads can be partially traced from stretches visible as cropmarks on aerial photographs or as earthworks, and lengths preserved in later boundaries. This would include a road running along the Nene valley between Titchmarsh and Water Newton. More speculatively, the existence of a route along the middle stretches of the Nene valley, linking the small towns at Duston and Irchester can be postulated although there is currently little physical evidence for its alignment.

Roads such as Watling Street can be viewed as being significant boundaries in the initial Roman conquest and consolidation of lowland Britain. This suggests a mid-late first century origin, and that it continued as a maintained route of strategic importance throughout the period. A similar

5.8 Part of the Roman timber bridge at Aldwincle. Reproduced by permission of the Historic Environment Team
© Northamptonshire County Council

argument can be made for the Gartree road. Other roads can only be interpreted and understood by reference to the network of larger nucleated settlements, although here a causal relationship between settlement centre and communication route (or vice versa) is difficult to prove. The towns are discussed separately elsewhere, but the identification of pre-Roman settlement at several of these sites (Duston, Towcester, Irchester) raises the strong possibility that parts of the Roman road network is based on earlier prehistoric communication lines.

The chronology of road creation and development of the network within the county is far from completely understood. Watling Street and the Gartree road can best be viewed within the context of the initial Roman conquest and consolidation of lowland Britain and to have continued as a maintained route of strategic importance throughout the period.

It is only in the Roman period that the creation of a permanent way necessitated major engineering operations. These include the causeway across part of the Nene floodplain north of the nucleated settlement at Irchester, recorded and partially excavated by the Oxford Archaeological Unit in Ditchford Quarry (Keevill & Williams 1995), or the extensive gravel metalled roads excavated south-west of Towcester (Brown and Woodfield 1983). Archaeological evidence for bridges across the river Nene has been recovered at Aldwinckle where gravel quarrying in 1968 revealed a timber bridge connected to a metaled roadway. The bridge had been re-built on at least three occasions and although no final date for its destruction could be determined, it was certainly in use between the 1st and the 3rd centuries (Jackson & Ambrose 1976). Other riverside constructions include a causeway at Irchester, and probable mills at Redlands Farm (Keevill 1992) and Towcester, Wood Burcote (Turland 1977). River-road intersections, such as the routes crossing the Nene north and west of Irchester, and Watling Street crossing the Tove immediately north of Towcester, would also have required bridges or fords, as was suggested for the road north of Irchester.

Perhaps surprisingly given the amount of development work on the gravels and alluvial deposits along the Nene there has been little research pulling together information on riverside installations and communications in the county. The potential for future discoveries may still be present at a number

of locations along the lower reaches of the valley (Jackson & Ambrose 1976).

SETTLEMENT LOCATION AND LANDSCAPE ORGANISATION.

Summaries of the evidence for rural settlement patterns, stability and shift in the location of settlement, and the basic layout of intervening land boundaries as a guide to changing patterns of social organization, are key to understanding Roman rural society in the county. Critical to this is some understanding of networks of settlement locally and regionally, rather than just individual sites. How far this is achievable is currently highly varied, but is already possible in some parts of the county.

Good information is currently available from the Raunds Area Project, a large scale survey and excavation work in the Nene Valley around Raunds and from work in advance of gravel extraction at Wollaston (Parry, forthcoming; Meadows, forthcoming). Away from the river Nene, a smaller survey around Brigstock examined an area that had been preserved from medieval plough damage within a deer park, while more recently there has been an extensive excavation and survey at Courteenhall (Foster, 1988; Buteaux, 2001). Generally, information from the north and west of the county and much of the clay lands is lacking. Both Raunds and Wollaston suggest some localized settlement shift during the late Iron Age or shortly after the conquest within long established bounded landscapes. Excavation on nucleated and dispersed settlements suggests a greater degree of continuity on the former, dating from at least the Late Iron Age. Such settlements are known at Duston and Stanwick though publication of the excavations at both is awaited.

Where excavation has been on a significant scale or carried out to more rigorous modern standards, results indicate that most villas within the county appear to have had late Iron Age predecessors (e.g. Ashley: Taylor & Dix 1985; Brixworth: Woods 1970; Piddington: Friendship-Taylor 1999; Stanwick: Neal 1989; Weekley: Jackson & Dix 1988). Until recently our understanding of non-villa rural settlements has been very poor. However, landscape orientated excavation and observation strategies as part of large scale developer funded projects, such as those at Wollaston, Crick and Courteenhall is now improving the situation (Meadows 1996 &

pers comm; Chapman 1995; Ovendon-Wilson 1997; Thomas 1998; Buteux pers comm). Although at an early stage, this work suggests that many of these settlements were relocated from nearby predecessors or were new foundations during the first and second centuries AD as rural settlement was reorganized within an existing bounded landscape.

Thanks to the quality and recent systematic mapping of aerial photography, information is available to assess the morphology of agricultural landscapes in a number of parts of the county. This is continually augmented by large-scale prospection ahead of modern development (e.g. Bramptons/Dallington: Cadman 1995; Ecton: Meadows 1993b; Upton: Buteux & Jones 2000) but the real need is to extend paleoenvironmental studies and link them to other material correlates of changing agricultural practice during this period. In order to develop a balanced and extensive understanding of how landscapes in the region developed, it will be critical to integrate analyses of boundary form and pattern, with environmental, artefactual and geochemical data that informs our understanding of land use. One approach to this issue is currently the subject of work at Crick, Wollaston and Courteenhall.

AGRICULTURE

The quality of our existing evidence for agricultural practice (as reflected in the structural evidence for periods of innovation, change or stability, alongside the palaeoenvironmental record, and patterns of land division and use) is also currently highly variable. Whilst excavations from the county have provided many dated examples of key changes in the organisation of agriculture, we still have very little detailed work on palaeobotanical and faunal remains of this period, especially away from the major river valleys or small towns/roadside settlements.

Synthesis of the published and unpublished environmental information is currently much needed as part of a regional overview, but it is already clear that few of the existing published excavations from the county contain any such information. Valuable results of preliminary work at Wollaston have demonstrated the presence of a significant area of probable viticulture in the middle Nene valley. During the examination of a 35 hectare gravel extraction site, a series of shallow, flat based ditches were uncovered running in parallel lines for over 6 kilometres and spaced 5 metres apart. Excavations

revealed post holes within the trenches which were interpreted as plant supports and analysis of the ditch fills produced vine pollen.

This work together with the extensive programmes of work at Stanwick villa, Redlands Farm and Courteenhall will eventually produce a much clearer picture of patterns of environmental change and agricultural regimes for the county. These key projects need then to be augmented by the additional datasets collected as part of smaller briefs and published accounts from other parts of the county (such as that from Croughton, Irchester, Aldwincle and Crick). Critically, however, there is still very little comparable environmental data from areas away from the Nene valley and gathering such information remains a high priority.

Sufficient information is currently available to study the structural development of Roman rural landscapes over significant parts of the Nene valley. Alone, such information tends to produce somewhat descriptive maps, which still often tell us little about the dynamics of agricultural land use in the Roman period. It is imperative if we are to understand the development of Roman agricultural life to develop approaches that integrate structural, environmental and artefactual data into models of land use, agricultural practice and exchange. With this in mind it is important to shift our thinking from an emphasis on solely structural and artefactual evidence to incorporate approaches that assist in the delineation of 'use areas'. In particular, this requires us to think of preliminary survey strategies (field walking, aerial photography, geophysics, geochemistry) and periods of active intervention (microtopography of stripped surfaces, environmental sampling and excavation) as providing highly significant landscape datasets for the study of the agricultural environment. Only when extant projects of this kind are completed and future opportunities for such work taken, will we be better placed to answer key questions about agricultural specialisation, centralization, the separate or similar development of upland, clayland or even potentially formerly wooded areas, and changing patterns of land use through time.

CRAFT PRODUCTION AND INDUSTRY

The nature and distribution of evidence for pottery and tile production, and the iron working industry are currently areas of real potential in Northamptonshire. A long tradition of work on the major regional Roman pottery industries gives reasonable data sets on the location of production sites, their date and technology, but is still poor on the context of production and the analysis of patterns of supply. Critically, earlier site based work on the upper Nene valley pottery kilns (e.g. Johnston 1969) needs synthesizing in order to fill a significant gap in our understanding of coarseware production, supply and use in the region (cf. Fulford & Huddleston 1991, 35 & 39). The study of tile production is, if anything, similar but worse and little recent consideration has been given to assessing the link between the two. This is particularly important in relation to the major excavated groups currently awaiting publication from Stanwick and Ashton, which have the potential to provide major synthetic studies for the Lower and Middle Nene valleys.

Iron production has been the subject of recent synthetic summaries and although information on the development and extent of the industry is still very fragmented, it appears that the importance Roman Iron production in the east Midlands has in the past been underestimated (Condron 1997, Schrufer-Kolb 1999, Bellamy et al, 2001). Earlier field walking surveys have provided good basic datasets on the patterns and extent of iron production sites across the county but much additional information is required if they are to be better understood. Primarily, these surround the need to better date the industry and begin differentiating between the locations of various stages in the process and the scale upon which they occurred. If much, or even a significant proportion of the sites currently known can be demonstrated to date to the Iron Age and, or Roman period this region, which includes neighbouring areas of Rutland and Lincolnshire, is likely to have been one of the most important centres for the industry nationally.

5.9 Excavation of an iron working site at Laxton. Reproduced by permission of the Roy Friendship-Taylor

Little is known about the economic and social context of the iron industry despite evidence being available from a number of earlier excavations. Dispersed patterns of iron smelting within the agricultural landscapes of the south of the county, around Silverstone (Mudd 2002), and in the Welland valley from Harringworth (Jackson 1981) and Wakerley (Jackson and Ambrose 1978). Evidence for more concentrated and potentially large scale iron smelting comes from nearby Laxton (Jackson & Tylecote 1988), but the wider layout and function of the settlement is still very poorly understood. Likewise, the unpublished excavations at Ashton strongly suggest that iron smithing was a significant element in the town's development and economy. Unfortunately, however, these have tended to be considered in isolation and a wider research framework that considers patterns of extraction, roasting, smelting, smithing and exchange is much needed if the role of this industry is to be understood.

Currently ample scope exists for assessing other potential industries as little or no work has been done. In particular, possible craft specialization linked to agricultural products such as textiles, horn, leather and bone is in need of examination, especially in relation to the still small number of important excavated groups from the small towns and larger villas.

RITUAL AND RELIGION, BURIALS & CULTURAL IDENTITY

Much recent work on Iron and Roman Britain has pointed to the evidence for the construction and maintenance of distinct regional identities, often at varying scales. In this respect, new projects would benefit from considering settlement architecture for example, as possible expressions of identity and status through time and space (e.g. a possible contrast between communities in the north east of county and those in the central south). Buildings clearly have practical functions but distinctive regional and chronological patterns are often caused by important social differences, an insight long recognized in architectural studies of later periods.

Portable material culture and identity has received much recent attention for the Late Iron Age, however this emphasis on possibly significant local differences has not been similarly pursued within Romano-British studies (e.g. Curteis 1996; Jackson

& Dix 1988). Such considerations are also valuable in considering the marked difference between nucleated/rural settlement assemblages as evidence for variation in social status. Likewise, the role of long term ritual traditions and religion in particular is important in this context, and consideration of the possibility of structured deposition and animal burial, the ritual associations of architecture, and human rural and boundary burial may all prove very fruitful.

Individual excavations have provided useful information on the more obvious material remains of Romano-British religious sites. At Brigstock, a circular and a polygonal shrine, both approximately 9 metres in diameter were located within 2 kilometres of the Gartree road. Most of the 278 coins and minature bronze objects (including a horse and rider, a table and an axe) were concentrated within the circular building. Within 8 kilometres of this site, a group of two polygonal, one rectangular structure and as many as three round buildings were located at Collyweston, (Greenfield 1963; Knocker 1965).

Substantial numbers of burials were encountered during excavations at Ashton and Laxton but these await publication. The possible religious function of some smaller Roman towns/roadside settlements is already suggested from survey evidence but little is known from excavation. At the heart of this is the continuing need to better examine religious foci within both rural and larger nucleated/small town sites such as Cosgrove, Titchmarsh, Irchester and Towcester. Many probable rural religious sites have come to light through metal detecting, and in the absence of any immediate likelihood of excavation, the analysis of such surface finds groups, preferably under controlled conditions, will remain the best option for their study. Evidence for such sites spanning the later Iron Age and Roman periods is now common, largely through the efforts of Mark Curteis (pers. comm.), but the establishment of a portable antiquities officer post provides further opportunities for the better recording and synthesis of this growing body of information.

Much excavated evidence is already available for other forms of settlement but a strong tendency to overlook evidence for ritual practice in such contexts, in contrast with Iron Age archaeology, has led to a potentially important gap in research. That such structured deposits did occur in domestic contexts is ably demonstrated by the articulated animal deposits discovered at Quinton, and needs

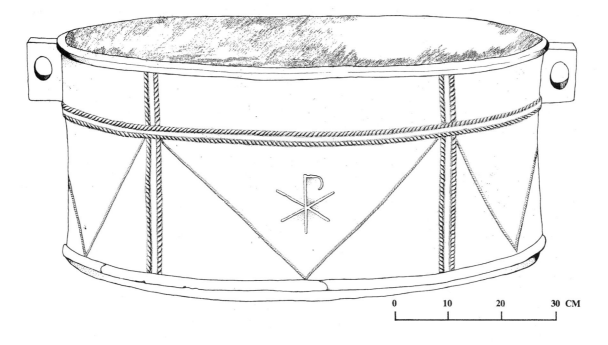

0   10   20   30 CM

5.10 Lead tank from Ashton, displaying a chi-rho monogramme.
Reproduced by permission of the Nene Valley Research Committee

to be considered in all future excavation projects on such sites (Friendship-Taylor 1974; 1979).

Evidence for specific religious traditions is somewhat limited by the lack of modern excavation on such sites. However, the discovery at Ashton and Rushton of lead tanks bearing the *chi-rho* motif, as well as the hoard of early christian church plate from Durobrivae, may well suggest the presence of significant late Roman Christian communities in the county.

Rural burials are sparse in number on any one site but commonly present and recent reviews of this phenomenon suggest some significant patterns in burial location and tradition (Pearce 1999; Taylor in prep). The excellent data from Ashton, where both substantial cemetery and boundary burial groups are recorded, alongside limited work at Laxton, provide a key opportunity to better understand later Roman urban traditions and compare and contrast urban-rural relationships with the traditions noted above.

6

The Anglo-Saxon Period

TONY BROWN AND GLENN FOARD

This account will present the archaeological evidence for three interlocked themes in the history of the Northamptonshire landscape: the dissolution of Romano-British society and its replacement with a tribal system, with a landscape which contained a fluid settlement pattern; the exercise of royal power in the form of the house of Mercia, and the imposition of a degree of stability; and finally, after the Danish interlude, and carrying forward the effects of that and the Mercian achievements, the development of a Midland common-field landscape which underpinned the economic expansion of the high Middle Ages.

TRANSITION FROM THE ROMAN PERIOD

Clearly the infrastructure of imperial government disappeared. The walled towns of Towcester, Irchester and Bannaventa (Whilton Lodge) ceased to function and some elements of the road system fell into disuse. The villas of the landowning class could not be maintained. Coins were no longer used and most of the industries which characterized Roman Britain and which are so clear in the archaeological record – stone quarrying, tile making and in particular pottery production – came to an end. All this has the effect of making the surviving Romano-British population archaeologically invisible; many of the peasant farmers could well have remained and been assimilated with the newcomers. What happened to the Christian communities attested archaeologically at such places as Oundle and Rushden in the face of the pagan Anglo-Saxons is quite unknown.

At the level of the individual site, the contribution which Northamptonshire has made to understanding the transition from Roman Britain to Anglo-Saxon England is growing. At Brixworth a genuine continuity of use is evidenced by the discovery that, in the post-Roman period, a room in a small villa was fitted out with two parallel rows of posts, presumably to support the roof (Woods 1970). Recent excavations at a villa site at Whitehall Farm, Nether

Heyford, have shown how in the 5th century the east wing was deliberately levelled. Two metalled stone surfaces were created, one to be used as a yard and the other as a base for a timber hall with substantial posts. At Redlands Farm, Stanwick, a very run-down villa building continued to be occupied into the 5th century at the same time as three sunken structures, of broadly the same type as those widely used by the Anglo-Saxons, were functioning 70 metres away. The number of instances of Saxon pottery turning up on Romano-British sites of all kinds is increasing, for example from the upper filling of a ditch associated with a recently discovered villa at Aynho, and from the topsoil over a temple at Cosgrove (Quinnell 1991): however the significance of these finds is by no means clear. One can point to sites which would if opportunity offered repay more extensive excavation. At Wollaston, there is early Anglo-Saxon pottery from the upper fills of ditches associated with a villa west of the village, and some sunken-featured structures and post-holes near by, but the evidence for what happened to the villa itself still lies unexcavated (Chapman and Jackson 1992). There has been nothing as yet to compare with Orton Hall Farm in the parish of Orton Longueville, in Northamptonshire until 1974. Here excavation in advance of road works has enabled the claim to be made that a large farm concerned with both grain and animal husbandry and in its final phases part of a larger establishment quite possibly in imperial ownership, was in the 5th century taken over in working condition by Anglo-Saxons, who continued to run it until a point early in the 6th century, gradually replacing Roman masonry buildings with their own timber ones as required (Mackreth 1996).

Taking a wider perspective, general arguments which turn upon the location of Anglo-Saxon sites in relation to Roman ones can be produced to suggest that the Anglo-Saxon takeover did in fact take place within a Romano-British framework. At Duston a small Roman town clearly occupied in the 4th century had close to it a mixed (but mostly inhumation) cemetery belonging to the period 450-

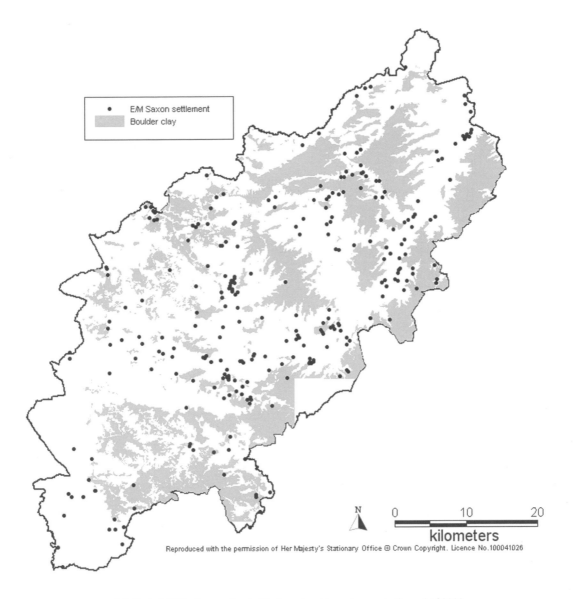

6.1 Early/Middle Saxon sites in Northamptonshire as known to the end of 2000

550, part of a country-wide pattern of quite early Anglo-Saxon cemeteries outside Roman urban centres. A more significant example comes from North Kettering, where a sizeable mainly cremation cemetery on Stamford Road, containing some urns considered to be early 5th century, but extending in date into the 6th, lay one kilometre to the south-east of another large Roman period settlement. The particular interest here is the place-name of the neighbouring village Weekley, which incorporates the Anglo-Saxon word *wic*, which in this case could derive from the Latin word *vicus*, meaning 'village'. The Anglo-Saxons who gave this name must therefore have appreciated the kind of place Roman North Kettering had been. Elsewhere a degree of continuity in the units of land exploitation might be suggested. The parishes of Stanford on Avon and Marston Trussel both have significant Roman occupation sites in the middle of them. Another possible example is in the north-east of the county, where a huge villa sits at the centre of the combined parishes of Cotterstock and Glapthorn, which in their present form are the result of the subdivision of an earlier, larger land unit.

There are instances in which deserted Roman sites were used for burial some point in the sub- or Anglo-Saxon periods. At Easton Maudit a villa had seven inhumation burials inserted into it. The old find of a skeleton with a gold ring and a spearhead from the villa at Piddington might be an Anglo-Saxon burial, and other better attested ones have been found in recent excavations. The skeleton with a spearhead beside it in one of the rooms of the bath house of the temple or villa on Borough Hill, Daventry could belong to this period. Such burials are not unusual, and while there is clearly a discontinuity at the level of the individual site, nevertheless the implication is that people were still living nearby, as was indeed the case at Easton Maudit, where a sunken-featured building was cut into one side of the villa

THE EARLY SAXON PERIOD (*c* 450-650)

One of the achievements of the 1970s was the recognition that the pottery of the Early and Middle Saxon periods could be identified in the ploughed fields of Northamptonshire in the same way as the long-recognized Iron Age, Romano-British and medieval material. Despite a great deal of fabric analysis, however, it has so far not proved possible to provide narrow dating brackets for the various types of wares. Up to the end of 2000 some 122 sites had been recorded in this way (Fig 6.1). About 25% of these coincide with Roman period sites. While there are a variety of ways in which this can be explained, continuity of occupation of some kind will be a possibility for a proportion of them. Field surveys regularly show the continuation of a trend visible in the late Roman period for a shift of settlement from the higher claylands to the lower and more easily worked permeable soils of the river valleys. During the years 1985 to 1990 the fields of the parishes of Raunds, Stanwick, Hargrave and Ringstead were

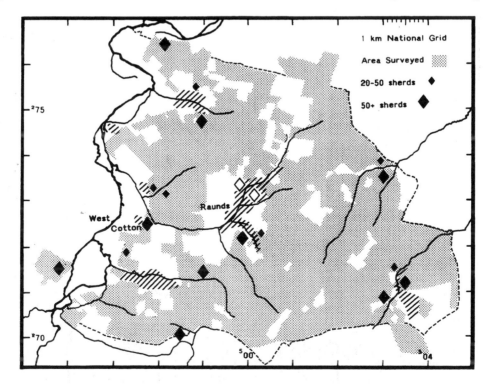

6.2 The Raunds area survey: distribution of early-mid Saxon surface scatters. Shaded areas show the extent of villages in the medieval period. Location of excavations at Furnells and Burystead shown by open lozenges. Reproduced by permission of Northamptonshire Archaeology © Northamptonshire County Council

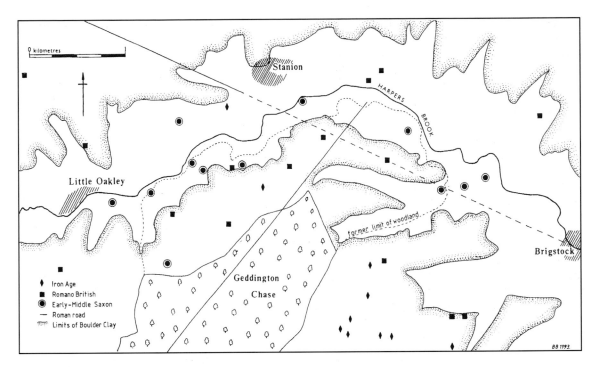

6.3 Early-Middle Saxon sites in the valley of the Harper's Brook. Reproduced by permission of Burl Bellamy

walked in a controlled way in lines at intervals of 15 metres, resulting in the discovery of 14 sites of this period, in this case hardly any coinciding with Romano-British ones but all on river gravels, quite often in pairs facing each other across a stream (Fig 6.2). To judge from the slight halo of contemporary pottery around them, the result of the deposition of domestic rubbish on cultivated land to manure it, these sites were farmsteads (Parry 1994). The survey gave a crude ratio of one settlement for every 2.9 square kilometres, in contrast with the figure of one settlement per square kilometre for the Roman period. Even taking into account the knowledge that not all Roman period sites were occupied at the same time the impression remains of a decline in population, quite possibly a continuation of one that was going on already. The ditches of Romano-British field systems, as at Wollaston, were allowed to silt up, and it is highly likely that from now on there was a greater emphasis on pastoralism.

The contraction of settlement from the clay-lands will have had the effect of permitting the regeneration of woodland and scrub on land previously under cultivation. This is not to say that the forests of Rockingham, Salcey and Whittlewood owed their existence entirely to regrowth in the Anglo-Saxon period; woodland must have existed here in the Roman period to underpin the iron and pottery industries. But that the area under some kind of tree cover did expand can be shown archaeologically in for example the area of Corby and Brigstock, where well-authenticated blocks of medieval woodland have Roman sites inside them. Outside the forests, areas bearing the names -*wold* or -*ley*, and therefore carrying tree cover of some sort in the Saxon period when the names were given, have in places Roman period sites and manuring scatters. An important exception to the lack of sites of the Early/Middle Saxon period in woodland areas comes from Rockingham Forest. Extensive fieldwork in a zone between the River Welland and the Willow Brook, in the parishes adjoining the Harpers Brook and around Easton-on-the-Hill, has revealed mounds and patches of iron slag as well as actual smelting furnaces. Charcoal from these has yielded C14 dates, providing clear evidence for a very substantial Early/Middle Saxon iron smelting industry which continued into the Late Saxon period and beyond (Fig 6.3; Bellamy 1994; Bellamy *et al* 2000-01).

Northamptonshire has produced the same range of structural remains known from elsewhere in Anglo-Saxon England: rectangular timber halls of various degrees of size and elaboration, with walls formed around posts set in post-holes or later on in trenches; and quite small sub-rectangular sunken structures, with post-holes at each end to support a roof. These were relatively humble ancillary structures for craft use, but they could be lived in; they are not generally thought to have had Romano-British antecedents. Large-scale excavations elsewhere in England have uncovered a variety of sites including well-organised groups of halls arranged to form farm units set within fenced enclosures; and large straggling sites with halls and sunken buildings in various proportions showing little obvious planning which represent a relatively small number of farms rebuilt as required in slightly different places. In Northamptonshire the largest area of early-middle Saxon rural settlement so far excavated is at Raunds; this shows this kind of site movement. Here work has taken place on both parts of a site divided by the Raunds Brook. On the western side, three sunken-featured buildings, four post-built structures, some pits, a kiln or hearth and various post-holes which could not be joined up in a meaningful way to make buildings, were found. A C14 date from the hearth gave a probable 6th century date. These buildings were abandoned after the mid-7th century and 100 metres to the south a residential hall 8½ by 4½ metres and at right angles to it another, larger, building were constructed, forming a kind of yard. This contained a circular timber structure, quite possibly a haystack for what looks like a farm. On the other side of the valley, there was certainly occupation at the same time. A great deal of pottery was found, including Ipswich and Maxey wares as on the site just described, but later damage meant that the contemporary ditches and post-holes could not be understood (Fig 6.4; Dix 1986-87).

Excavation has been able to show how the scatters of pottery found during fieldwalking can indicate settlements. At Brixworth, a parish subjected to intensive fieldwalking which has produced over 19 Anglo-Saxon sites, a small pottery scatter (seven pieces) indicated a site which on excavation turned out to contain a boundary ditch, seven similarly aligned post-built buildings and four sunken structures besides numerous post-holes, pits and hearths. The site, to judge from decorated pottery fragments, began in the 5th century and continued

in use possibly into the 8th (Ford 1995). This was probably a single farm. At Upton forty-five sherds covered a sunken building, several post-holes and possible boundary ditches. This formed part of a much larger area of dispersed or shifting occupation (Shaw 1993-94: Ford 1995). In 1965 an unusually large sunken building 9 by 5½ metres excavated in advance of road works, was, on the evidence of the 60 loom weights inside it, clearly a weaving shed (Jackson *et al* 1969). At Courteenhall the excavation of four Anglo-Saxon scatters produced virtually no features – there was one sunken-featured building – but analysis of the precise location of the pottery finds led to the conclusion that despite the lack of structural evidence temporary, short-lived occupation had in fact taken place. Sunken-featured buildings are by no means uncommon in Northamptonshire. At Grendon, four examples could have been associated with furnaces used for the smelting of bog ore for iron, and a group of at least three found on Northampton Sand at Briar Hill, Northampton can be linked with a group of sites in the Hunsbury Hill area where a smelting furnace and various pits, ditches and post-holes relate to the exploitation of the local ore. Anglo-Saxon pottery has been found in the hill fort (Fig 6.5; Jackson 1993-94, 1995)

Until the second half of the 7th century the Anglo-Saxons in this part of the East Midlands were pagans. Northamptonshire has some 58 pagan cemeteries, almost all of them brought to light through chance discoveries made by workmen digging for minerals or stone or during building work in the 19th or earlier 20th centuries. They are therefore badly recorded. On the basis of the information which has survived, none of the Northamptonshire cemeteries was particularly large. Kettering, Stamford Road and Duston certainly had over 100 burials, but none is known to have approached the thousand or so occasionally known from cemeteries in Norfolk, Suffolk and Humberside (Meaney 1964). It is clear that both inhumation and cremation were practised from the earliest days of the period, and there are many mixed cemeteries, but cremation was more popular in the 5th century. All the known cemeteries lie on permeable geologies and so match the distribution of Early/Middle Saxon sites and in some cases it looks as if they lay close to the settlements they served. At Raunds excavations 100 metres south of the church have revealed the edge of a probably 6th-century cremation cemetery which

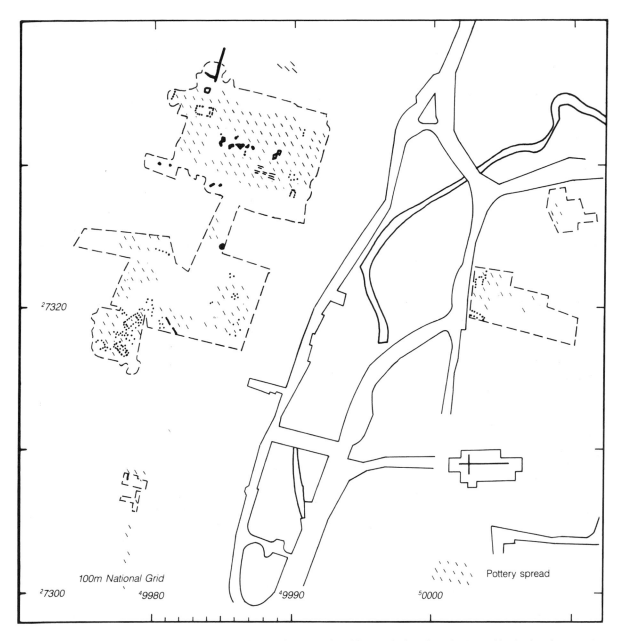

6.4 Raunds, early Saxon occupation, 6th-7th centuries. Reproduced by permission of Northamptonshire Archaeology
© Northamptonshire County Council

would have belonged to one of the settlements described above. At Upton it is possible that a reticella bead (a polychrome ornament formed of glass rods wound around a core, and a high status item) and a swastika brooch, both surface finds, could derive from a cemetery which served the early/middle Saxon settlements. Some burials made use of features derived from the prehistoric past. At Pitsford fourteen cremation urns were found in 1882 in the possible Neolithic long barrow known

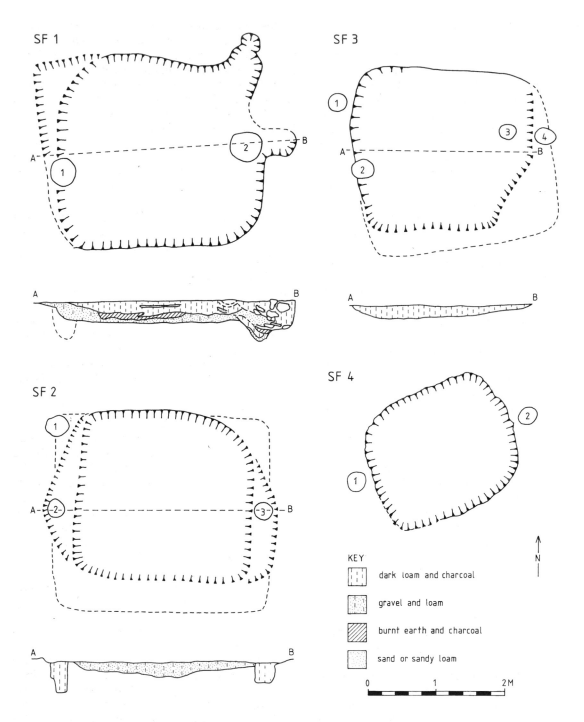

6.5 Sunken-featured buildings, Grendon. Reproduced by permission of Northamptonshire Archaeology
© Northamptonshire County Council

as Lymans Hill. At Borough Hill, Daventry, an inhumation burial of the late 5th-early 6th century with a brooch, buckle, pin and glass beads came from one of the barrows. Recent excavations ahead of road widening at Tansor found the inhumation burials of a woman and a child set in a circular Neolithic or Bronze Age mound. The rather small number of grave goods – beads, silver wire rings, a silver pendant and a plain pot – suggest a 7th century date (Chapman 1996-97).

In the *Ecclesiastical History of the English People* the Venerable Bede (*c*673–735) identified with precision the particular areas of Denmark and northern Germany from which the Angles, Saxons and Jutes came. During the last century the pioneer of pagan Anglo-Saxon pottery studies, J N L Myres, showed that there were sometimes quite striking parallels between pottery found in cemeteries in England and that discovered in the home areas of the invaders, thus in his view enabling the territorial origins of the occupants of some cremation cemeteries to be located. The work has not been without its critics, but nevertheless it is still worth while looking at what he has to say about Northamptonshire cremation urns, because his conclusions about the mixed origins of the settlers here in the 5th century is borne out by the metalwork included in their inhumation burials in the 6th. He thought that some pots with line and dot decoration and with chevrons from the cemeteries at Kettering and Brixworth were of 5th century date and resembled vessels from the lower Elbe region, from which the Saxons came. A pot from Barton Seagrave decorated with facetting he regarded as similar to vessels from this area and from the Weser-Ems coastline, also Saxon. But the Kettering cemetery also produced pots with decoration like vessels of early 5th century date from the Danish island of Fyn and from Schleswig, and so Anglian. The general picture derived thus from the funerary pottery and from the size of the cemeteries so far known is of relatively small groups with traditions originating in a number of north European regions. He was able to point to knobbed pots (*buckelurnen*) from both Kettering and Barton Seagrave which used identical decorative stamps and schemes to those employed on pots from a 6th century cremation cemetery at Girton near Cambridge, evidence maybe of the transference of decorative ideas between regions by women, the traditional makers of pottery, on marriage (Myres 1977).

This mixture of cultural traditions appears again when one considers the metalwork placed in the inhumation cemeteries of the later 5th and 6th century. This shows a highly stratified society concerned with the expression of status, group identity and lineage. Certain men were given weapons, swords being the most prestigious; very few burials of this date range from Northamptonshire had these, and the records, which suggest sword burials at Badby, Cransley and Thorpe Malsor, are early and not very reliable. Others might be given shields and spears, the traditional indicators of free status, or just a spear or a knife; other burials might be unaccompanied. The types of these objects from Northamptonshire male graves tend to belong to the same broad classes as are found elsewhere in southeast England. The ornaments found with female burials are different. The collections of jewellery from richly furnished graves show how women, presumably of a certain status, had a folk costume consisting of a dress fastened at both shoulders with brooches, with underneath it a shift with long sleeves closed at the wrist with fasteners (a fashion derived ultimately from Norway) and held to the dress at the front by a third brooch. Women who lived in the Saxon areas of the Thames Valley had similar overdresses but different undergarments which did not require wrist-clasps; and whereas Anglian women preferred cruciform and certain types of annular brooches, as well as some types of the small-long brooch (a cheap variant of the cruciform brooch), Saxon women used round brooches, particularly saucer-shaped ones, and different forms of the small-long. In Northamptonshire, an Anglian area, we find graves in which both Saxon and Anglian types occur, although the latter predominate. As an example may be cited the overwhelmingly inhumation cemetery of 6th-century date excavated at Wakerley. The majority of the 85 burials were female, and few people were over 45. The jewellery consisted mainly of annular, cruciform and small-long brooches, with poor graves having brooches of the swastika variety; these were all types characteristic of the East Midlands. But there were also four circular brooches belonging to the tradition of Saxon England (Fig 6.6). Of the male graves, the 18 burials just with spears belonged to people aged 17 to 25; the burials with spears and shields (10) were of older men, 25–35, the difference in equipment perhaps an indicator of this. The name of the settlement to which the cemetery belonged could

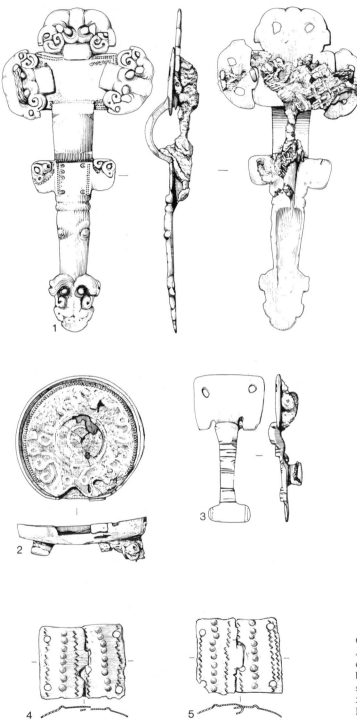

6.6 Wakerley cemetery, grave 74. A mixture of Anglian and Saxon jewellery. No. 1 is a florid cruciform brooch and No. 3 is a small-long brooch, both Anglian types; No.2 is an applied saucer brooch of Saxon derivation. Nos. 4 and 5 are wrist clasps. Reproduced by permission of Dennis Jackson

1. The Iron Age mirror from Desborough (photo: British Museum)

2. The Stanwick long barrow during excavation (by permission of Oxford Archaeology)

3. Grave goods from a Beaker burial at Stanwick (by permission of English Heritage)

4. The beaker round barrow at West Cotton, Raunds during excavation (reproduced by permission of Northamptonshire Archaeology © Northamptonshire County Council).

5. Two Iron Age coins: A Gallo-Belgic E stater (left) and a Whaddon Chase type stater, both found during recent fieldwork at Harpole (photo Mark Curteis)

6. The unique lead torc from the Brackmills burial (reproduced by permission of Northamptonshire Archaeology © Northamptonshire County Council).

7. Reconstruction of the Piddington villa (photo by Roy Friendship-Taylor)

8. The cellar of the villa at Piddington. Note the windows at the end of the building
(photo by Roy Friendship-Taylor)

9. The church at Brixworth

10. The church at Earls Barton

11. Conjectural reconstruction of the Blisworth plateway (painting by Brian Collings)

12. The ornate office range of the Footshape Bootworks, Barrack Road, Northampton

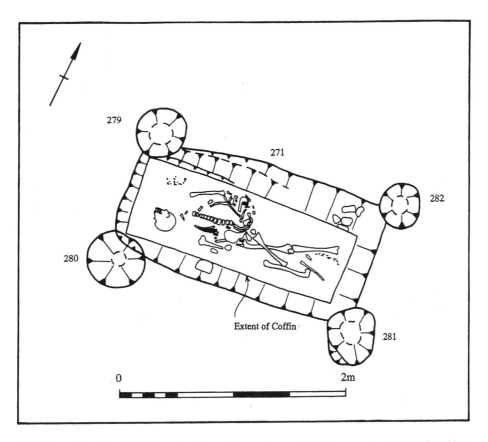

6.7 Great Houghton, late 7th century inhumation cemetery with timber mausoleum. Reproduced by permission of Northamptonshire Archaeology © Northamptonshire County Council

have been Boseley, the name borne by a field some 950 metres away to the west, which has produced some Anglo-Saxon pottery (Adams and Jackson 1988-89).

It was during the 7th century that the kind and also the quantity of jewellery deposited with women changed. Brooches are much less common and we get wire rings, necklaces and pins, sometimes fastened together, all part of a country-wide style of female dress based on aristocratic models derived from late antique prototypes and indicative of an important shift away from a tribally-based society. A small inhumation cemetery of this type containing eight sparsely furnished burials, some with silver wire rings, lay 200 metres to the north-west of the 6th-century example at Wakerley (Jackson and Ambrose 1978). In 1996 a small inhumation cemetery (23 burials) was excavated south-west of Great Houghton. The burials were unfurnished and carefully orientated east-west; a C14 date would

indicate a late 7th century date. These were almost certainly the graves of Christians (Fig 6.7; Chapman 2000-01). At Whitehall Farm, Nether Heyford, recent work has uncovered an inhumation cemetery (five burials so far); one of them, of a young man in a semi-crouched position, was accompanied with a sword and iron knife, clearly a member of the warrior class. Carbon-14 gives a date somewhere in the late 7th to late 8th century; the sword burial was aligned east-west, cutting through an earlier north-south one, and this has led to the suggestion that we may be seeing here evidence for the transition to Christianity.

THE MIDDLE SAXON PERIOD (c. 650-850)

The Christianisation of this part of the Midlands came about because of political changes. In 653 the pagan Mercian king Penda made his son Peada

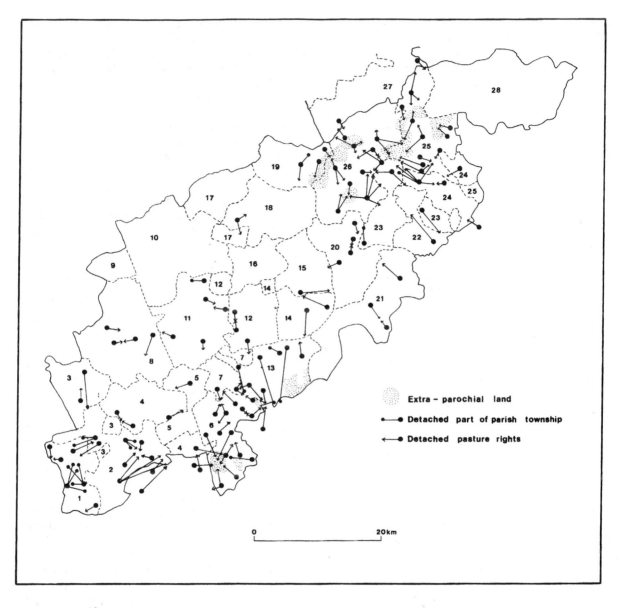

Extra - parochial land

Detached part of parish township

Detached pasture rights

0   20km

Key to hundreds:

1. Sutton	8. Gravesend	15. Orlingbury	22. Navisford
2. Alboldstow	9. Alwardsley	16. Mawsley	23. Huxloe
3. Warden	10. Guilsborough	17. Stotfold	24. Polebrook
4. Foxley	11. Nobottle	18. Rothwell	25. Willybrook
5. Towcester	12. Spelhoe	19. Stoke	26. Corby
6. Cleley	13. Wymersley	20. Navisland	27. Witchley
7. Collingtree	14. Hamfordshoe	21. Higham	28. Uptongrene

6.8 Northamptonshire: hundreds, and detached rights of townships and parishes.
Reproduced by permission of Glenn Foard

princeps (*ie* sub-king) of the Middle Angles, a group of peoples inhabiting the East Midlands; the price of a marriage between him and a Northumbrian princess was the acceptance of a Christian mission in Middle Anglian territory.

A key instrument used by the Mercian kings to maintain control over their territories was the monastery; these in addition to religious activities fulfilled important functions in the machinery of government. One of the greatest in the whole of England had been established in the late 7th century at Peterborough. In Northamptonshire nothing is left of the monastery at Oundle, which was according to his biographer Eddius the location of Wilfrid's death in 709. Nor are there remains at Weedon, founded by Werburgh, the daughter of the 7th-century Mercian king Wulfhere, although a ditch containing sherds of Ipswich ware has been located. At Brixworth, however, where a monastery was established from Peterborough in perhaps the 7th century, there survives one of the best preserved churches of late 8th to early 9th century date in the whole of north-west Europe (Colour plate 9). Excavations in the vicarage garden have uncovered part of a lay cemetery of this date and a length of the ditch which demarcated the monastic precinct on the western side. Very detailed analysis of the building stones of the church has shown how it was constructed out of re-used materials, presumptively of Roman origin, taken from a wide area, including tiles and stone fragments with dowel holes, one with a fragment of an inscription (Cramp *et al* 1977; Sutherland and Parsons 1984).

It is now that the range of available evidence - scrappy references in historical sources from the 8th century, place-names, back-projection of information from Domesday Book, the general distribution of natural resources and the structures of medieval ecclesiastical government – permits a beginning to be made in understanding the administrative organization of the region (Foard 1985). The units of government and land exploitation which emerge from this vary in size. Some were large: Bede refers to the *provincia* of Oundle, his word for a kingdom or sub-kingdom, and the land unit around King's Sutton seems to have been substantial, extending well beyond the present county boundaries.

Within these major units were other centres, such as Fawsley, Brigstock and Yardley Hastings, which had access to a variety of natural resources and had around them places which owed dues and services

based on these, many of which could be subsumed in the Old English word 'soke'. Irthlingborough is an example of such a centre. It is known that Offa was there in 780, because it was at *Yrtlingaburg* that he confirmed a grant by the *dux* (ie sub-king) of the South Saxons to St Pauls of Earnley, Sussex. Clearly there was a royal establishment here, named after a fortified place, which was presumably the focus of a royal estate which could provide the food and other resources necessary to underpin the activities of the king and his entourage. Just where this fortified place might have been was became clear in 1986 when trial excavations through the defences of a hill-fort revealed by aerial photography (see Fig 4.2) showed that this originally Iron Age site had been reoccupied in the Anglo-Saxon period (Dix 1986-87).

At the time of Domesday, some three hundred years later, Irthlingborough appears as part of the soke of Finedon, a place-name name which incorporates the Old English word *thing* , a meeting, and thus the 'meeting place on a hill'. This 'soke' had extensive dependencies north of the Nene but also several south of it in Raunds, Rushden, Irchester and Knuston. In Domesday Book these places were components of a substantial estate centred on Higham Ferrers, evidence perhaps of a once very large unit of administration on both sides of the river. Higham means the 'high *ham*' or home farm, indicative of its function as a central place. On its northern outskirts, aerial photography, fieldwalking, geophysical prospection and finally excavation have revealed an oval ditched enclosure over 100 metres across, largely empty, with to the north-west and south timber structures of the Early and Middle Saxon periods (Spandl 1996). The whole thing looks as if it was intended for the management and collection of stock, not inappropriate for an estate focus at a time when pastoralism was important. The site also shows how the origins of significant physical elements in these centres can sometimes be taken back by means of archaeology to a period far earlier than we might suspect from the historical sources alone.

Two outstanding richly furnished graves take on their full meaning when viewed against the Middle Saxon administrative background. In 1876, during ironstone digging at Desborough, an inhumation cemetery of 40 graves was found within a rect-angular earthwork. The graves were very poorly recorded, but no one could miss the fact that one of

CLASP, DESBOROUGH.

6.9 The Desborough necklace reproduced from Archaeologia, 1880

them contained one of the most remarkable pieces of jewellery to have survived from this period, a necklace consisting of alternating gold and garnet pendants separated by gold wire spacer beads, with an equal-armed cross of sheet gold tubing hanging at the centre (Baker 1880). The significance of the cross is that it is without much doubt a symbol of Christianity, but the obviously high status of the piece is entirely appropriate for someone associated with the fortified residence (Deor's *burh*) within the territorial unit described in Domesday as the royal manor of Rothwell.

Still more significant was the male inhumation burial found in 1997 during gravel extraction beside a Roman road which ran along the southern parish boundary of Wollaston. An oval grave contained an expensive pattern-welded sword within a wooden scabbard. A bronze hanging bowl, an item of high-status feasting equipment, had been clearly an heirloom when deposited in the grave. Most important was the very rare iron helmet, with a simple crest in the shape of a boar (Fig 6.10).

This is an exceptional grave of princely status; it belonged to the later 7th or early 8th century and its

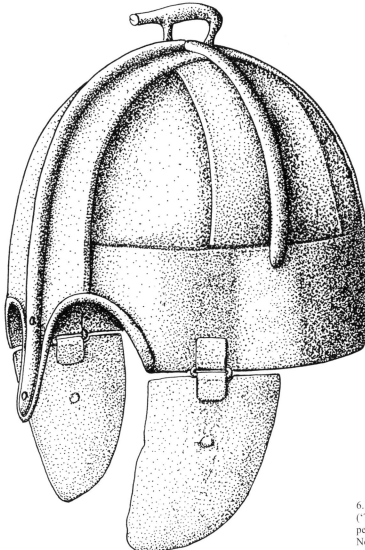

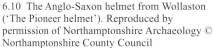

6.10 The Anglo-Saxon helmet from Wollaston
('The Pioneer helmet'). Reproduced by
permission of Northamptonshire Archaeology ©
Northamptonshire County Council

location on the southern boundary of the Hundred of Higham Ferrers would indicate a person associated with the soke belonging to Higham Ferrers and Irthlingborough or just possibly the princely house of the *provincia* of Oundle. A burial in this position was making a statement about territoriality. The statement might originally have been enhanced by a barrow, but this if it existed did not survive (Meadows 1996-97).

The most spectacular excavated structural evidence for the Middle Saxon period comes from Northampton. Evidence for early Saxon settlement has been found in the south-western segment of the medieval walled town in the form of sunken-featured structures, some incompletely preserved post- and trench-built buildings, a scatter of early pottery, some of it stamped, going back to the late 5th to early 6th centuries, a couple of early brooches and a few fragments of glass vessels. On this evidence, early Saxon Northampton looks like an unremarkable rural settlement. But large-scale excavation during urban redevelopment from 1980

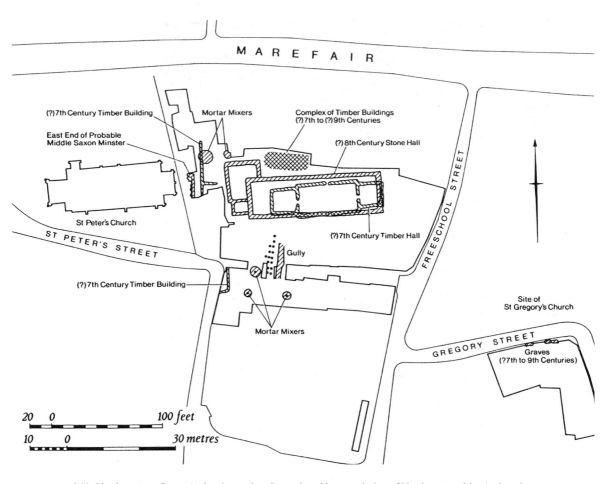

MAREFAIR

(?)7th Century Timber Building

Mortar Mixers

Complex of Timber Buildings
(?)7th to (?)9th Centuries

East End of Probable
Middle Saxon Minster

(?) 8th Century Stone Hall

FREESCHOOL STREET

St Peter's Church

ST PETER'S STREET

(?)7th Century Timber Hall

(?)7th Century Timber Building

Gully

Site of
St Gregory's Church

Mortar Mixers

GREGORY STREET

Graves
(?7th to 9th Centuries)

20   0   100 feet
10   0   30 metres

6.11 Northampton, Saxon 'palace' complex. Reproduced by permission of Northamptonshire Archaeology
© Northamptonshire County Council

to 1982 has shown that at a point in the mid-8th century a very imposing timber hall was built on a site east of St Peter's church (Fig 6.11).

The structure, 29.7 by 8.6 metres overall, consisted of a central hall with annexes at both ends; there were opposing doorways in the centre of each of the long sides. The building had been extremely accurately set out using a module of 1.85 metres (six feet); the bottom of the foundation trench did not depart from the level by more than two centimetres. There were other quite substantial timber buildings to the north-west, but not enough remained of them to appreciate their plans. Then, c. 820 the building was demolished, to be replaced with a remarkable rectangular structure, 37.6 by 11.4 metres, constructed of ironstone and limestone slabs taken

from elsewhere, with some Roman tile. There was evidence for wall plaster with a white lime wash on one side, probably from the inside. At a later date two rather less substantial stone structures had been added on the west. Also, between the hall and St Peter's church was found the square east end of what can reasonably be regarded as the predecessor of the church, constructed in the same way as the additions to the hall. Equally remarkable were five mortar mixers, most of them circular basins 2 to 3 metres across, lined with wattlework and operated by a beam carrying paddles (Fig 6.12).

The site was interpreted at the time as a royal palace, on the basis of analogies with comparable, undoubtedly royal, sites here and abroad. This interpretation would fit in well with general notions

6.12 Northampton,
Saxon 'palace' complex:
8th century mortar mixer.
Reproduced by permission of
Northamptonshire Archaeology
© Northamptonshire County
Council

of the consolidation of royal government in the *regiones* of the Middle Angles during the Mercian supremacy (Williams *et al* 1985). It has recently been suggested however that the site should be regarded as a monastery (Blair 1996). That there was an ecclesiastical connexion is undeniable. St Peter's church is clearly an integral part of the layout, and, since it had parishes subordinate to it in the Middle Ages, Upton and Kingsthorpe, it would qualify as a minster church, one served originally by a group of priests responsible for a wide area. There is also the location of St Gregory's church to be considered, only some 50 metres to the east of the halls, on the same general alignment and so producing the kind of overall axial plan known from monastic sites elsewhere. That St Gregory's was an early ecclesiastical site is shown by the 7th-9th century C14 dates obtained from its graveyard. However, the evidence in favour of monasticism is not absolutely conclusive and it is notoriously difficult to distinguish in this period between monastic sites and high-status secular sites. The name of the place, *Ham tun* , 'home farm' or more significantly, 'central residence', is not encountered until 914; however it is unlikely to have been new at that date and probably predated the Danish invasions. The name is more in accord with notions of secular authority than monasticism.

An increasing number of villages in Northamptonshire have yielded pieces of Ipswich Ware, a superior type of pottery imported into the region and which began to be made in the late 7th/early 8th century. It appears on high-status sites, for example the 'palace' at Northampton, the monasteries at Brixworth and Weedon, significant places within the territorial unit surrounding Irthlingborough (Irthlingborough itself, Higham and Finedon) and at royal manors such as Passenham. But it is also making an appearance in certain villages, including as we have seen Raunds. Raunds at Domesday was in part a berewick of Higham, a detached part of the lordly demesne, concerned with the production of grain. Maybe therefore the settlement associated with this function was already in the 8th century on the site of the present village. Many Northamptonshire villages have produced evidence of Middle Saxon occupation; these sites were the foci around which the Late Saxon and medieval villages were formed. The pottery derived from the excavation or fieldwalking of Middle Saxon sites outside these villages does not contain pieces in Late Saxon fabrics – they had been deserted before *c*850 when these pottery types began to be used. In some cases furlong and field names have preserved the names these places had, more often than not containing the element 'cot' or 'cote' ie cottage, an indication of their subordinate position. It was in the Middle Saxon period therefore that the process began whereby settlement started to concentrate on the places which became medieval villages. There are a number of villages which have embedded in their plans the outline of an oval enclosure, which in the light of the example from Higham Ferrers could

go back to this period or before. There are good examples at Badby, Brixworth and Brackley. At Daventry the oval formed by the street pattern, and within which the church stands, has to the north of it occupation of 6th-century date. At Grafton Regis the medieval village was arranged around the periphery of an enclosure which had occupation of the Iron Age and the Roman and Early/Middle Saxon periods inside (Brown 1991; Brown and Foard 1998). Such layouts may result from the greater and more systematic demands being made by the agencies of royal government and by the church, with its monasteries and minsters. Such demands would have prompted more intensive exploitation of resources as well as a greater definition of rights and obligations within defined territories. The conditions for the creation of the Midland champion landscape were being created.

THE DANES

In 873 the kingdom of Mercia collapsed in the face of Danish invasions. Following the wars with the Wessex of Alfred, the boundary between the areas subject to the Danes and to the English was fixed along Watling Street. Northampton became the focal point for one of the Danish armies. Place-names in Northamptonshire ending in *-by* and *-thorpe* are concentrated east of this line and show the reality of the Danish presence. As part the process of conquering the Danelaw Alfred's son Edward the Elder constructed fortified *burhs;* the *Anglo- Saxon Chronicle* tells us that in 920 one of these was made at Towcester. The Danes of Northampton and Leicester attacked this and failed. Later in the year Edward went to the royal manor at Passenham and remained there while Towcester was given a stone wall; the Danes of Northampton as far north as the river Welland thereupon acknowledged his authority. It was the combining of this tract of Danish territory with a number of Saxon land units west of Watling Street which formed what was to become the county of Northampton.

Archaeological material which might be attributed to the fighting between English and Danes is scanty. There are battleaxes and spears from Borough Hill, Daventry, and a stirrup and other finds from Finedon bridge. The refortification of Towcester seems to have entailed the refacing of the remains of the massive Roman wall and evidence for this may perhaps be seen in the form of the town wall's robber

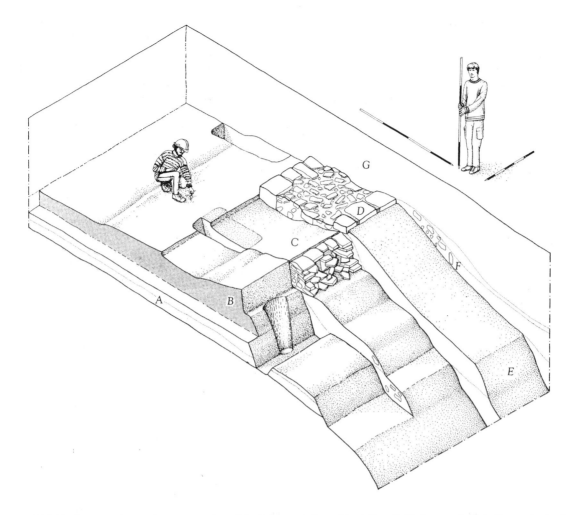

6.13 Northampton: isometric reconstruction of the defences at Green Street. Key: B. Timber revetted late Saxon clay bank C. Later limestone revetment D. 12th century town wall. Reproduced by permission of Northamptonshire Archaeology © Northamptonshire County Council

trench. A defensive ditch could also have been dug at this time (Woodfield 1992). As for Northampton, in 1954 Alderman Frank Lee pointed out in a famous article how the layout of certain streets in the south-western corner of the medieval walled area seemed to define an earlier enclosure of some 80 acres and suggested that this indicated the outline of the Saxon fortified town. Until recently excavations along this line have been inconclusive, but in 1995-6 the south-western defences were located in Green Street. They initially consisted of a clay bank 6 metres wide and over 2 metres high, with a timber revetment and a wide ditch in front; the revetment was later replaced in stone (Fig 6.13). At this point the defences were cut by a metalled road and there were the remains of a timber gatehouse on its southern side. This had been the original access road from the west; the present principal east-west street, Marefair, is the result of a reorganization of the street system when the much more extensive medieval defences were brought into being. The dating of the pre-Conquest defences depends on pottery and is imprecise. The earlier 10th century is suggested, but it is not possible to say whether the construction date falls within or just outside the period of Danish control (Lee 1954; Chapman 1998-9).

THE LATE SAXON PERIOD
(*c.* 850 to MID-11TH CENTURY)

The Late Saxon period brings to the fore aspects of the archaeological record which show that we are clearly entering the medieval world. The formation of the county, first heard of in 1016, entailed also the creation of subordinate units, the hundreds, which in some cases cut through the areas dependant upon the earlier soke centres. The population rose. The open fields can be recognized for the first time, as can the parishes and villages with which we are familiar. The 168 mills recorded in Domesday attest a significant concern with grain production. There is also a greater use of money, an expansion of trade both internal and external and as a result an approach to urbanism. Most of these things may well have had their roots in earlier centuries, but they become visible now in sharper focus and more developed form. A common factor in both rural settlements and field systems is the application of techniques of planning on a large scale.

At Northampton, the Middle Saxon stone hall was abandoned; its walls were robbed for their stone at various times in the 10th century. Much humbler structures appear in this area; there were several sunken-featured buildings, one in the ruins of the hall, and the slots and post-holes of timber buildings, which were loosely arranged around a courtyard entered by a gate. Similar structures appear wherever excavations take place in the south-west of the historic core of the town. Anglo-Danish Northampton seems not to have been a densely built-up place. There is no doubt however about the nature of the activities which went on there. Furnaces, slag, crucibles, turnings and fragments of sheet metal attest the working of iron and copper alloy. The hard grey pottery known as Northampton Ware was manufactured; a fragmentary kiln has been discovered. There is evidence for the working of bone and antler and items of equipment indicate the manufacture of textiles. A site north of Marefair produced crucibles for the working of silver, of particular interest since we know that, from the reign of Eadwig (955–959), Northampton was the location of a mint. Internal trade is indicated by the presence of pottery from Stamford, Thetford and Leicester. A number of stone hones from Norway have been found. All these discoveries are indicative of urban activities and it is therefore not surprising to find Northampton referred to in 1010 as a *port* or place of trade (Williams F 1979; Williams J H 1979, 1982; Williams and Shaw 1981). But commercial activity was growing generally in the Late Saxon period and by the time of Domesday Book (1086) markets are mentioned at Higham Ferrers, Oundle and Kings Sutton, all of them important centres earlier in the Anglo-Saxon period

The common fields of medieval England fell into a number of types. Northamptonshire was in the heart of the Midland system. The dispersal of land throughout the township (the smallest unit of communal land exploitation); the maintenance always of one of the great fields as fallow, for grazing and the retention of soil fertility; the standard farm units (yardlands or in Latin virgates) with their fixed sizes and rights in the keeping of fixed numbers of animals, all show how the system was intended to achieve self-sufficiency and the regulated sharing of resources. The parcelling-out of the arable was achieved by means of the ridge and furrow which until recently was such a familiar feature of the Northamptonshire countryside (Hall 1995). This regularly oversails the early and middle Saxon pottery scatters found during fieldwalking and so post-dates them. Also, the dark, shelly pottery known as St Neots ware, introduced into this area from the late 9th century and appearing in greater quantity from the mid-10th, and which is commonly taken as a marker for the start of the late Saxon period, only appears in ploughed ridge-and-furrow fields as a generalized manuring scatter derived from the villages from which were worked. This suggests that the fields and their associated settlements did not come into being before the late 9th to 10th centuries. The physical components of these fields were not static, and there is evidence to indicate that in places the original plough ridges had been much longer. Also, where sufficient documentation exists, it can sometimes be shown just how carefully these fields were laid out. For example, the two townships in the parish of Daventry were originally rated at twenty hides (a unit used for the calculation of tax liabilities). Each standard hide had four virgates, and each standard virgate thirty (taxation) acres. This would give a nominal taxation rating for the two field systems combined of 2400 acres. But the unusually extensive medieval and later documentation shows that that was the number of acres the field systems actually contained, in real terms; the Anglo-Saxon surveyors had laid out a system of exactly the size they wanted (Brown 1991).

But exactitude and planning extended beyond this into what might be called the social organization of a field system. There are places, for example Great Doddington and Earls Barton, in which the land belonging to different classes of owner or tenant – the lord, freemen and villeins or customary tenants – was laid out in separate blocks in the fields.

The archaeological evidence makes it clear that the process of manorialisation was well under way in the Late Saxon period. Estates were held by lords who were maintained by the produce of demesnes worked by villeins, as well as by dues and services from other tenants, a development which reduced the cohesion of the sokes described earlier. The excavations at Raunds provide an example of this (Fig 6.14).

Here, after apparently a gap in the occupation sequence, the Early/Middle Saxon farm on the western side of the Raunds Brook was replaced at a point between the later 9th and early 10th century, and so within the Danish phase, by a set of four rectangular post-hole buildings grouped around a yard; one of these, well built and with opposed doorways in the long sides, was a residential hall. Subsequently a trapezoidal ditched enclosure was made along the southern side of the yard, with entrances aligned with those of the hall. One of the post-hole buildings lay inside the enclosure. The site at this time looks like a peasant farm. But around 950-975, and so after the English conquest, a dramatic change took place. A ditch was dug at least 230 metres long running north-south and extending outside the excavated area in both directions. At the northern end of the site, this formed the western side of a ditched enclosure an acre in area (0.4 ha), within which was a long timber structure with foundation trenches 37.4 by 4.8 metres, in the northernmost part of which was a hall. This was probably from the beginning, but certainly later, separated by a ditch from domestic parts of the same range. An empty enclosure to the south, again attached to the north-south ditch on the west, was probably for stock. To the south again, and still linked to the long boundary ditch, was a series of rectangular enclosures, some of them containing timber buildings. There can be little doubt that the structures at the northern end of the site represent a manor, the residence of a lord and the place from which his demesne farm was exploited. The size of the structures, the way in which the hall is marked off from the domestic buildings and above all the known subsequent history of the site – it can

be identified with confidence as the manor held by the king's thegn Burgred in Domesday Book, to become known later as Furnells after the de Furneus family who held it in the 12th century – all combine to show that manorialisation has taken place. The buildings to the south of the manorial complex might have been the farms of the tenants (Cadman 1983; Dix 1986-7).

On the opposite, eastern, side of the valley, were more rectangular ditched enclosures in series, also containing timber buildings. The enclosures were on the same general alignment as those on the western side and apparently part of the same phase of major reorganization. What we are looking at is the foundation of what became the medieval village.

Other examples of late Saxon manorial structures are known in Northamptonshire. At Sulgrave the Norman ringwork was found to have below it a hall of sill beam construction, with a central hearth and benches set against one of the walls. There was a service room and detached kitchen at the western end and a solar block, for the private use of the lord and his family, at the eastern end. Perhaps early in the 11th century a free-standing stone building, 7.6 by 3.6 metres, was added north of the hall and an attempt made to fortify the site with a bank and ditch (Davison 1977). The use of stone at this time for a secular building is of great interest. At Nassington, excavations inside the Prebendal Manor House by its present owner (while at the same time living in it) have revealed the post-holes of a structure dateable to c.1000, but the full plan was not recoverable. It apparently had no relationship to the manorial hall of sill-beam and post-in-trench construction which was built in the subsequent century (Foster et al 1989). At Yardley Hastings, small-scale excavations north of the present manor-house and church have uncovered part of a rectangular post-in-trench building of the 10th-11th century, which however overlay a ditch containing pottery of the 7th or 8th century, as well as fragments of mortar, indicative maybe of an earlier high-status building at the centre of the soke of Yardley (Jackson and Foard 1993-94).

West Cotton was a small medieval settlement, originally with its own field system, 2½ kilometres to the west of Raunds, close to the River Nene. Its partial excavation in advance of a major road scheme has shown that it was an entirely new foundation of the mid-10th century, at about the same time as the creation of the manorial layout at the Furnells site. Like the Furnells site, it was very precisely

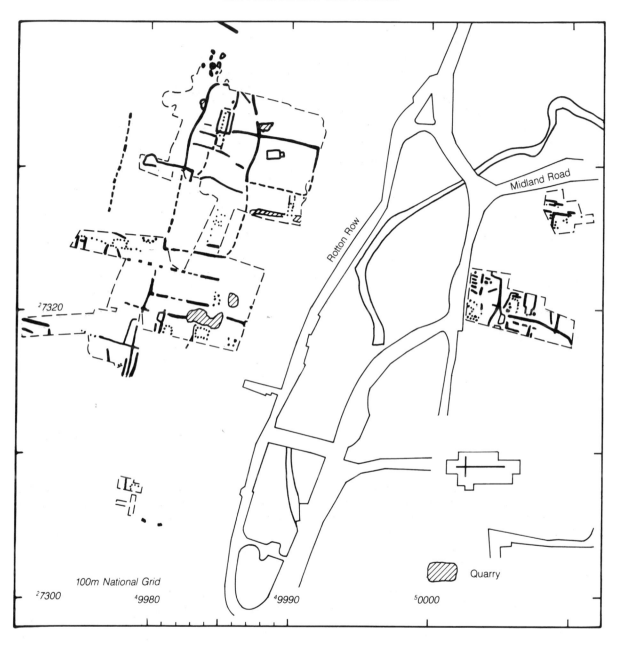

6.14 Raunds, late Saxon phases, 9th-11th centuries. Reproduced by permission of Northamptonshire Archaeology
© Northamptonshire County Council

planned, a near-square of six acres divided into one-acre ditched plots. The northernmost part of the site was occupied by a long timber building rather similar in plan but smaller than the manorial range at Furnells, consisting of a hall with an attached domestic range to the west. There were two empty half-acre enclosures on the south. To the south of these could have been a similar set of buildings and enclosures. The eastern part of the site, substantially undug, on the evidence of domestic rubbish, might

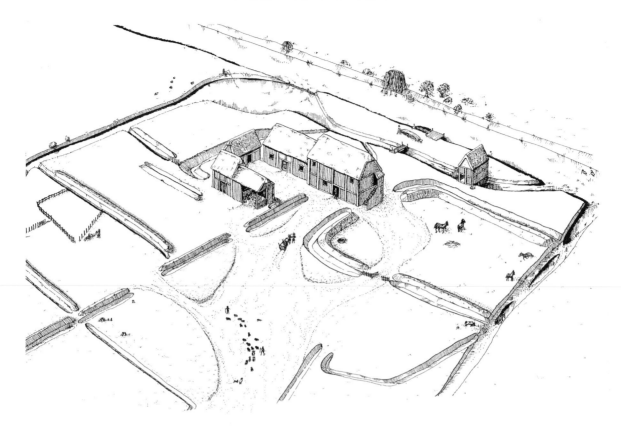

6.15 West Cotton: late Saxon timber buildings and watermill. Reproduced by permission of Northamptonshire Archaeology
© Northamptonshire County Council

have contained peasant tenements. What we seem to have here are the holdings of people of lesser social rank than the manorial lord of the Furnells site, but nevertheless members still of the landowning class. To the north-west of the northern holding was a watermill, at first of undershot type but replaced early in the 11th century by a horizontal wheel and quite probably one of the mills recorded for Raunds at Domesday (Fig 6.15; Dix 1986-87; Windell *et al* 1990).

The West Cotton site provides evidence for the growth in population thought to have taken place during the Late Saxon period. The taking in of land for occupation can also be demonstrated at Daventry, where the site north of the church lay empty for over 300 years; it was then subjected to a phase involving the digging of boundary ditches and pits and the construction of a timber buildings (Soden 1996-97). At Naseby, the settlement known as Nutcote attached to the south of the village was

laid out at this time on the evidence of the dating material found in the boundary ditches which demarcated the plots (Mudd 1995).

Northamptonshire contains several churches with Anglo-Saxon masonry still surviving, mostly of 10th or 11th century date, as at Brigstock and Nassington, both of which, like St Peter's at Northampton, stood at the centre of large dependant land units and may have originated as minsters (Franklin 1984). But most of the parish churches of the county were not like this and started life as one of the appurtenances of a rural manor. Sulgrave is almost certainly an example; the parish church is near to the manor house, is axially arranged in relation to it and has a Saxon triangular-headed doorway re-set in the tower. The Furnells site at Raunds provides a better example. Here a tiny single cell church of stone, only 8 by 3½ metres externally, was built around 975 to the east of the manor house, overlapping the eastern side of the manorial enclosure and making

6.16 Stone crosses and grave slabs, Stowe Nine Churches. Nos 3 and 4 are from crosses of late 9th-early 10th century date; no.5 could have been part of a grave slab of 9th century date; nos 6 and 7 are similar in style and could have belonged to a tomb, shrine or cross of the 9th or 10th century. Reproduced by permission of Paul Woodfield

necessary the cutting of a new boundary further west. A small chancel with a bench for clergy was added; there is evidence for a bell cote from the start. The graveyard, in due course demarcated by ditches, contained 360 burials, including one with a decorated stone cover and possibly a standing cross, interpreted as the grave of the Saxon lord who established the church (Boddington 1996). Such associations with lordship, in the form of patronage, may well explain some of the ten or so Late Saxon cross fragments which still remain in Northamptonshire churches (Fig 6.16).

The celebrated tower at Earls Barton, of 10th or early 11th-century date, is an even more spectacular example of a manorial church (Colour Plate 10). The lowest storey of this, with its monumental western doorway and double windows, is shown by the crosses set on its western and southern faces to have been for religious use, representing the minute nave of the church belonging to the lord of the manor. The storeys above this could well have held bells, and also had a defensive function; but the nature of the tower as a symbol of lordship was probably paramount, since the possession of one was one of the indicators of thegnly status. The tower is placed in a very prominent position at the end of a spur defended on the north by a rampart fronted by a deep ditch, within which the lord's residence probably lay. The name of the place is indicative of the high rank held by him (Audouy et al 1995).

Northamptonshire has a dozen or so of the documents known as to the Anglo-Saxons as landbooks, which record the grant of land by the king usually but not exclusively to ecclesiastics. They can be used by historians for a variety of purposes, but their archaeological interest resides in the fact that a number of them contain clauses which define the land by means of points set along its boundaries. Quite often the points can be identified and the boundaries reconstructed. When this has been done, as has proved possible in the case of the three sets of boundary points of 10th and 11th century date belonging to the area around Badby, one can see precisely how parts of the landscape looked at that time (Brown et al 1978). The main point to emerge is the similarity between the Late Saxon landscape and the present-day one: many of the roads and tracks, the location of bridges and of woodland, and even certain hedge banks, still remain much as the Anglo-Saxons described them. The physical links between our world and that of the Anglo-Saxons are closer than many people imagine.

7

Medieval Northamptonshire

GLENN FOARD

THE SHIRE

The shire, administered from Northampton, was defined in the late Saxon period and remained largely unchanged in extent until the late 19th century. It included the Soke of Peterborough and several hamlets now attached to Banbury in Oxfordshire. Most of the county looked to Northampton and the Nene valley as its core. On the north east, Peterborough was an important satellite centre which was however an integral part of the county because on its north, east and south, unlike today, it was encompassed by a vast tract of largely unoccupied fenland. On the north west, west and south west the peripheral areas of the county looked, as today, towards adjacent counties, with the towns of Stamford, Market Harborough, Rugby, Banbury and Stony Stratford being the dominant centres.

Northamptonshire was administered through 27 'hundreds' in 1086. While various major estate centres controlled the hundredal administration, the hundred moots or meeting places were typically in isolated locations. Six of these were possibly associated with prehistoric burial mounds and others with distinctive topographical features such as groves, and most may prove to have been significant pagan religious sites. Each hundred comprised a number of townships, the smallest administrative unit, usually coincident with the territory of a single village and its land, although many aspects of administration were applied at a manorial level. Purpose-built moot halls are only typically found in towns where separate market courts were held, and in the three self governing boroughs, Northampton, Brackley and Higham, where borough courts were held. Apart from the possible example at Kings Sutton, there is no standing medieval example of a court house, but the sites of a number of moot halls are known in market places in the main towns. Lockups are occasionally found with the markets, but there is no surviving example of medieval date. The vast majority of manors had lesser punishment places including stocks, pillory and ducking stool:

a number of examples of the former survive, some probably of medieval origin. Some manors also had the right of a gallows but only a few sites are known, typically on main roads away from the settlements and sometimes set on mounds.

LANDSCAPE PHASES

The medieval landscape of the county evolved through three main phases. It originated in the period 900-1000, characterised by re-planning of the field systems and rural settlements, associated with a process of manorialisation and accompanied by the development of Northampton as a major urban settlement. This was firmly based upon a phase of major capital investment during the 10th century and many of the major trends that characterise the medieval, in demography, economy and society have their origins at this time. The second phase, from 1000 to the early 14th century saw continuing, rapid agricultural intensification and expansion onto all but the most marginal land with an increasingly intensive exploitation of woodland. In addition the specialisation and intensification of all forms of activity is reflected in a progressive 'formalisation' of the landscape. Accompanying this there was major demographic and settlement growth and large scale town foundation. This reflects an intensification of the market economy, which penetrated to the very heart of rural life. In this the towns were crucial, both as the conduit for much of the growth of local commerce and at the other extreme regional and international trade. Also of importance, but generally neglected in recent study, were the developments in communication and especially of industry in both rural and urban contexts: on these communication a good deal of the urban expansion must have been based. The third phase began in the early 14th century when demographic growth and agricultural intensification had reached a limit. The famines of 1315-22, compounded by an increasingly wet and cold climate, took a major toll on population and led to a brief but significant economic recession. There

7.1 Early hundreds, hundredal manors and hundred moots

had been a partial recovery, both demographic and economic, by the 1340s but then, with the arrival of the Black Death in 1348-9 and successive visitations of the plague in the following decades there was a dramatic demographic collapse, particularly in the years 1361 and 1368-9. There was shrinkage of villages and abandonment of marginal agricultural land, a massive economic recession with decay of most market villages and decline of the small towns and of Northampton itself, reflecting the major decline in commerce and industry. The 15th century saw the first stages of a demographic and economic recovery which led to a distinctively post medieval world. Most importantly in landscape terms there was a major agricultural restructuring. Although much land will have been temporarily abandoned through lack of tenants, especially with migration of tenants from marginal to vacant tenements in wealthier villages, only limited areas reverted permanently to heath and furze. The major agricultural changes of the 15th century involved a reduction in the intensity of exploitation and in particular a conversion to sheep pasture in selected, mainly marginal, townships, in response to changes in grain prices only indirectly linked to the demographic decline. The increasing specialisation in sheep farming, beginning in the 15th century and accompanied by enforced depopulation and enclosure of certain townships, was paralleled by an increase in the amount of pasture in unenclosed townships. There were a handful of attempts at founding new markets but with little success. Commercial activity after the Black Death was to be far more tightly concentrated in the main towns and a very few villages without the wider network of market villages that characterised the 13th and earlier 14th century.

THE EVIDENCE

The medieval period is the earliest for which we have significant survival of detailed documentary evidence and of historic buildings to complement the archaeological record. The archaeological evidence is characterised by a lack of consistent information on monuments of most classes. Though large numbers of archaeological monuments are known, the vast majority, such as mill, manor, peasant tenement and grange, have only been identified from documentary sources. Neither has there been much synthesis of the evidence for medieval Northamptonshire since Steane's study from 1974, completed well before most of the major 20th-century excavation and survey projects were underway (Steane 1974). There are the introductions to the various RCHME volumes and the essay in the RCHME Atlas (RCHME 1980) while a few specific themes have received their own studies, notably open fields and rural settlement (Hall 1995; Lewis et al 1997). However, without

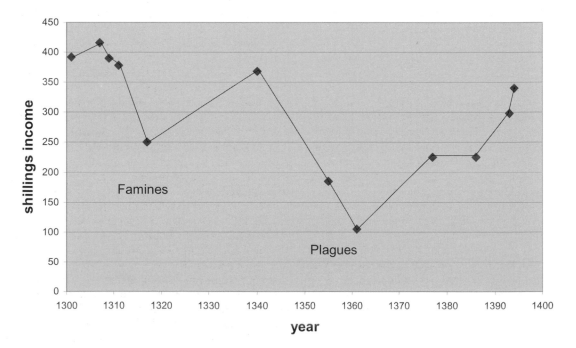

7.2 Graph of Peterborough market income

much more such work it is difficult to judge how representative our excavated examples actually are of the medieval landscape as a whole. Only through extensive mapping from documentary sources has it been possible to begin to address these limitations to provide here a coherent story, drawing also upon the unpublished historic landscape projects conducted by Hall, partly in association with Northamptonshire Heritage (eg Hall 2001).

Most major earthwork sites were surveyed by RCHME in the 1970s-80s, with additional work by Brown and others, while Hall has conducted a unique but as yet largely unpublished countywide survey of Northamptonshire's medieval and post medieval open field systems and other associated land use (Hall 1995). This evidence has recently been presented and analysed for a quarter of the county in the Rockingham Forest Project (Foard et al 2004) (see Fig 7.3). A range of other ground and aerial survey has taken place on earthwork and ploughed sites, including the recording of patterns of manuring as defined by pottery scatters at Raunds and the definition of the extent and character of the medieval iron and charcoal industries in Rockingham Forest. Recently, the Extensive Urban Survey has reviewed all archaeological and much of the documentary and topographical evidence for all smaller medieval urban settlements and market villages in the county (Foard et al 2001), complemented by other work by Laughton (Jones et al 2000). In addition, a major research project is currently under way by the Medieval Settlement Research Group to study the character and evolution of Saxon and medieval settlement and land use for part of Whittlewood Forest in Northamptonshire and Buckinghamshire. This will provide a complement to the study of the largely nucleated settlement and champion landscape examined in the Raunds Area Project (Jones 2000; Parry forthcoming).

A range of major excavations have taken place in both the Raunds area and in the medieval town of Northampton. There have been seven other major excavations of medieval monuments ranging from complete tenements to monastic sites, while a further 15 less extensive but still significant excavations have taken place on other monuments, including various excavations in the pottery production villages of Stanion, Potterspury and Yardley Gobion. There have been at least 72 other minor excavations. Despite this, the vast majority of the medieval monuments in the county and most types of site and

themes have never seen any significant excavation. Intensive investigation, required through the planning process in advance of development, looking at a wide range of sites, particularly in medieval rural and urban settlements, is beginning to raise the level of knowledge of small towns towards that already achieved for Northampton. There are however many important themes which have received relatively little investigation. For example industry, with the exception of pottery production, has not seen systematic study either in a rural or an urban context.

The ceramics of the county are however relatively well studied and a countywide ceramic type series has been compiled, accompanied by an assessment of the current state of knowledge and the priorities for future investigation and enhancement (Blinkhorn 1996). This ceramic sequence means that it is possible in most parts of the county to provide fairly close dating of stratified evidence from ceramics alone. However carbon 14 and perhaps even archaeomagnetic dating will be critical in certain issues, as for example in the identification of iron bloomeries of late Saxon and medieval date from earlier furnaces, because in most cases these remains lie outside medieval settlements and there is very little associated ceramic evidence. For historic buildings the use of dendro-chronology will also be of importance, but at present only a handful of such dates have been obtained for medieval buildings in the county.

Countywide architectural surveys have been conducted by the RCHM in the early 1980s on the country houses (RCHME 1996) and on the medieval churches, though unfortunately the latter has yet to be published. In contrast the survey of vernacular buildings was restricted to a small part of the north east of the county (RCHME 1984). In addition there have been detailed, but as yet unpublished, studies of the historic buildings of Oundle by Heward, while there has been a review of the county's larger medieval secular buildings (Woodfield 1981). However the vast majority of the vernacular buildings in Northamptonshire have not been surveyed and so we know little of the lesser medieval buildings that might survive. There will be few if any from the 11th to 13th centuries other than churches survive. A significant number of manor houses remain from the 14th and 15th centuries, but only a handful of lower-status buildings have been identified. Occasional discoveries are being made, as with a recent identification of a small medieval hall house at Gretton. On the basis of the 677 structures surveyed by RCHM in north east Northamptonshire it seems probable that something of the order of 125 medieval houses may survive countywide, but as few as 40 of these are likely to be of below manorial status. However, as the RCHM study excluded any substantial small town it is possible that the numbers surviving in several settlements, notably Higham Ferrers and especially Oundle, might significantly inflate this figure.

Documentary sources are sparse before the 13th century, though various key documents exist in addition to the Domesday Survey, particularly for certain monastic and royal estates (eg Martin 1978 and 1980). From the mid 13th century onwards the sources become increasingly common both at an estate and countywide level. However there is great variation in the quality and quantity of medieval documentation between different manors and townships, with the royal and especially some of the monastic estates being exceptionally well documented while many of the estates of lesser secular lords are often very poorly documented. There is a high level of continuity, particularly in plan form of settlements, of tenurial structure and of many individual monuments through to the post medieval. Thus, there is a high potential for the use of post medieval documentation, particularly maps and detailed surveys, to provide a topographical framework for both documentary as well as archaeological study of the medieval period. Such reconstruction has been completed for each of the small towns in the county and a few villages, but far more comprehensive coverage is required (Foard et al 2001).

AGRICULTURE

Intensive mixed farming in the form of a common field system was established in the late Saxon period for each community across almost the whole county. The manorial and each of the tenants' land was typically distributed through much of the field system in long narrow cultivation strips now represented by

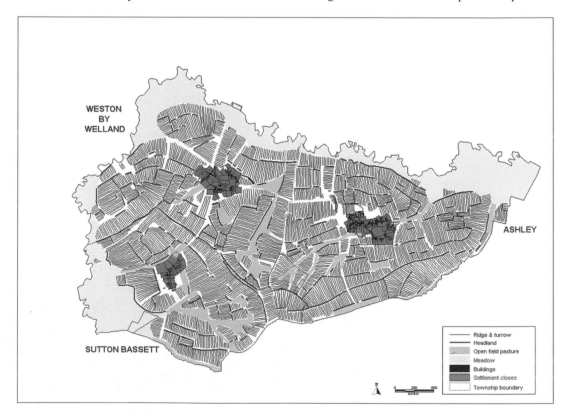

7.3 Open field township in the Welland valley (Foard et al 2004)

the earthworks known as ridge and furrow. In most cases a two or three year rotation was practised, changing between cereals and fallow. Common pasture on the arable after harvest and on the fallow was supplemented in many townships with hay and then after mowing by pasture on the floodplain meadows which were too wet to plough or, where it existed, pasture and pannage (seasonal feeding of pigs on acorns) in woodland and on heathland. Indeed many of the townships seem to have been laid out to exploit this range of resources. Many of those in the Nene Valley for example originally stretched from river meadows up to woodland on the boulder clay watershed or had detached portions of land within more distant woodland. There was very little pure pasture retained within the field systems themselves. Domesday shows this system in place countywide with a dense distribution of water mills already reflecting the high intensity of grain processing which would characterise medieval Northamptonshire. The timing of the transition to intensive mixed farming can probably be dated both

by the archaeological investigation of these mills and through investigation of the rapid alluviation that took place in the river valleys as ploughing destabilised the soils across vast tracts of the county. Excavations at Raunds and elsewhere seem to show this beginning in the 10th century, but far more research is needed in other lesser river catchments countywide to confirm this picture (Robinson 1994).

While some of this land use change may have represented the clearance of woodland, much of the marginal boulder clay land had probably previously been pasture or lightly wooded 'wold'. In some other regions of medieval England such extensive tracts of downland, heath or wood pasture were never cultivated, for there the marginal land was not presumably as suited as the boulder clay to intensive cultivation. By 1086 probably the only land remaining in the county for conversion to arable was the woodland, which then survived in just two main areas, in Rockingham and Whittlewood/Salcey forests. Between the 11th to 13th centuries these saw

7.4 The floodplain meadows of the Nene at Irchester revealed by winter floods.
Reproduced by permission of The Historic Environment Team © Northamptonshire County Council

extensive assarting (clearance for agriculture) to accommodate the rapidly growing rural population. At first these new lands were probably integrated into the common field systems but later assarting apparently resulted in independent land holdings, some containing their own separate hamlets and farms. At the same time there was increasingly intensive exploitation of the best agricultural land at the heart of the common field systems, the main peasant farms being subdivided to support increasing population. There was also intensive manuring to maintain land fertility, as can be seen by the concentration of pot sherds from domestic rubbish scattered on the fields, particularly close to the settlements (Parry forthcoming).

Excavations at Raunds and elsewhere have also begun to provide an insight into the range and relative

importance of crops and animals produced in this mixed farming regime from the late Saxon through to the late medieval (Robinson 1994). A surprising additional contribution to the understanding of the agricultural economy is also beginning to come from study of the crop and weed types preserved in the smoke blackened thatch of a small number of our medieval buildings. Several examples of such buildings are known to survive in the county, best exemplified by the case surveyed at Great Doddington. It is important that we identify all the rest before modernisation leads to the destruction of this unique evidence for a long lost agricultural economy (Letts 1999).

Meadow was a discrete component of many open field systems which was located on the alluvial floodplains of the river valleys. It probably came into

7.5 One of the best preserved and most easily visible areas of ridge & furrow near Crick.
Photo: Glenn Foard

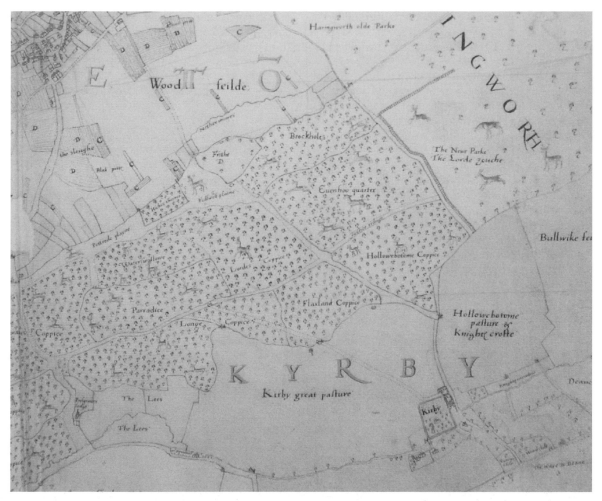

7.6 A landscape in Rockingham Forest in the late 16th century showing deer park, coppice woodland, open field and pastures. Reproduced by permission of Northamptonshire Record Office from the Finch Hatton Archive (NRO FH272)

existence as a result of the large scale alluviation in the late Saxon period, the land no longer being suitable for cultivation due to the periodic flooding. Much more needs to be done to recover evidence about the meadows from pollen preserved in waterlogged deposits in buried river channels. The high rent value of the meadow reflected its great significance in providing grazing and hay for the support of stock in an otherwise intensively arable landscape, since continuing alluviation probably maintained a high level of soil fertility despite annual cropping for hay. Only the common pasture of the woodland and the small areas of heathland and tiny areas of marsh or 'mor', seem to have provided any comparable grazing potential outside the open

field systems for the townships which lacked access to the extensive meadows of the main river valleys. This relative lack of common pasture contrasts dramatically with some other regions of England, outside the 'central province', where there were vast tracts of common pasture on downland or heathland on which communities could graze their stock.

Northamptonshire's field systems have exceptional survival of both documentary as well as archaeological evidence. The latter is best seen in the townships of the north west of the county like Great Oxendon and Lilbourne. Hall has conducted a survey integrating documentary with archaeological evidence to reconstruct the varying pattern of medieval field systems across the whole county.

This nationally unique study, when published, will provide a remarkable insight into the nature of the agricultural landscape and rural economy of the whole county (Hall 1995). It will also reveal important clues as to the origins of the field systems, for it was the establishment of intensive mixed farming which produced the massive increase in the production of grain which made possible the urbanisation of medieval England.

WOODLAND HEATH AND MOOR

Heathland was never extensive in Northamptonshire, being concentrated in four main areas: on Northamptonshire Sand and Ironstone immediately north of Northampton and around Guilsborough; on limestone south of Brackley, part of a wider heathland stretching into Oxfordshire; and in the north of the county near Easton on the Hill, part of a much more extensive heathland mainly within the Soke of Peterborough (Hall 1997). Some heaths have produced extensive evidence of prehistoric and Roman settlement and field systems and even early-middle Saxon settlement, for example on Brampton Heath, suggesting that the transition to heathland may only have occurred in the Saxon period. Substantial areas of heath were undoubtedly converted to common field during the medieval period, but even at the height of agricultural expansion in the early 14th century some areas remained under heath because it was such poor quality land and because of its value for pasture and other products. With the recession of the mid 14th century the extent of heathland expanded again as a result of desertion of the poorest ploughland, only to be lost to agriculture once more following parliamentary inclosure in the 18th and 19th century. For the small number of townships which had rights over the heathland it was probably an important source not only of pasture but also of fuel (turf & furze) in place of those provided elsewhere by woodland. A few rabbit warrens and deer parks, as at Long Buckby, were also laid out on the heathland by medieval lords. Whereas on poor sandy or limestone soils there was a reversion to heathland as a result of the recession of the 14th century, some marginal clay land reverted to 'furze', areas of common pasture covered with varying density of gorse. A good example is seen in the 1810s at Brayfield on the Green, recorded on the Ordnance Survey Surveyors Drawings in the British Library. These furzes were also lost to agricultural

improvement in the 18th and early 19th century and so their distribution can only be reconstructed from detailed documentary research. Both heathland and furze probably developed as a result of low intensity grazing on land that had been abandoned for arable during the recession. However, unlike the reversion in the 5th or 6th centuries AD it seems that sufficient grazing continued to stop a regeneration of woodland.

Woodland was the second major land use in medieval Northamptonshire after arable farming (Foard 2001). Extensive areas of woodland lay largely on boulder clay, in Rockingham Forest between the Nene and the Welland, and in Whittlewood/Salcey Forests between the Nene and Ouse. Despite the late Saxon and medieval clearance, even by the early 14th century, large tracts of land remained covered by trees. Throughout the medieval period this had a major impact on the character and development of settlement and the economy in those regions of the county. The extent of woodland in the medieval period is difficult to reconstruct but can be estimated from the mapped distribution of post medieval woodland combined with the evidence from Domesday and of medieval assarting. With the increasing pressure on land the management of the woodlands also became more intensive with the laying out of coppices enclosed by banks and ditches. The coppice wood was periodically harvested and then dead hedges constructed and maintained on the banks for a few years to protect the re-growth from the browsing of deer and stock. For communities in these regions, the woodland was important not only for wood products but also for grazing of stock. Indeed some tracts of woodland may have been cleared through intensive grazing, for some common pastures of the post medieval contain extensive distributions of charcoal hearths (see below) showing that they had been wooded at some time in the medieval period. However by far the greatest impact on the woodlands was clearance for agriculture. Early in the medieval this appears to have continued by the incorporation of land into the common fields of existing nucleated settlements. By the 12th or early 13th century however woodland clearance seems to have resulted in land held in severalty and with some of these areas being farmed from new isolated settlements. These ranged from large manorial establishments, of which Biggin Grange in Oundle was by far the largest, to minor farmsteads.

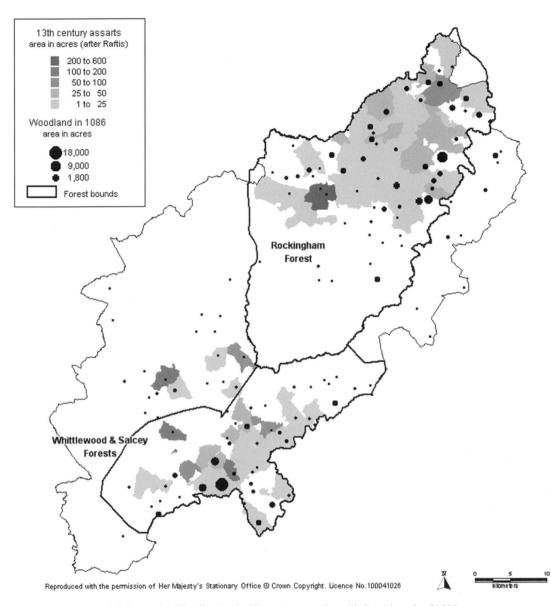

7.7 Domesday Woodland and 13th-century assarting with forest bounds of 1286

HUNTING FORESTS AND DEER PARKS

The main woodland areas became royal forests after the Norman conquest, administered for the king primarily for the management of deer, though the territories also encompassed large areas of arable land and settlements (Pettit 1968; Steane 1973a). The forests were progressively expanded in the 12th and 13th centuries, but in 1299 the forest bounds were redrawn to encompass a much smaller area, concentrating mainly on the surviving woodland. In addition to royal hunting in the forest, which is documented as early as 1086 in Rockingham and Whittlewood, there were a number of private hunting preserves in the forests, most notably Geddington Chase and Yardley Chase, attached

111

7.8 Remnants of woodland in the heart of the medieval forest, around Lyveden.
Reproduced by permission of The Historic Environment Team © Northamptonshire County Council

to major medieval manors. However much of the management and hunting of deer by the 13th century, by both the crown and other lords, was in clearly defined deer parks mainly laid out within the woodland. A few parks were created in the 12th century but most were established in the 13th and some in the earlier 14th century, at the height of intensification of the exploitation of the medieval landscape. A few more were established in the later 15th century (Steane 1973b). Although some deer parks may have decayed in the late medieval period, most were not disparked until the post medieval. Hunting lodges were constructed in most parks while some manors, such as the royal manors at Geddington and Rockingham, were developed as major hunting lodges. There were also a number of small medieval parks adjoining manor houses or other residences, as at Fotheringhay Castle with its Little Park, which may have served a similar recreational function to the post-medieval parks associated with country houses. These and a few

other parks, such as the Queens Park at Brigstock, were created from agricultural land. A few parks were also created on heathland, but most were within woodland, with areas being cleared for lawns for both grazing and the hunt. The continuing discovery of small numbers of parks suggest that a significant number still remain to be identified while many more require definition of their boundaries and identification of their lodges. The earthworks of the pales, now surviving just as a bank with an internal ditch, but originally surmounted by a deer-proof timber fence, vary enormously in scale, from features up to two metres high as at Biggin near Oundle to almost non existent banks as at Grafton Regis. A few were even constructed with stone walls rather than timber pales, as at Moulton Park, but the only surviving examples are probably of post medieval date, as with the remarkable 2 metre high wall surviving around part of Harringworth Park. A number of park lodges are known as earthworks, for example the moated Old Lodge in Brigstock Great Park, while at least two have surviving medieval lodge buildings, at Higham Park and Harringworth Park.

RURAL SETTLEMENTS

Medieval Northamptonshire was characterised by a highly nucleated settlement pattern, usually with a single nucleated village within a single township. There were some hamlets with their own land unit, however other hamlets or farms lay within the same township as a nucleated village (Brown et al 1975). A dispersed settlement pattern existed in just three small areas of the county, in the Lyveden valley in the south east part of Rockingham Forest, at Hartwell in Salcey Forest and in the southern part of Whittlewood forest. The latter two were part of a wider pattern of dispersed settlement in north Buckinghamshire. This pattern may prove to be the result of late colonisation of woodland, but there are hints, in the concentration of hamlets

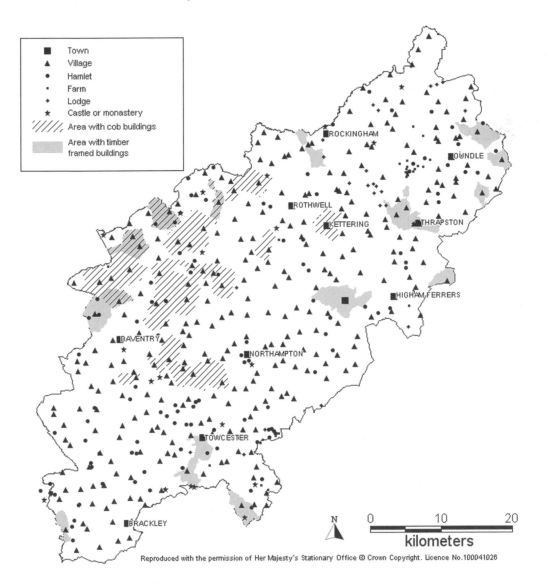

7.9 Medieval settlements with areas of known cob and timber frame construction indicated

around Towcester, that in part there may be earlier origins that will cast light on the whole process of settlement nucleation in the Saxon period. Occasional castles, manors, churches and monastic sites of medieval origin, due to strategic and other considerations, also lay in isolation. The only widely-distributed dispersed components of the settlement pattern were the medieval water mills and, mainly in the woodland zones, the deer park lodges. The settlement pattern of the open field landscape is relatively well known, due to the high level of nucleation and the ease with which old enclosed land can be identified from post medieval sources. However, in the woodland areas, especially in Whittlewood, where there were extensive areas of ancient enclosure and large areas of land never incorporated within open field, a significant number of isolated farms and one or two hamlets probably await identification.

The size and wealth of settlements in the medieval period can be assessed from Domesday and the various 14th century national taxations, with the 1524-5 subsidy providing a final assessment for the period (Lewis et al 1997). This shows a pattern of higher wealth in the townships on the permeable geologies, particularly in the Nene and Ise valleys where there was extensive good quality agricultural land and access to meadow. In contrast the boulder clay capped higher ground was generally poorer and had a lower density of population, as were the townships of the north west which lacked both meadow and woodland resources.

Although there are notable exceptions, like Raunds and Warmington where there has been intensive excavation or like Irthlingborough which has exceptional documentary sources, the settlements themselves have yet to reveal much of their history and character. The large number of deserted and shrunken villages provide extensive evidence of the character of medieval settlement without the confusion of later occupation, but it must be remembered that they are unrepresentative: these tended to be smaller villages or hamlets on the more marginal land (Allison et al 1966). Earthwork surveys have been conducted on most of these sites, revealing the plan form. Occasionally, as at Blatherwycke and Catesby, aerial survey in very dry conditions can add remarkable detail of buildings and tenements, but only where the buildings had stone foundations. Where cob or timber framing was the norm for building construction then the evidence

from the earthworks is far more difficult to interpret and, as at Clay Coton, may not yield clear results even from excavation. Those deserted sites which have been damaged by ploughing can yield extensive surface scatters of pottery telling something of their origin and growth, but only one or two of the ploughed sites, such as Newbold in Catesby, have been systematically field-walked. Equally few sites have seen any significant excavation, the most complete examples being the tiny hamlet of West Cotton in Raunds (Chapman forthcoming) and the unpublished excavations at Faxton.

Excavations have taken place within surviving villages, in an attempt to provide a more representative picture of medieval settlement than that derived from deserted sites. However these have usually addressed restricted issues of village origins, as at Warmington, and industrial production, as at Stanion and Weldon. Even where major excavations have taken place within living villages, as at Rraunds, the evidence has been mainly from deserted areas with surviving earthworks. Investigation of occupied areas, during redevelopment or infilling, produces far poorer results but is important in completing the picture of the topography and chronology of settlement development. The settlements which have seen major decline, such as Fotheringhay, are likely therefore to be the ones where future investigations have the greatest potential.

Detailed documentary research on settlements such as Irthlingborough and Kettering has shown the great complexity of our nucleated settlements with varying function and status of tenements. At Kettering for example, in 1400 the virgate tenements were concentrated in one part of the settlement. In contrast in Irthlingborough, in addition to the manor of the Abbot of Peterborough, there were a number of subsidiary manors with tenements concentrated in different ends of the village and interspersed with a number of freehold tenements. While a great deal of the expansion of the 11th and 12th centuries may have been accommodated by infilling, within the framework of regular but often unoccupied plots that had been laid out in our villages with the Great Replanning of the 10th century, later growth seems to have required the addition of new rows, sometimes called Newlands. Such rows are identifiable because they are wholly of cottagers or other tenements with little field land. Expansion was also achieved by the subdivision of virgate (often circa 30 acre) or even carucate (circa 120 acre) farms to create a

7.10 Excavations of medieval tenements at West Cotton. Reproduced by permission of Northamptonshire Archaeology © Northamptonshire County Council

larger number of smaller holdings of half or even quarter virgates. This shows how unrepresentative the excavation of just a few tenements may be in a village which may have comprised as many as 50 or 100 (Foard, in preparation).

Few if any medieval peasant houses are likely to survive in the county, though there are a few late medieval examples of the homes of the wealthiest farmers. Until the 12th or 13th century, most buildings apart from important manors and churches are likely to have been of timber with earth set posts or sill beams. At Raunds, in the heart of the stone area,

7.11 A hollow way running south from Kirby Hall with peasant houses and farms on either side.
Reproduced by permission of The Historic Environment Team © Northamptonshire County Council

Furnell's manor was only rebuilt with stone from the late 12th century. Post-medieval standing buildings provide a broad guide to the likely zones of medieval building traditions after this transition; the types comprised stone, cob and timber frame roofed with thatch, stone slate and tile. The limited number of excavations in the county can be related to this pattern though the evidence from some excavation is equivocal. At West Cotton complete construction in stone is indicated for peasant buildings in the 13th century. At Faxton cob building is attested from the 12th-13th century when a transition was noted from timber construction, while in the 14th century some stone buildings were identified.

Northamptonshire, with its large number of well preserved earthworks sites of deserted and shrunken villages, is well placed for the study of the dramatic changes which began with the famines and then the plagues in the 14th century. There are a few places like Catesby where the combined study of extensive late medieval documents and well preserved settlement remains provide a valuable insight into this period of recession, depopulation and reorganisation of the agricultural economy. However it is unclear what proportion of tenement clearance was due to the impact of the famines and plagues rather than the major losses known from conversion of arable to sheep farming in the 15th century.

MANORS AND APPURTENANCES

The driving force within the medieval rural landscape was the manor. As a result of subinfeudation, manors increased substantially in number during the medieval period. The vast majority of the manor sites still remain occupied but only a small number have surviving medieval fabric from either the manor itself or the ancillary buildings. A significant number of manor sites do survive as earthworks, but many more especially of the smaller manor are likely to remain unrecognised within our village earthworks. Most of the substantial surviving medieval secular buildings are manor houses (Woodfield 1981), but only one standing medieval manor house has been subject to major excavation, Nassington Prebendal Manor (Baile 2002). Although an important manor originating in a royal estate centre and held in the medieval period by the Bishops of Lincoln, the site

7.12 Shutlanger manor house. Photo: Glenn Foard

has revealed what is likely to have been a common story. It originated in the late Saxon period and was rebuilt and expanded throughout the medieval. A similar sequence but of somewhat lower status has been revealed in the excavation of Furnell's manor at Raunds and of another probable manorial site at West Cotton in Raunds. Furnell's showed the whole grouping of buildings with a hall with associated rooms, detached kitchen/brewhouse, dovecote and an associated church and cemetery. What was not clearly resolved from the Furnell's or the West Cotton excavations was the issue of the scale and character of the structures associated with the demesne farm. Medieval documents from other manors reveal the range of buildings that are to be expected, including beast houses, barns, granary, malt house and sometimes even a horse driven malt mill, most if not all of which may be expected to lie in an associated courtyard adjacent to the main residence. Other components might lay adjacent such as the gardens and orchards or more distant still, such as the sheepcote, rabbit warren and fishponds. At Higham Ferrers there was even a vineyard. Demesne farm complexes appear to survive in good condition on a number of earthwork sites, such as Mallows Cotton, but individual items such as dovecotes or sheepcotes are rarely identifiable. As yet, no demesne farm courtyard with a wide range of buildings has been excavated, although a small number of ancillary buildings were examined in major excavations at West Cotton near Raunds. Recently the barn, malting and dovecote of a subinfeudated manor have been excavated at Irthlingborough. The character of these manorial sites can be seen from a handful of surviving medieval buildings across the county, such as the manor houses at Shutlanger and Nassington, the medieval barn at the de Bray manor at Harlestone and the dovecote at Nassington.

Unlike deer parks, the warrens established for breeding rabbits could lie close to the manor, as with the stone walled 'conigree' adjacent to Higham Ferrers castle. This was large enough to also contain

7.13 Fishponds at Braybrooke. Reproduced by permission of The Historic Environment Team
© Northamptonshire County Council

fishponds providing better protection for both from the depredations of peasant poachers, though some warrens lay at the very edge of the township as at Whiston (Brown 1974). There are many known but many more to be discovered and, unlike the deer parks, they were not concentrated in the peripheral woodland zone. At Fotheringhay for example the 'pillow mound' in which the rabbits were to burrow was laid out on top of ridge and furrow, the Master of the College there having laid out the warren on top of former common field strips adjacent to the village (Foard et al 2001). Rarely did these warrens have lodges, probably because they were both small and often close to the manor itself, but a handful of medieval warreners' lodges are known. There is a similar association of warrens to woodland and heathland as seen with deer parks but there are also significant numbers in association with settlements and on enclosed open field land.

Fish from both river fisheries and, increasingly during the medieval period, from specially constructed fishponds, were a significant component of the demesne economy. Fishponds have been subject to detailed study through earthwork survey because they produce physical remains out of all proportion to their relative importance (Steane 1970). In contrast, the fisheries in the rivers, which may have had a far greater importance to the demesne economy have received little attention, being known archaeologically only from the weights for the eel traps which were typically associated with mills. Most manors constructed fishponds but the scale of fishponds varied enormously from the major complexes such as Braybrooke and Harrington to the tiny moated ponds such as that belonging to Higham Ferrers College. Fish were also bred in moats and other man made bodies of water such as mill ponds. The proliferation of fishponds during the medieval period is yet another example of the intensification of the rural economy.

MONASTIC HOUSES AND ESTATES

In 1066 there was just one monastic house in Northamptonshire, the great fenland abbey of Peterborough. The Abbot was then one of the major landowners in the county, while various other abbeys such as Ramsey, Crowland and Evesham had important estates in the Northamptonshire. In contrast, by the later medieval period, there were 65 monastic houses across the county. Of these 16 were abbeys or priories, 21 hospitals, 15 hermitages and 7 secular colleges, while hermits and anchorites are also recorded in a number of Northamptonshire parishes. These lesser monastic sites were progressively established and endowed by manorial lords and other wealthy residents, the trend being for smaller establishments as time progressed, finally shifting in the later medieval

period towards the foundation of secular colleges, chantries and even of grammar schools rather than monastic establishments. The main concentration of monasteries was in Northampton and its suburbs, where there were 16. The other main towns in the county generally included several monastic houses, mainly hospitals, except where the manor was owned by a major monastery, as with the Peterborough Abbey manors of Kettering and Oundle and the Crowland manor of Wellingborough.

There were extensive antiquarian excavations on Canons Ashby priory (Audouy 1991) and Pipewell Abbey and lesser work on Fotheringhay College and Higham Ferrers College. Major modern excavation, as yet unpublished, have been completed on Grafton Regis hermitage (Parker 1981) and recently on the church, ancillary buildings and especially the cemetery of St James's Abbey in Northampton's

7.14 St John's Hospital, Northampton.

western suburb. Extensive earthworks survive for the sites of Pipewell Abbey and Perio Hospital near Southwick. Following the dissolution in the 1530s a number of the monasteries were converted into country houses, as at Delapre by Northampton and at Catesby, but in every case later demolition or conversion means that all standing evidence has been destroyed. There are however surviving buildings at St John's Hospital Northampton, St John's Hospital Brackley and Higham Ferrers College, while there are parish churches which were integral to several other monasteries, including Canons Ashby priory and several of the Colleges, as at Irthlingborough and Cotterstock.

The estates of monastic houses are generally the best documented of medieval estates and the national surveys of 1291 and 1535 provide a unique picture of the distribution of these estates. Though in some respects they may have been atypical, they offer a high potential to explore various aspects of the medieval demesne economy, especially through the integrated investigation of central house and dependent holdings through both archaeological and documentary evidence (Page 1936). However only Badby Grange has yet been extensively excavated although other sites appear to survive as earthworks at Cold Ashby and Braybrooke.

THE CHURCH

Although Domesday mentions only one church in the county, the recording of priests in 59 other manors almost certainly indicates the presence of other churches. However many more churches must have been omitted from the record: churches with Saxon work, such as Greens Norton and Earls Barton, are in manors for which no priest was recorded. More than 380 churches and chapels are known from documentary, architectural and archaeological evidence to have existed in Northamptonshire by the end of the medieval period. Of these only four lie isolated outside a medieval settlement, at Great Oxendon (Fig 7.15), Harrington, at the important fair site at Boughton Green and at Wadenhoe next to a probable manorial site. Excavations have taken place in at least 24 churches, but of these only two were major antiquarian excavations, at Canons Ashby and Irthlingborough, with just two major modern excavations at Brixworth and the nationally important excavation of both church and cemetery at Raunds Furnells (Boddington 1997). Although the

RCHME have studied all the standing churches in the county, detailed architectural analysis has taken place only at Brixworth and on Earls Barton tower, both to examine Saxon fabric (Richmond 1986).

Manor and church were typically closely related, with the devolution of manorial authority frequently being accompanied in the late Saxon period by devolution of ecclesiastical authority, the lord often constructing the church immediately adjacent to the manor house, as at Furnell's manor in Raunds. In a few cases the Saxon pattern seems to have survived through the medieval period, where the fragmentation of the authority of old minster churches was never completed. Hence at Towcester for example a large parish encompassed a number of separate settlements, some having their own subsidiary chapel but other hamlets lacking any church or chapel. In most cases however the ecclesiastical arrangements, which had become largely fixed by the 13th century, were of a single township and village with a single parish. Although manorial authority was frequently fragmented below this level, this rarely occurred with parishes: only 11 villages are known to have had two churches. Of these 7 had two separate parishes (Aldwincle, Barnwell, Blatherwycke, Cranford, Irthlingborough, Maidwell, Rushton, and probably Raunds). The others are subsidiary chapels at Warmington, Weedon Bec and the standing buildings at Harringworth and Charlton, and it seems likely that some additional chapels will be identified in future in other villages. Urban churches represent a distinctive group. There are four towns with more than one church: Northampton had nine churches and at least two chapels, with multiple parishes; Brackley two churches and two parishes, Oundle two or possibly three chapels in addition to the parish church, all in one parish, and Higham Ferrers an additional chapel in one parish.

Accompanying the churches there were rectorial farms for the support of the priest, comprising a large tenement, typically adjacent to the church, with land in the common fields and other rights as well as the income from tithes. Many of these rectories were appropriated by monastic houses, who diverted most of the income to their own house and appointed a vicar, who had a much smaller glebe and the income of just the small tithes, to provide for the spiritual needs of the parish. None of these rectories or vicarages have been examined archaeologically.

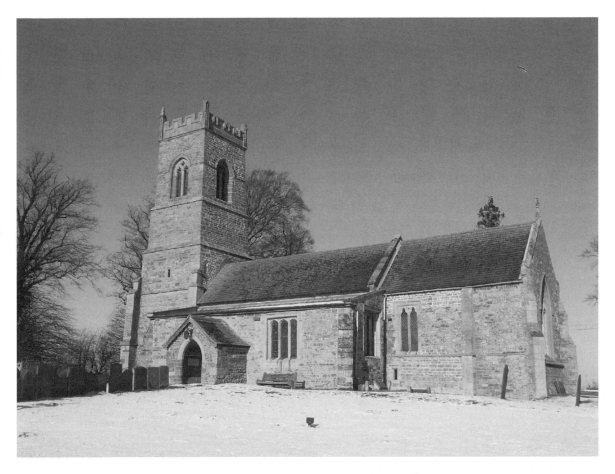

7.15 Great Oxendon Church. Photo: Glenn Foard

While most medieval churches continue in ecclesiastical use today, the best archaeological survival is likely to be in the small number of churches, like Furnell's in Raunds, which were deserted in the medieval or even the post medieval period, as with Catesby in the 16th and Clopton in the late 19th century. In some cases, as at Catesby, Boughton Green and Brackley St James, the abandoned churches continued to have functioning churchyards into recent times but there are at least 28 deserted churches, while other undocumented early medieval churches similar to that at Furnell's probably await discovery. A few isolated finds of burials within medieval settlements, as at Titchmarsh, may indicate sites of such chapels, while others lie in some of the deserted villages in the county. The combination of well preserved church and cemetery in association with extensive settlement remains as at Blatherwycke or Sulby may offer the greatest potential for the integrated study of a church and its community, both the buried population itself and their farms.

TOWNS, COMMERCE AND COMMUNICATIONS

Commerce must have expanded rapidly in late Saxon and early medieval Northamptonshire, and with it came urbanisation. Periodic fairs are likely to have been the earliest commercial foci of the Saxon market economy, before the first towns were re-established in the county. Some fairs will have been located at hundred moots or other religious sites. Only one possible early fair site can be suggested at present, that at Boughton Green, associated with a

7.16 Settlement remains at Blatherwyke, visible as parchmarks.
Reproduced by permission of The Historic Environment Team © Northamptonshire County Council

7.17 Towns, markets, villages and major roads

holy well and turf maze which are almost certainly of pagan origin. Other fairs were possibly at major estate centres, where the earliest documented markets and fairs are found. Many new annual fairs were established in response to the rapid growth in the medieval economy in the 12th and 13th centuries, almost all located in towns and market villages. They continued to serve an important commercial function enabling large scale exchange of often specialised goods, though there is little documentary evidence for them other than their foundation charters and records of the tolls collected by the lord. However it was the proliferation of weekly markets which was the most important indicator of the speed and extent of commercial development countywide. They were intimately linked to the development of towns, though as the 13th century progressed more and more markets were founded in settlements which never succeeded in making the transition from village to town. In 1086 one borough and three other market settlements were recorded in the county. By 1349 there had been attempts to found markets in a further 36 places (Goodfellow 1987). Though a few grants were apparently never implemented and some markets failed very quickly, the majority did function if only in most cases on a very modest scale. While most of these settlements remained just market villages a small number, especially the earliest foundations, developed as true towns. The competition was intense. While Northampton in the later 13th century considered its exclusive hinterland should extend 12 miles, as far as Wellingborough and Towcester, the lesser towns will have mainly served a territory of about 7 miles radius. Any new town foundation attempted within this zone usually led to failure. Of the 13th-century foundations there were only two that were successful in the long term, Wellingborough and Kettering ultimately supplanting their neighbours.

At the conquest Northampton was the county's only borough and probably its only true town (Foard 1995). It expanded beyond the defences of the Saxon *burh* with the planning of a new borough soon after the conquest and then subsequently expanded along the major roads and also along new subsidiary streets, possibly part of a regular, planned growth. This growth saw the transformation of the town with a new commercial focus around the market place, just outside the gates of the original *burh*, accompanied by a realignment of the major road system with a new bridge on the London road. However significant parts of the area encompassed by defences in the early 12th century seem to have remained largely undeveloped. The first comprehensive overview of the industrial and commercial base of the town is in 1524, which reveals the textile (broadcloth) and leather trades represented 17% and 25% of trades respectively (Dyer 1978). However the service, distributive and food trades comprised 40% of the occupations

7.18 Higham Ferrers market place and medieval market cross. Photo: Glenn Foard

of Northampton, showing the importance of basic marketing for the county and particularly the town's immediate hinterland. In contrast, farming comprised just 6% of the occupations. Despite the importance of the cloth industry in the 11th to 13th centuries, there is little significant evidence of that industry from excavations. This may in part be because the industry was concentrated in areas of the town which have not been the subject of modern excavations, as is suggested by the presence of the Scarlet Well, so named from the effect of the dyers activity there.

Borough status was granted to several other towns which grew out of villages in the 12th and 13th centuries, notably Higham Ferrers and Rothwell, but only one new planned town became a self-governing borough. This was Brackley, which had risen by the 13th century, through the profits of the wool trade, to become by far the largest and wealthiest of the county's towns, after Northampton. The non agricultural tenants of other towns such as Oundle and Daventry were also granted burgage tenure with its various freedoms, but these settlements did not achieve self governing borough status (Brown 1991). In contrast Wellingborough and Kettering, where the artisan cottagers were never granted any special freedoms, grew rapidly at the expense of their adjacent boroughs of Higham Ferrers and Rothwell. All of the towns, even Northampton, retained their open fields and in some of the small towns there were as many tenants employed in agriculture as were involved in commerce and industry.

There are just two market settlements where extensive archaeological remains survive as earthworks, the shrunken settlement of Rockingham and the deserted Lower Catesby, neither of which were much more than market villages. Most of the county's market settlements and especially the true towns are still occupied today, some having been intensively redeveloped in the 19th and 20th centuries. The topography of these settlements is sometimes complex but for some settlements it can be reconstructed in detail from documentary sources, revealing clear evidence of the nature and

7.19 Daventry market place in the 1970s. Photo: Glenn Foard

chronology of urban growth. With such evidence it is then possible to effectively target archaeological investigation when redevelopment takes place and in Brackley, Oundle, Daventry and Towcester this has begun to reveal important information about the character of the county's medieval urban settlements (eg Soden 1996). The most intensively studied town still remains Northampton where tenement rows in a number of streets have been excavated (eg Williams 1979).

The wool trade was probably the most important commercial activity in Northamptonshire, with some merchants directly involved in international trade. This brought high wealth for some merchants, notably in Northampton and Brackley, which was invested in substantial town houses and, particularly in Northampton, will have contributed to the construction of the town's defences, monastic houses and churches. The county was also a producer of broadcloth and this also formed a significant component of the urban commerce. It is not yet clear how quickly trade in leather and leather products grew, forming the foundation for its dominance of the county's industry and commerce in later centuries. The towns also of course provided a wide range of goods and services to their local hinterlands with the larger towns having the widest range. Hence we find in Northampton and Brackley the trades range from ironmongers to goldsmiths.

The market place with its shops and market stalls was the focus of commercial activity and attracted to it many of the major houses and in the late medieval period the inns and alehouses, where many of the deals were struck. Particular goods were typically segregated into sections of the market place with wool markets and drapery rows being represented in various towns as well as the ubiquitous butchers rows. Market places probably started as large open areas but rapidly saw infilling with the construction of rows of permanent shops and of temporary stalls. The stalls became increasingly permanent and some shops were later converted into tenements. Market halls were set on the market place, but no medieval example survives in the county and unfortunately the remaining shop rows and market halls were cleared away with the Improvement Acts of the 19th or earlier 20th century. Only in Higham Ferrers and Northampton do significant rows still survive on their medieval footprints, but it is highly improbable that any medieval structures will survive in either case.

While commerce was the initial and core function of all the towns it did not have major labour requirements: only if a settlement also developed a significant industrial base would it grow into a substantial town. Hence several of our towns, such as Thrapston, have been successful since at least the early 13th century as local trading centres but remained smaller than the wealthier villages. While Thrapston and Rockingham were filling gaps between older established towns and never threatened their neighbours, others like Brackley were successful and supplanted neighbouring centres. Only in Northampton and Brackley has excavation yet begun to reveal significant evidence of industrial activity in urban tenements and this must be a target for future urban excavations.

Urban decline began in the county well before the Black Death, as excavations in Castle Lane Brackley have shown. Northampton and other towns in the region were suffering in the later 13th century from the flight of the cloth industry to rural areas. Decline was dramatically compounded by the agricultural crisis of 1315-22 and finally by the massive recession which accompanied the successive plagues from 1349 onwards. Urban decline is seen not only in the desertion of numerous tenements and some shops and stalls in the successful towns, but also and even more clearly in the collapse of the village markets, particularly in the second half of the 14th century. The attempts at re-founding some markets in the later 14th and 15th centuries may indicate a limited revival, as with the establishment of a new market in the village of Brigstock in 1466-7, but they were few in number and only two had even limited success. The major recovery probably did not come until the 16th century.

A knowledge of the pattern of communications contributes to a full understanding of the process of urbanisation, being essential to a towns' interaction with their hinterland and its links into wider national and international trade. It will also of course be important for the understanding of other issues such as the strategic location of castles. Hence Clifford Hill, the largest castle motte in the county, was constructed to control the Clifford where the road between the important towns of Bedford and Northampton crossed the Nene, an early medieval precursor to Billing Bridge. There seems to have been a major enhancement of the road network perhaps when the *burhs* were established in the early 10th century or soon after, for a network of new roads, some named as portways, is recognisable linking the major towns in the region. When these routes are studied in detail they appear to avoid many villages and, as at Brackley and Grafton Regis, to cut across the early road network yet elsewhere they are followed by the medieval township boundaries. Later in the medieval period more modest changes included the upgrading of fords to bridges, some lords promoting their towns through the construction of bridges and diversion of major roads to pass through their town, as for example at Oundle. Unfortunately the road network of the county was transformed in the 18th and 19th centuries with turnpiking and parliamentary enclosure. As a result the pattern of local and national roads is now poorly understood and any study must begin with the reconstruction from documentary sources of the pattern of major roads prior to the 18th century from sources such as Ogilby's Itinerary of 1675 and the late medieval Gough map. This can be refined using evidence of medieval bridges (Goodfellow 1985) and of hermitages, hospitals and chapels, which were in many cases associated with major roads, to begin to reveal the major medieval road network (Foard, in preparation).

Though the possibility has been often suggested, no convincing evidence has been demonstrated from archaeological or documentary sources for substantial water borne trade along the Nene above Wansford, prior to canalisation in the 18th century. In the 15th century, when a scheme was being considered to open navigation to Fotheringhay, it was specifically stated that the Nene was not navigable above Wansford due to the presence of bridges, of which there were numerous medieval examples between Wansford and Northampton. None of the other rivers in the county are of sufficient size to have supported river transport. Water transport was however important for the county in terms of the export trade, through road links to ports outside the present county. Throughout the medieval period London is likely to have been the dominant port through which Northamptonshire's engaged in international trade, continuing London's pre-eminence as the *wic* serving Mercia in the Saxon period. However the new ports on the Wash at Boston and Kings Lynn, together with the latter's fenland transhipment port of Holme, will have become key outlets especially for international trade from the eastern half of the county.

INDUSTRY

Medieval industry in the county was briefly reviewed by the Victoria County History in the 1920s but otherwise it is largely a neglected subject both from a documentary as well as an archaeological perspective, with the notable exception of the pottery and, thanks to recent work, the iron industry. The most important industry in the medieval period was probably cloth manufacture with leatherworking increasing in importance by the late medieval. Iron production was clearly important in the 11th and 12th centuries but had disappeared by the end of the medieval period. The scale, range and significance of all other industrial production is poorly understood, as is the degree to which the industries were urban as opposed to rurally based. The only countywide data is as late as 1777 which, although prior to industrialisation, may be massively different to medieval Northamptonshire. It does however show that of the four most common trades even the most urbanised, shoemaking, only 45% of production was in urban settlements, though several urban settlements could be dominant with for example Northampton and Wellingborough having 20% and 16% of all shoemaking respectively. For weaving and woolcombing, a textile industry that was by far the dominant single industry in the county in 1777, the figures were 28%, 22% respectively. The evidence of the trades recorded in the various towns from medieval documentary sources would suggest a broadly similar pattern, though there may be major exceptions, such as Northampton prior to the late 13th century when it appears to have had a major broadcloth industry. There are of course certain industries which were almost wholly rurally based due to the location of the raw materials, as with the processing of agricultural produce, such as malting which has been examined archaeologically at Raunds, and the various stone industries.

Broadcloth production may have provided the main industrial base for the growth of medieval Northampton and some or most of the small towns, but its is unclear how significant it was on a national or regional scale. Broadcloth required fulling, tentering and dyeing and, until the introduction of water driven fulling mills in the mid to late 13th century, fulling was by hand and so will have been conducted within the settlements. Under restrictive practices of the guilds, it continued thus for far longer in some boroughs, probably including

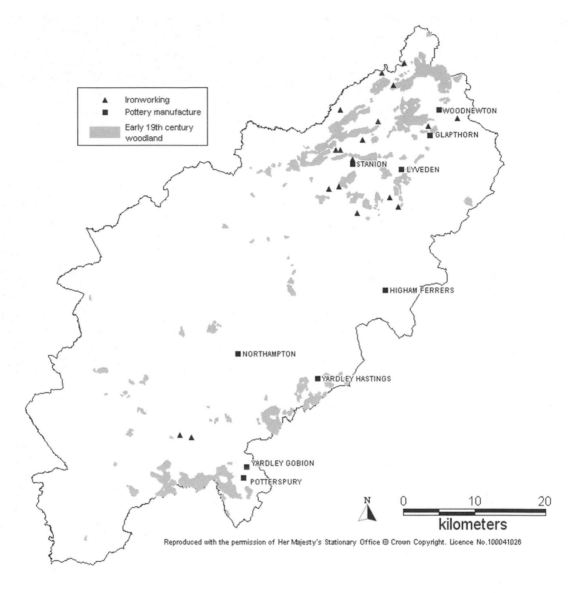

7.20 Medieval Ironworking and pottery production with early 19th century woodland

Northampton, even after the introduction of the fulling mill. This may explain the later 13th-century flight of the industry into the villages and small towns from Northampton and other major towns including Leicester, Stamford and Coventry. Archaeologically fulling mills and dyeworks should be relatively easily identified, though their small numbers within the medieval landscape of the village may render them difficult to locate without documentary evidence.

Scarlet Well Street, Northampton probably locates dyeworks in Northampton, perhaps significantly in the north west part of the town which showed the greatest degree of depopulation in 1610. Post medieval dyeworks are also known from documentary sources in Brigstock and Wellingborough with only the late 13th century dyeworks in Kettering known from the medieval documents outside Northampton. Similarly medieval fulling and tentering is known

7.21 Evidence of charcoal burning hearths at Brigstock. Reproduced by permission of The Historic Environment Team © Northamptonshire County Council

from documentary evidence in Northampton, but medieval fulling mills have been identified in documentary sources from only a handful of other places, including Wellingborough and Kettering. Other textile production undoubtedly existed on a smaller scale in various place for there is archaeological evidence of production at West Cotton and records of flaxlands in places such as Higham Ferrers and Kettering, while linen shops are recorded from 14th-century Higham Ferrers. Leatherworking may have overtaken cloth production as the most important industry in the county by the 16th century, as it certainly had in Northampton, but the scale of the industry in the medieval period is not well understood. Leather was tanned and processed in the county not only for production of shoes but also for gloves and other goods. Medieval street names in Northampton record industrial specialisation in a number of areas of the town, Tanner Street lying in the south west corner of the towns. However as yet only very limited excavation evidence has been recovered here for the medieval tanning industry.

In 1086 Northamptonshire had a substantial iron industry centred on Whittlewood and Rockingham forests and this continued into the 12th century and beyond (Foard forthcoming; Bellamy et al 2001). Large scale iron production required vast quantities of fuel and hence the forests also supported a major charcoal burning industry. The iron industry had decayed by the end of the medieval period but the chronology of and reasons for the decline is not understood. The charcoal industry has been extensively mapped through aerial survey while recent work has provided C^{14} dating to the late Saxon and early medieval period for major slag heaps in Rockingham forest. An ironworking tenement of the 12th century has been excavated at Lyveden, furnaces at Stanion and Little Weldon while there was an unpublished amateur excavation of a probable forge site in Great Weldon village. In contrast to the Roman period however there is no evidence to suggest that the forges or other reprocessing in the important iron industry was focussed in Northamptonshire towns, the medieval forges being

7.22 Medieval pottery from the kilns at Stanion. Reproduced by permission of Northamptonshire Archaeology.
© Northamptonshire County Council

in forest villages like Weldon and Geddington. Other metalworking is recorded from documents in several urban settlements but the only extensive archaeological evidence for other metalworking is again in a Rockingham Forest village, the copper and lead working recently excavated at Southwick.

While early medieval pottery production was, at least in part, urban based and has been demonstrated in Northampton, from the 12th century onwards major pottery industries existed in Whittlewood and Rockingham forests (Foard 1991). Another production site is expected in the south west of the county and there is an outlier at Yardley Hastings of the north Buckinghamshire industry. There is a single urban kiln of the late medieval known from Higham Ferrers. There have been various excavations of kilns at Stanion, Yardley Gobion and Potterspury, but only at Lyveden has there been the extensive excavation of a complete potter's tenement (Steane et al 1967-75).

In particular villages the production of building materials, notably high quality stone and stone slates, were important components of the economy (Steane 1967). Weldon was a major stone producer exporting stone for the construction of major buildings in the county and beyond, and in the south of the county Helmdon was another important centre. Stone slate production was most intensively developed at Collyweston and Easton on the Hill, but other production centres are known including from the Northampton and Brackley areas. In the post-medieval period both at Weldon and Collyweston the quarrying took place in the open field, with at Weldon even cottages apparently being constructed in association with the quarries. Whereas the landscape around Weldon has been largely destroyed by modern mineral extraction, extensive quarry earthworks survive at Helmdon, Charlton, Collyweston and Easton, but because most of the industries continued through to the 18th or 19th centuries it is unclear which earthworks, if any, relate to medieval production.

Corn mills were an almost ubiquitous manorial appurtenance with 168 already recorded in 1086 and many more constructed in later centuries. The appearance of windmills to supplement the

7.23 A stonemason depicted in a stained glass window from Helmdon. Reproduced by permission of
The Historic Environment Team © Northamptonshire County Council

water mills is seen increasingly with the growth of population and arable agricultural production from the 12th century onwards. A third type of mill is also recorded on some manors, the horse driven malt mill. There are a number of windmill mounds surviving as earthworks and a few levelled sites recognised from cropmarks. However, as many mill sites continued in use into or were newly built in the post medieval, so medieval water and windmills are difficult to identify. In addition some watermills existed for other industrial purposes, related to full-

ing and possibly also forges for the iron industry. There have been complete excavations of a water mill at West Cotton and a windmill at Lamport.

MILITARY

Excavations at Sulgrave have suggested that the defences of some medieval sites may have originated prior to the conquest but most, although sometimes constructed on earlier manorial sites, were almost certainly new constructions representing the imposition of Norman control in the century or so following the conquest. Only a handful of castles continued in military use after the 12th century and even less were newly constructed, the best example being Barnwell. However, a number of the sites, such as Towcester, continued as manorial sites long after they ceased to serve any defensive function. Northamptonshire had at least 36 castles and fortified manor houses and a further seven are suggested by place-names or unconfirmed archaeological evidence. It was only in the early 1970s that Thrapston Castle was identified and hence several other sites may still await identification, as for example at Irthlingborough where an 18th-century document refers to the Castleyard. It is likely that significantly more fortified manor houses have yet to be located. Most of the castles were originally of earth and timber but three, including Northampton, were probably constructed from the outset in stone with some of the others acquiring stone walls at a later date. However with the notable exceptions of Rockingham and Barnwell, all that survives on most sites today are the earthworks. The best known site is however Sulgrave where there have been extensive excavations. In contrast to the castles, little is known of the fortified manor houses, except for the extensive antiquarian excavation of a site in Titchmarsh.

Rockingham castle was built by the king while Northampton and Higham Ferrers were constructed by the earl of Northampton and William Peverell. These are well documented and Northampton, though now largely destroyed, has been examined in detail (Giggins 1999; Klingelhoffer 1984). In contrast, most other castles are poorly documented including several which are completely unrecorded, possibly because they were erected in the civil war of 1139-1141. The undocumented sites however include several castles like Castle Dykes which had substantial stone structures and like Weedon Lois which was an important estate centre.

7.24 Barnwell castle. Reproduced by permission of The Historic Environment Team
© Northamptonshire County Council

Most castles were located in settlements and probably in most cases replaced an undefended manor at an important estate centre. Often, as at Brackley and Rockingham they also controlled important roads. However a few seem to have been located in isolated sites for purely strategic reasons, as with Castle Dykes, Clifford Hill and Fineshade. All the main towns in the county, except those held by monastic houses, seem to have had a substantial castle (Northampton, Brackley, Towcester, Thrapston, Higham Ferrers and possibly Rothwell) as do a significant number of the market villages (Rockingham, Fotheringhay, Long Buckby, Lilbourne, Culworth, Wollaston, Barnwell). This seems to be a clear reflection of the coincidence of castles with manorial centres of major lords who were the main driving force behind market and town foundation.

Although many towns in the county had castles, only Northampton had town defences. The late Saxon *burh* defences at Towcester may have survived into the medieval period but there is no reason to believe they were maintained. In contrast the Saxon *burh* at Northampton was replaced by one of the most extensive circuits of stone defences and gates anywhere in England, probably by the Earl of Northampton in the early 12th century. Most of the circuit survived to be depicted on John Speed's map of 1610, except on the west and south west sides, where recent excavations have revealed the course and character of late Saxon and the medieval defences (Chapman 1998).

In 1264 Northampton's defences were put to the test and found wanting, during the rebellion of Simon de Montfort when the town was stormed by forces loyal to the king. A monument related to the siege was found in the town in the 19th century but no other evidence related to the siege has been recovered. There were two other major military actions in the county in the medieval period. Rockingham Castle was taken back by siege by the king in circa 1220 but the scale of the action is uncertain and while no other sieges are recorded, it is possible that the second castle at Lilbourne, on the hill overlooking the village, represents a siege castle.

There were two major field engagements in the county in the medieval period, during the Wars of the Roses. The Battle of Northampton, on 10th July 1460, took place in the area of Delapre Park and saw the king captured by the Yorkists. The presence of an earthwork called the Battle Dyke, possibly a park pale, used in the battle as a defensive position for the Lancastrian camp, provides a potential for a substantial buried archaeological feature. Recorded in later terriers of the field system, if located the dyke has the potential to provide a key topographical focus for the investigation of the battle. Extensive artefact distributions from the battle may also survive across the park, but there has been no survey to confirm the potential. The other major action was the Battle of Edgcote, on 26th July 1469. The exact location of the battle is disputed but there is a high probability that the traditional site on 'Danesmoor' is correct: archaeological survey is required to confirm the site. A mass grave recorded in the 19th century on the edge of the village might represent battle-related burials (Smurthwaite 1995; Haigh 1997).

8
Post-Medieval Northamptonshire (1500-1750)

DAVID HALL

THE COUNTRYSIDE

Open field, familiar as ridge and furrow, was the predominant form of agriculture at the beginning of the period. There was still 97 percent of the county open in 1500, falling to 23 percent by 1800. Nearly all of the remainder was thereafter rapidly enclosed, only one place, Lutton, remaining open until 1866 (Hall 1997 363).

The operation, management and social structure of open-field holdings are available from copious records (Hall 1995). In most parts of the county, farmers were tenants of the landed gentry or lesser lords of the manor who owned estates comprising most of one or more parishes. In the north-west, however many farms were freehold by the mid 18th century. Practical aspects of farming organization are indicated by open-field orders made at manorial courts. Details of farming work, such as yields and stock breeding, are recorded in 17th and 18th century glebe books and tithe books of clerics who farmed in hand.

Ridge and furrow has been fast disappearing over the last 50 years, caused mainly by ploughing. By 1992, 85 percent of the ridge and furrow surviving in 1940 had been destroyed, irrespective of whether there was a lot or little in 1940 (Hall 1993, 24). In January 1999, new vertical photography of the

8.1 Ridge and Furrow overlain by enclosure hedges at Braunston. Reproduced by permission of the Historic Environment Team.
© Northamptonshire County Council

43 best preserved townships in the East Midlands showed that many had lost ridge and furrow. Overall the total amount of recorded ridge and furrow fell from 7,640 ha in c.1990 to 6,761 ha in 1999. This loss (11.5%) highlights the vulnerability of the monument class.

The landscapes of hedged fields resulted from enclosure over many centuries. Of the 390 townships in the historic county (pre-1964, including Peterborough) 65 percent were parliamentary (1733-1901) and 35 percent were non-parliamentary. The term 'parliamentary' refers to enclosure processes that included commissioners, which differ from places where Parliament ratified a private agreement between a few parties.

The non-parliamentary enclosure profiles are; 15th century 3% (of 390); 16th 13%; 17th 15%; 1700-32 2%. A further 2% were enclosed privately after 1732 (Hall 1997, 398; fig 4). The early enclosures lie in a patchy north-western swathe from Banbury to Rockingham Forest. Many small and deserted townships are included, some that had late monastic enclosure. They lie in the part of the county that had up to 90 percent open field arable. This is the region most likely to be converted from arable to pasture because of its great shortage of grazing. Lack of pasture had partly been accommodated before enclosure by introducing a high percentage of leys, often more than 35 percent, within the fields (Hall 1995, 22-27).

Details of each township enclosure and the subsequent infilling of plots are very varied. Early enclosure was usually made for sheep farming and had large fields. These were further subdivided, mainly during 1750-1850, as the economy changed to mixed farming with arable crop rotation in the enclosed fields but retaining some closes under permanent pasture.

The mechanics of Parliamentary enclosure have been fully described by Tate (1967) and several Northamptonshire details are available (Hall 1997, f.n. 17, p.354). The social aspects of enclosure are the subject of ongoing research. Recent work by Neeson (1993) is by no means the final, or an accurate, account. Enclosure was the beginning of a change from small to larger farms that has gone on to the present day. The fate of the small landowner in the Corby area after enclosure has been studied by Moore-Colyer (1997, 1999). Many opted out of farming, probably often by choice.

Forests and woodland are an underrated part of the Northamptonshire landscape. Many thousands of acres of woodland survive, much of it under the management of the Forestry Commission. There was much more woodland in the 18th century than now, when it had not changed a great deal since the late Middle Ages, except for some disparking during the Commonwealth period. Most woodland removed since 1825 was pulled up in the 1860s, after formal enclosure, which took place from 1798-1856. There were further inroads during the 20th century with wartime aerodromes and clearance for agriculture.

The forest consisted of coppices, plains, ridings, lawns and lodges, most of which have medieval origins. Veteran oaks surviving in lawns and elsewhere are in need of protection. All woods under the management of Forest Enterprise have been surveyed for archaeological remains. The Forestry Commission is currently supporting a scheme to replant woodland in the forests of Oxfordshire, Buckinghamshire and Northamptonshire. Whittlewood Forest has had its historic landscape mapped by Northamptonshire Heritage and South Northamptonshire Council (Hall 2000). It is now possible to develop a management policy for the area with suggestions for restoration of woodland to its former location, should this be required.

The management of crown woods is very fully recorded from the 16th century. Only a few details can be found for coppice sales in private woods, e.g. Farthingstone in the 16th and 18th centuries (NRO Th 2047). Very little historical evidence exists about industrial activity, such as charcoal burning. A moderate amount of new woodland was planted on some of the large estates (e.g. Althorp and Easton Maudit), where ridge and furrow is visible beneath the trees. Modern woodland records are held by the Forestry Commission, and include woodland diaries.

PARKS & GARDENS

The gardens of Northamptonshire cover a wide range of types and some have major archaeological remains. In scale they vary from the extensive works of the great houses to the gardens of farmhouses. As well as private gardens, there are those of public institutions, 19th century and later, such as workhouses, hospitals and asylums, municipal parks and cemeteries, although these have had little study so far.

A few earthwork gardens where a great house no

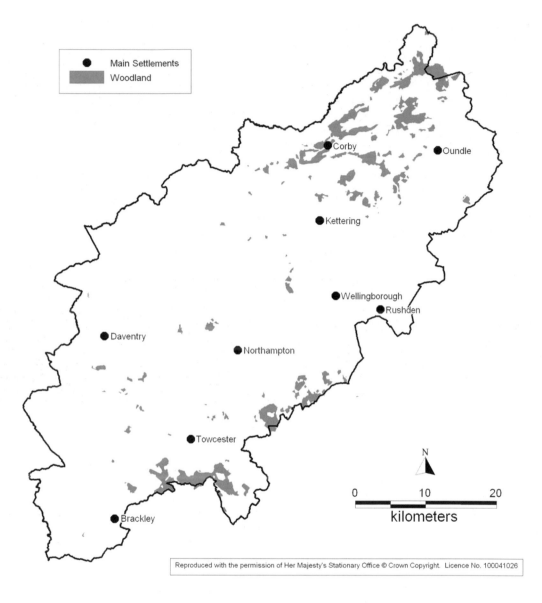

8.2 Eighteenth-century woodland.

longer survives, such as Wakerley and Harrington, are scheduled monuments. Some gardens are protected because of their association with monastic or manorial sites. Scheduled sites are the only ones that are preserved. More difficult to manage are gardens currently in use (the majority); these are likely to change or be put to a different land-use. Since there is no protection, gardens can be destroyed by horticulture or agriculture without notice. The surviving documents are varied; e.g. the extraordinary scheduled terraced gardens at Harrington have no known record (Fig 8.3).

Gardens have research value because they relate to the wealth of the owners and their social status, and reveal changing fashions. Documentary work is required on the evolution of gardens in relation to the

8.3 Terraced gardens at Harrington. Reproduced by permission of the Historic Environment Team.
© Northampton County Council

social structure of the county. Archaeological study of gardens should include those with good historical records, although in some cases, archaeology is the only source of information about major gardens, e.g. at Paulerspury.

SETTLEMENT

Villages in Northamptonshire were mostly nucleated. Medieval dispersed settlement in the Whittlewood and Salcey Forest regions had shrunken so much by the 18th century that it cannot be distinguished from dispersed farmsteads in enclosed landscapes, except by fieldwork.

The population in the post-medieval period was predominantly rural and changed little before 1800. Some gentry families were accused of depopulation and conversion of arable to pasture in 1517, e.g. at Deene (NRO Bru A.iv.19). Bridges (1791, ii, 163) notes that Easton Maudit had a reduced population due to enclosure (c.1639).

Population estimates for c.1720 (Bridges 1791) show the major towns clearly. Earlier databases are available from the 1524 Lay Subsidy and the 1676 Compton Census. More detail is available from the county hearth tax returns. A full report on Northamptonshire towns (Foard forthcoming) will enable the chronology of change to be studied in detail.

Northampton saw growth but its size was still smaller than the 13th century town, areas remaining undeveloped within the walled area. Ten towns survived the 14th century recessions while other places survived as market villages or were revived in the 15th century. There were also new market village foundations, notably Brigstock, and re-foundations in the 16th century at Kings Cliffe, Aynho and Weldon. Welford market was moved to West Haddon. Village markets filled minor marketing niches in thinly populated areas of the county distant from the main towns. None ever grew to significant size and most failed fairly quickly, except for Rockingham,

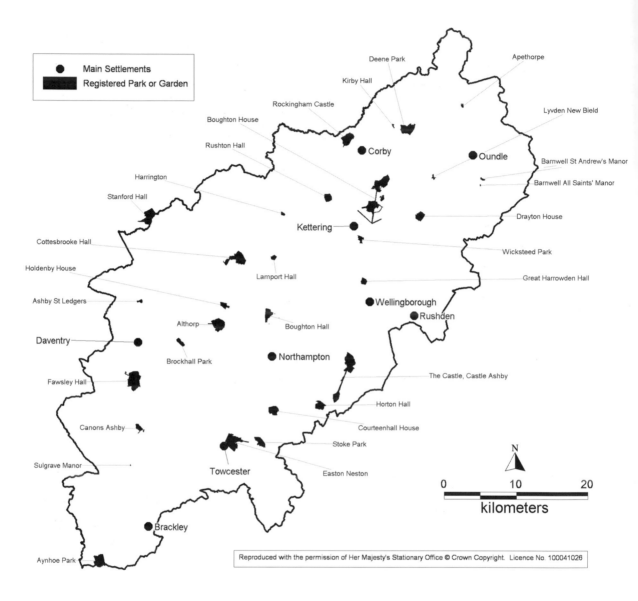

8.4 The locations of parks and gardens on the English Heritage Register.

which had a high population for its acreage suggesting non-agricultural functions. Rockingham is significant for the study of small settlements because all the buildings and tenements around the market place were demolished and cleared in 1645. Extensive earthworks remain, providing a major archaeological resource.

The dominant towns were those that had been important in the 13th and 14th centuries. Kettering continued to eclipse Rothwell, and Wellingborough to eclipse Higham Ferrers. This was based both on the transfer of general commercial functions but also, during the 17th and 18th centuries, upon the first stages of large-scale specialisation in the textile and shoemaking industries.

Wool trade existed early in the period, but was

8.5 The relative sizes of market settlements in 1524

probably in decline, with a transition, during the 16th century, from wool to leather. The wool market at Oundle was infilled before 1565 while leather searchers were appointed to Higham market in the mid 16th century, and by the later 17th century there was a significant leather fair at Rothwell.

Kettering and Wellingborough saw major development in the later 17th and 18th centuries with the specialisation and intensification of the worsted and shoemaking industries respectively. Other small towns, Oundle, Daventry, Brackley, Thrapston and Towcester, remained as the main commercial and service centres for their district, shown by the range of specialist services provided in 1777, such as attorneys, surgeons etc (Hatley 1973). While Thrapston, like Rockingham, served

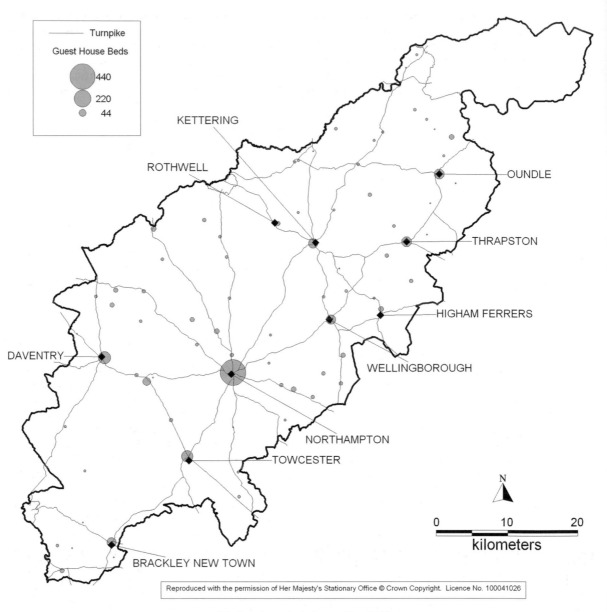

8.6 Guesthouse beds & turnpikes, 1800

marketing functions and the ubiquitous agricultural component, the other towns had a broad but limited industrial base, with no concentration on a major industry or trade. Oundle had a 16th century glove-producing trade, which continued to 1777, but never provided the basis for development to compare with the 18th century specialisation at Kettering and Wellingborough. Northampton retained a broad and substantial industrial and commercial base; the 1524 subsidy reveals the importance of the broadcloth and the leather trades, the last a specialisation that intensified by 1777, moving increasingly to-wards shoemaking. The service, distributive and food trades comprised 40% of the occupations of Northampton in 1524, showing the importance of marketing. The textile and leather trades represented

17% and 25% of all trades respectively. Farming comprised just 6% of the occupations.

By the later 17th century, Towcester and Daventry, sited on major routes, specialised on servicing major through traffic. Other towns, including Northampton, Wellingborough, Kettering and Brackley also had significant trade from important through routes, shown by the numbers of guest beds and stabling for horses in 1686. The scale of commerce at towns can be assessed from the number of alehouses and inns, which represent accommodation provision for visitors, though the impact of servicing through traffic needs allowing for.

Small towns were based around the marketplace, with rows of shops and stalls. There was development of permanent structures in the main towns with shops fronting market places, as well as a continuation of market place infilling. Apart from recent work in St Giles' Street, Northampton (Shaw 1997), no significant excavations have examined the development of Northampton or of any other town in post-medieval Northamptonshire.

Communications and the scale of transport activity on particular roads can be mapped from the records of alehouses (1630), guest beds and stabling (1686 and 1800), The last two are related to major roads recorded on the maps of Ogilby & Morden, and the later turnpikes (Fig 8.6).

There were substantial changes in the road network in the 18th century as a result of turnpiking which have distorted the early post-medieval road network. Mapping of the pre-turnpike road pattern is necessary to understand both urban development and the potential of through traffic for the support of service industries. The impact of the development of coaching in the later 17th and 18th century and its effect on towns such as Towcester and Daventry needs study.

The English Civil War has several sites of interest in the county (Foard 1994). Northampton, a major parliamentarian garrison of national importance, was defended during 1642-1647. Major defensive works were made around the town and the castle and the south and west bridges were fortified. There is no earthwork survival of the town defences but they are well documented. Areas outside the walls near St Andrews and St Edmunds were cleared of houses. Reconstruction of the likely circuit of defences from documentary evidence has been completed and needs testing archaeologically. Earthworks at the castle site probably include some Civil War works.

Rockingham was an important parliamentarian garrison 1643-1647. Buried archaeology is likely, and there are some documentary sources including a plan of the defences of the motte, but no detailed study has been made on the earthworks or the historical record. Towcester was a royalist garrison for the main army during October 1643 to January 1644. Refortification occurred mainly along the Roman defences with the castle-motte earthwork re-used as an artillery platform. Two sections made over the Civil War ditch revealed little archaeological evidence.

Grafton Regis was the site of a minor royalist garrison during October-December 1643, fortifying a country house. It has high potential for well preserved buried archaeology and the documentary record of the siege is good. Musket balls are scattered on the surrounding land, where there is absence of modern development and scope for analysis of details of the military engagement by metal detecting.

At Naseby a major battle of the highest national importance occurred (Fig 8.7). Extensive artefact scatters have been recovered. Burial sites are known and others are likely to exist, though none has had modern excavation. Extensive action and possible subsidiary skirmish sites have been located. Naseby can be used to study the nature of actual deployments relative to the ideal of the military manuals. It also represents one of the best testing-grounds for the development of the archaeological study of Civil War battles because of the excellent documentary and historical topographical record, and the lack of modern development. Evidence has been lost by uncontrolled metal-detecting for musket balls, and the site should be protected by scheduling.

INDUSTRY

Northampton had a significant production of leather and shoes in 15th and 16th centuries. Tanners were recorded at Rushden in 1462 for fouling the brook with lime and tanning bark. Higham Ferrers had an officer who checked leather quality by 1539 and thereafter until the 17th century. Butchers were to bring hides as well as meat to the market or meat could not be sold, showing that hides and leather were considered important (Hall and Harding 1985, 229-32). The leather trade comprised 25% of the occupations in Northampton in 1524 compared to 17% for the textile industry. Morton (1712, 23)

8.7 The Monument marking the Naseby Battlefield

noted that 'mighty numbers' [of shoes] had been sent to foreign plantations and to the army in Flanders.

Curriers and Whittawers cured skins to give a supple product suitable for glove production etc. Tanners supplied the shoemaking and other leather trades. In 1524 there were 15 tanners in Northampton and 5 curriers and whittawers. By 1777, all three were concentrated in urban centres.

It is not yet known how important the leather industry was at the beginning of the 16th century. Whether it already concentrated on shoes or if it was primarily urban based. The relationship between the development of shoe production and the production of leather from pastures in the county remains unknown and whether there was a significant shift from wool to leather.

A broadcloth industry was well established in Northamptonshire in the Middle Ages. It required fulling of cloth followed by stretching or tentering. The location of the industry can be approximately identified from the distribution of fulling mills and of tentering areas, and suggests a concentration of the industry in the Nene Valley between Northampton and Fotheringhay. The distribution relates reflects the availability of water-power and continued until the mid 18th century but had ceased by 1777. The pattern is supported by the distribution of dyers, with dyeworks known at Brigstock before 1725, Wellingborough in 1767, and Northampton had seven dyers in 1524 and two in 1777. In 1524, the broadcloth industry in Northampton was second only to the leather industry. It appears to have been supplanted before 1777 by worsteds.

A worsted industry was introduced into Kettering

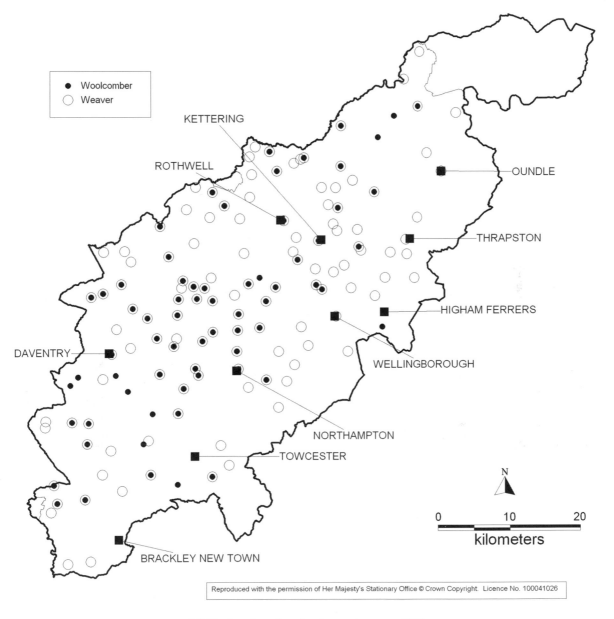

8.8 The Location of woolcombers and weavers, 1777

in the mid 17th century (Randall 1970, 1971). There were no woolcombers recorded in Northampton in 1524 even though it then had a significant textile industry, but by 1777 there were 19 woolcombers with 59 weavers. It comprised two main components: woolcombing, the processing of wool into yarn, and weaving to produce finished cloth. The process did not require fulling and tentering. In 1777 the industry was concentrated in the north-west of the county, with much woolcombing at Long Buckby and nearby, and weaving being centred at Kettering. This suggests that the production of the wool was in the west of the county, where there was early enclosure, but it is not known what proportion of the

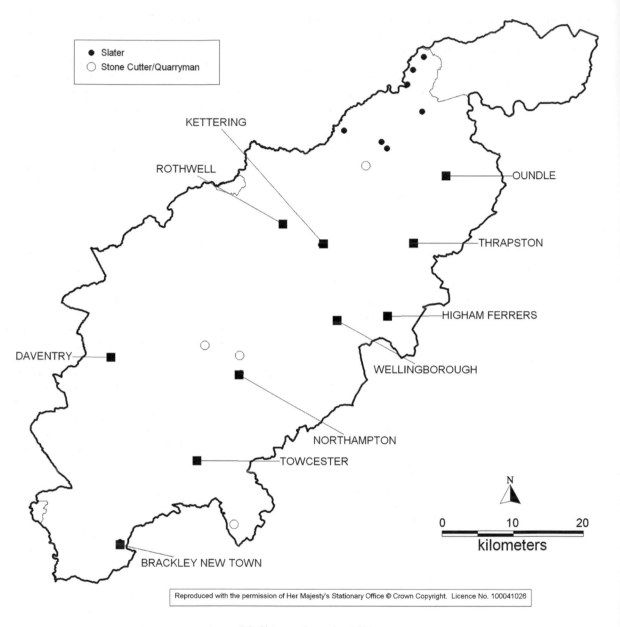

8.9 Slaters and quarries, 1777

wool was imported. It is possible that the worsted industry developed in the north west of the county where the broadcloth industry was not practicable because of lack of watermills for fulling.

Building materials used in the county were wood, stone, brick and cob. Wood was available in forests and the early enclosures. Northampton had many wooden buildings before the fire of 1675, but they are now rare being mainly concentrated in north-western villages

The greater part of the county lies on a limestone belt. Good quality stone came from the well-know quarries at Easton on the Hill, Weldon and Harlestone. There were, however, local stone quarries in most parts of the county except the north-west. Good quality stone was needed for jambs, quoins and dressings, but the famous quarries were by no means the only suppliers. King's Cliffe was used for Burghley in the 1580s (Till 1997). Parry (1987) has discussed Helmdon stone, and Hudson and Sutherland (1990) describe many Northamptonshire building stones.

In the 17th century, Raunds 'marble' was much esteemed (Morton 1712, 107), and quarries at Maidwell are described in 1806 referring to the quality of stone and lime produced from them (NRO IL 2892). One of the quarries, Dale stone pits, still visible on the ground, was called *standelvis* in 1316 (NRO FH 3021).

Slates likewise are sourced from many local quarries as well as the large and better known ones such as Collyweston (Figure 6). At Higham Ferrers a *slatt pit furlong* is recorded in 1567 and 1789; on the ground there is a depression in the field surface with small pieces of thin flatstone scattered about. Tiles from Newbottle and Charlton are frequently referred to in 15th-century manorial building-accounts at Preston Capes (NRO Knightley court rolls A iv, 8 & 24).

The distribution of stone slates on extant buildings reveals three regions. The main one is in the north-east of the county, centred on Collyweston and Easton on the Hill but there are other lesser foci picked out by the 1777 list. Two other regions seen in surviving buildings suggest minor slate production, at Northampton and at Brackley in 1777.

Collyweston and Easton on the Hill have quarry pits and associated working areas surviving as earthworks. The historical record of this subject has not been assessed, and work is needed to identify quarries and working areas in all the production centres. The draft enclosure maps of both places give detail of the small quarries. Some of the limestone quarried was burnt to prepare quicklime for mortar. Closely related were 'mortar-pits' used for poorer quality mortar. They were often located where a natural clay contained lime that conferred good binding properties.

Early brick buildings are rare because of the ready availability of stone. Another contributory reason was the shortage and expense of fuel needed to make bricks. Early brick was used for chimneys, hearths and in high status buildings like royal park lodges and episcopal palaces. The manor house at Edgcote had brick in the 15th century (imported from Calais: Driver 1997, 320). At Easton Neston, in 1511, bricks used for chimneys were probably made on site. There was a brick making family called West in the Cleyley Hundred during the 17th century; they were possibly itinerant brickmakers, but their activities leave little trace on the ground or in documents. Fawsley dower house is made of early brick and Yardley Hastings rectory is a Queen Anne brick structure. Towcester had brick buildings in the 18th century, and there were kilns of the same date at Brigstock, and Boughton (Kettering), probably using fuel from the nearby forest. Brick-making did not occur on the large-scale until coal was available via canals.

Cob is a method of construction using solid earth walls lying on a low stone plinth, rendered to prevent weathering. The current distribution of cob buildings is very much at the north-west of the county where building stone is in short supply (Seaborne 1966). There may have been such buildings elsewhere, but they have long been replaced by stone or brick.

Ceramic production was not a very important activity countywide. There was production of coarse-wares at Glapthorn into the 16th century (G. Johnson forthcoming) and potting continued at Potterspury into the 18th century, by that time only making coarseware that did not weather very well (Bridges 1791, i, 316). A kiln at Paulerspury yielded pottery dated to the 17th century (Hall 1974). It is not known when these wares were superseded by products from major centres such as Staffordshire.

BUILDINGS

Buildings demonstrate many aspects of the past. As well as their intended functional structures, they throw light on commercial and industrial activity, indicate the wealth of the builders, reveal building patterns of vernacular architecture, and the show the varied use of building materials.

The spatial organization of great houses and their relationship to the surrounding landscape needs study, such as the impact on the environment and the size of land-holdings. Economic and social aspects of running a large house are also of interest, since the staff often formed a community separate from nearby villages.

Research into the history of farming in the county as revealed through buildings is needed. The resource of surviving farm buildings and farm-houses is extensive, however, the current level of

8.10 19th century labourers cottages at Sywell

threat is high, since this category of building is probably being lost to demolition and conversion at a greater rate than any other type. Some villages have historical surveys made building-by-building, e.g. Mears Ashby (1577), places in the Kettering and Raunds areas (1730s) and much of the Grafton Regis Estate (1720s). Many historic farmhouses are listed, but the associated farm buildings tend not to be. They need recording and are currently even more threatened because of low farming returns. They have potential for understanding agrarian history, and the adaption of buildings to more mechanized farming during the late 18th and early 19th century.

Specialized building types associated with rural trades and small traditional industries are of interest. These buildings are at high risk of loss and may contain much useful information. Some buildings can be identified because they were used for very specific purposes, e.g. granaries might have very hard, smooth lime-ash floors. Buildings belonging to butchers, blacksmiths etc, have received little attention. The large number of surviving buildings offers a high potential for further study and it is necessary to decide how to select suitable samples.

Rows of purpose-built labourers' cottages are mostly of country estate origin. A late 18th century example survives at Achurch. Many estate villages have a high proportion of labourers' cottages of 19th-century date, e.g. at Strixton and Sywell. Squatters' cottages are referred to at Abthorpe and King's Cliffe in documentary records, but it is doubtful if any survive. Cattle End, Silverstone, seems to have been built as encroachment in a forest riding.

Only a few early shops survive; an 18th example in the Drapery, Northampton, is listed, and there was one until recently at Kings Sutton. A possible 15th shop occurs in Towcester, and Higham Ferrers offers potential because shop sites have not been cleared away for road widening. Inns measure the wealth of towns in terms of visiting commercial activity, and even where altered, outbuildings and stables can often be identified. The buildings of tradesmen such as butchers and bakers probably can be identified if not too much changed.

Medieval churches are well recorded in terms of architectural history and their archaeology is con-trolled via the faculty system for any structural alterations. However, details of the fabric of churches are not satisfactorily recorded. No system of recording Nonconformist buildings exists and there is currently a problem with redundant chapel conversions, some of which have buildings dating before 1750.

There are a very few pre-1750 industrial buildings, such as the pin factory at Long Buckby. This was a small scale activity that used an existing barn. Likewise whip-making at Daventry and the work-shops of the woollen industry in the north-west are unlikely to have had many purpose-built structures.

Buildings hold information about economy and industry and about social matters. It is essential to decide what to record, and to engage planning consents to determine research objectives. Research based on the analysis of buildings can confirm from the physical evidence what relates to data

8.11 An early nonconformist chapel at Creaton. The earliest chapel on the site dated from 1694 while the core of the current building was constructed in 1793.

from written sources. It can also extend the depth and scope of understanding suggested by historical documents. For some buildings, where no written records survive, the physical information is the only data source

Buildings fall naturally into two groups, those dated and those undated. Many listed buildings are dated (usually qualitatively) in their description to within 25 years or so. From these examples it is possible to attribute dates to unlisted buildings on stylistic and contextual grounds. Although for most management purposes this is adequate, for research it is necessary to have accurate dating. This can sometimes be provided from documents. Dendrochronology has not yet been much utilized in Northamptonshire; it is more difficult to apply in this county than other regions. A sample needs 80-100 rings because timber that grew on claylands has less annual ring variation than material from elsewhere, so necessitating the development of local sequences. Funding needs acquiring for this work, as it is now a major research tool. A sampling policy also needs establishing to create the local dating sequence.

9

Northamptonshire in the Industrial Period 1750-1960

JENNY BALLINGER

INTRODUCTION

Industrial archaeology is different to the study of other archaeological periods, primarily because many of the archaeological monuments of the industrial age are still in existence today. Factories, schools, chapels and transport networks often continue being used for their intended purpose, whilst other buildings have been converted for alternative uses including domestic residences and social and recreational facilities. Therefore there are a wider range of sources and techniques which can be used to study the industrial period. The analysis of standing buildings and surviving industrial landscapes can be used in conjunction with below-ground archaeological investigation and the study of the prolific number of documents related to the process of industrialisation to develop a full understanding of the industrial age. The detailed study of the physical remains of the period has not yet fully matured, and therefore the potential of many of the sources has not been completely realised.

Until recently industrial archaeology focused on industry and technology with a particular emphasis on the 'great achievements' of the 'industrial revolution'. In recent years the focus has changed to the study of the 'industrial period' (the period following 1750) or 'the archaeology of industrialisation'. This development has ensured that the wider social and economic consequences of industrial development (including the impact on settlements, transport networks, social, administrative and cultural facilities) have been considered in an archaeological context.

Northamptonshire has a great deal to contribute to the 'archaeology of industrialisation' as the process of industrial development in Northamptonshire was very different to that in the central and north west regions of England. The traditional perception of industrialisation in Britain is that there was an Industrial Revolution, however archaeologists and historians have questioned whether industrial expansion in Britain was actually a 'revolution' (Berg 1994; Beckett and Heath 1988). Industrial development began in the early 18th century, but accelerated from 1750 onwards with a number of key inventions relating to the production of iron, the use of steam to power engines and developments in the textile industry. Many areas of the country were, however, largely unaffected by these sweeping changes. Northamptonshire did not undergo substantial industrial development until the mid 19th century, by which time national legislation to improve the living and working conditions of industrial workers had already been passed, and a wide range of social and administrative organisations had been established. Northamptonshire therefore largely avoided the worst of the social and economic problems (including poverty, overcrowding and a wide range of health risks) usually associated with industrialisation and urbanisation.

NORTHAMPTONSHIRE 1750-2000

Northamptonshire remained a largely rural county between 1750 and 1850; settlement outside the county town was based in the nucleated villages and market towns which had been established in the medieval period. Dispersed farmsteads were also beginning to appear in the centre of the fields created by parliamentary enclosure. Industry was primarily craft based and carried out in the homes of individual workers. The main industries in Northamptonshire were boot and shoe making, lace-making and the weaving and woollen industry. There were also local specialisms for example wood turning in Kings Cliffe and whip making in Daventry. Northamptonshire was effected by the transport revolution of the 18th and early 19th centuries which saw the establishment of turnpike roads and canal and river navigations. These were of considerable importance in developing communications links both within and outside the county. The central geographical position of Northamptonshire meant that the county benefited considerably from both the coaching era in the 18th and early 19th centuries and the developing canal network. Administration remained based around the hundreds and parishes which had been established in the late Saxon period and modified in the Elizabethan era, however changes were beginning to be made. The most significant development was the establishment of the Poor Law Unions in 1834, which revolutionised the procedure for dealing with the poor.

The period following 1850 in Northamptonshire was characterised by rapid and continuing change. The two main features were the large-scale development of the boot and shoe industry and the widespread process of urbanisation. The boot and shoe trade had been a cottage industry in the 18th century and had begun to increase considerably in the early 19th century. The large-scale development of the industry in the county was, however, linked to the process of mechanisation after the sewing machine was introduced in 1857. Large numbers of boot and shoe factories began to be developed in the main towns in the county (Northampton, Wellingborough and Kettering) and in many of the villages. Settlements with a substantial boot and shoe industry underwent a considerable growth and many former villages became industrialised towns by the end of the 19th century. The population graph of Northamptonshire as a whole shows a steady rise in population, continuing a trend from the early 19th century. However the populations of individual settlements, noticeably Northampton, Kettering and Rushden, underwent a phenomenal growth during the second half of the century. Ironstone quarrying also became a major industry in the late 19th-century and employed a considerable proportion of the population of the county. The development of the railway network through the county from the 1830s onwards had a major effect on communication systems. The Midland Railway line, in particular, appeared to have a major impact on settlement and industry in the area.

A large number of local government functions including school boards, burial boards, boards of health, sanitary authorities, town councils and urban and rural district councils were developed during the late 19th and early 20th centuries. Schools, hospitals, local government offices and cemeteries were established by these organisations. The urban environment of the county was characterised by the development of large mixed zones added to the original core of settlements. These zones contained a mixture of houses, shops, factories, schools, chapels and social clubs. The rapid rate of social change in the period following 1850 was clearly instrumental in developing a form of working class consciousness. During the late 19th century a number of working class movements developed in Northamptonshire including the temperance movement, a large number of co-operative societies and a network of working men's clubs.

A further change has been experienced in North-amptonshire in the latter part of the 20th-century. The county has seen the decline of its two main industries: ironstone quarrying and the manufacture of boots and shoes. The former industry has ceased completely, whilst the latter remains in existence with a few key firms still in operation, but the scale of the industry has declined considerably. The railway infrastructure has also been considerably depleted, with the closure of a large number of branch lines in the 1960s. The main lines through the county have, however, remained in operation. The central location of the county has remained important to its development. The county has good communication links with the M1 motorway passing through its boundaries and the recent development of Daventry International Rail Freight Terminal. Distribution is one of the key industries in the county, in addition to light engineering. Northamptonshire is also part of the extended commuter belts around London and Birmingham. Other developments have included the expansion of the leisure and service industries, the growing importance of information technology and the segregation of commerce, business, sport and leisure from domestic life. The latter can be seen in the physical development of the county with the creation of specialised housing estates, industrial estates and out-of-town retail and entertainment complexes. The changes that have occurred in Northamptonshire in the past 40 years have been mirrored across the Great Britain. There is now a far greater homogeneity of our social and economic life and greater uniformity of the built environment than ever before. This period is often viewed as the post-industrial age with significant developments being based on information technology. The developments are best seen in a national or even global context and therefore are not discussed further here.

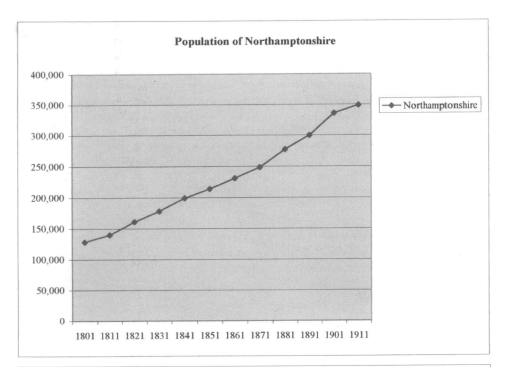

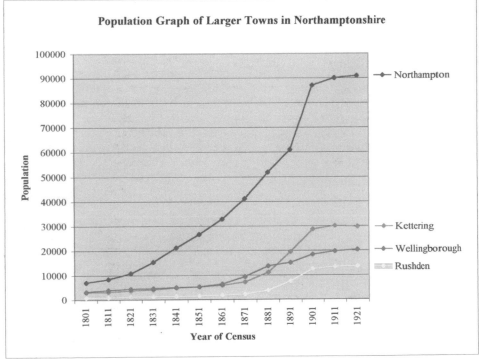

9.1 Population graphs for Northamptonshire as a whole and
Northampton /Kettering/Wellingborough/Rushden

INDUSTRY

Craft industry

There were a number of industries operating in Northamptonshire in the early part of the period (between 1750 and 1850) including the woollen industries (weaving and woolcombing), lace making, silk making and the boot and shoe trade. Industries were based in different geographical areas of the county; the Kettering area was renowned for its weaving industry, Wellingborough had a large boot and shoe industry at this early date and Long Buckby was a major centre for woolcombing (Hatley, 1973).

Industry was primarily craft based. The majority of work was conducted within a domestic setting. It is not known whether workers houses had any special adaptations as many buildings would have been of low status and poor construction and therefore do not survive. There was a large weaving industry in the Northamptonshire, but there are few known surviving examples of 'weavers windows' which are so much in evidence in other areas of the country. There were some large individual manufactures in the county in the 18th and early 19th centuries including a bell foundry at Kettering, a carpet factory at Burton Latimer (Ballinger, 1999), the cotton mill in Northampton and woollen mills at Burton Latimer and Brigstock (Raybould, pers comm). Little archaeological work has been conducted on 18th century industry in Northamptonshire.

Boot and shoe manufacture

Large-scale manufacturing began in the county in the mid 19th-century. The boot and shoe industry quickly became a specialism in Northamptonshire. Boot and shoe making had been an important craft industry in the county in the 18th and early 19th centuries, but the industry underwent a massive expansion in the period following 1850. The pivotal factors in the expansion of the boot and shoe trade were the mechanisation of the industry following the introduction of the sewing machine in 1857 and the establishment of the factory system between 1857 and 1895. There was initial resistance to the factory system in the county, but by the 1870s a substantial number of factories were well established in towns and villages. Domestic manufacture and the factory system existed side by side during this period. A substantial expansion in handworking was required to meet the increased requirements of the factory system. The majority of small outworkers workshops date to the late 19th century (Cooke et al 2000).

Nineteenth century boot and shoe factories were typically rectangular brick buildings of three storey construction. The factories were designed to combine both hand and mechanised processes under one roof; clicking, closing, lasting, making and finishing were all undertaken in the buildings which also had to provide storage space and office accommodation. A wide range of architectural styles and details were employed on boot and shoe factories. Many early factories were of simple utilitarian design, but architectural embellishment was increasingly used. Polychromatic brickwork (the use of red, blue, and yellow bricks) was frequently used to decorative effect and the principle entrance was often given elaborate treatment (see Colour Plate 12). Some of the larger factories were designed in Italianate styles. Single storey factories with office ranges to the front and rows of north lit sheds to the rear began to be erected from the 1890s onwards. Manfield's factory on the Wellinborough Road, Northampton is believed to be the earliest example. Single storey buildings were also erected in Higham Ferrers, Rushden, Long Buckby, Raunds and Kettering. The architect Sir Albert Richardson designed the John White Shoe Factory in Lime Street, Rushden (a two-storey building) in 1938.

There was a large supporting industry for the boot and shoe trade in the county. Tanning and leather dressing and preparing were major elements of this and the manufacture of specific elements of boots and shoes including heels, lasts, laces, uppers, ink, wax, buttons and buckles, Dubbin and polish were also a substantial offshoot. Companies also existed for the specialised manufacture of machinery, tools and even cardboard boxes for the shoe trade.

A county-wide survey of the boot and shoe industry and its component parts has been undertaken by English Heritage. A rapid survey of all surviving boot and shoe factories, workshops and warehouses was undertaken to establish the range and diversity of buildings relating to the industry. Over 400 surviving buildings were recorded in towns and villages across the county, only a sample of garden workshops were recorded due to their prolific numbers, with up to 2000 in Kettering alone. Record sheets for each individual structure surveyed during the project and a report summarising the findings have been produced. (Cooke et al, 2000)

Other manufacturing

Northamptonshire was of national importance for the production of boots and shoes, but there were a number of other industries, which were of economic importance in the county. Clothing manufacture was concentrated in a number of towns along the Ise Valley including Kettering, Rothwell, Desborough, Burton Latimer and Wellingborough and there were also factories in Brigstock and Cottingham. The manufacture of stays and corsets appeared to be a particular local specialism. There has been no substantial archaeological or documentary work conducted on the clothing manufacturing industry in Northamptonshire, but the buildings are very similar in style and function to those in use by the boot and shoe industry.

Brewing and malting became a substantial trade in Northamptonshire in the 19th century; prior to this period brewing was primarily a domestic industry or conducted on a small commercial scale by landlords

and publicans. The growth in commercial brewing began in the late 18th century; simply increasing the size of the equipment used could expand the scale of production. Technological developments such as the use of the thermometer and the introduction of the saccharometer (to calculate fermentation, beer strength, duty and pricing), wort coolers and beer pumps facilitated commercial operations. Improved transport links brought a wider range of markets within reach of the brewers. Northamptonshire, like most counties, had a number of large commercial breweries based in the traditional market towns of Wellingborough, Kettering, Brackley, Towcester and Oundle. The large commercial brewers in the county were family based. The Smiths at Oundle, the Dulleys and Praeds of Wellingborough, the Phillips of Stamford and Northampton and the Phipps who originated in Towcester were all Northamptonshire families who had a substantial stake in the brewing industry in the 19th and early 20th centuries (Brown

9.2 Albion Steam Brewery, Northampton. Photo: NCC 2001

9.3 Rice's Eagle Foundry, Southbridge Road, Northampton. Photo: NCC 1999

and Wilmott 1998). A detailed business history of all known breweries in the county, from the late medieval period to the present day, has been produced, but it is not known how many of these buildings survive. There were also a substantial malting industry in the county particularly in Wellingborough and Oundle. The Maltings, North Street, Oundle were subject to detailed recording in 2000 prior to conversion of the building to flats. The building is shown on an inclosure map of 1810 and was at this date in the ownership of John Smith Senior (who later traded as John Smith Oundle Brewery Ltd) and ceased operation as a maltings in 1966 when it was sold to Oundle School. Few documents survive relating to the building, but evidence for at least six phases of development were recorded (Heaton, 2000).

A number of foundries and engineering works were established in the county during the 19th century. Foundries were attached to some of the iron smelting works in the county, but the majority were separate establishments, which specialised in the production of castings. Initial survey work has been conducted on foundries in Northamptonshire involving a combination of documentary research and a description of the surviving buildings and products (Starmer 1981).

Northamptonshire Industrial Archaeology Group has recorded the working practices of a number of foundries, many of which have now ceased operation. Engineering works were usually established with a particular market in mind. A large number of firms provided machinery for the boot and shoe trade, but there was also a wide range of other specialisms. Charles Wickstead manufactured children's playground equipment in his works at Kettering; the products were tested and used at Wickstead Park as well as being distributed all over the country. The Nene Side Iron Works in Thrapston, owned by Smith and Grace, was responsible for the production of a number of innovative products including a screw boss pulley and a V-drive belt and was successful on a national basis. The company ceased production in 1994 following a fire at the premises and the site was derelict for several years before being re-developed as a housing estate. The manufacture of lifts began in the county in 1910 with the establishment of the Abbey Works in Northampton by a London based company Smith, Major and Stevens. The company merged with Express Lifts in 1930 and ceased operation in Northampton in 1996. The lift-testing tower, a famous landmark in Northampton, was erected in 1982 and is a listed building.

EXTRACTIVE INDUSTRIES

The absence of coal seams in the county contributed significantly to the slow process of industrialisation in Northamptonshire. The lack of coal was a real geological shortage rather than a lack of initiative or entrepreneurs in the county. There were reports of possible coal seams at Poddington and Irchester, although the quality of coal was poor, and the Great Central Coal Mining Company was established to mine for coal at Kingsthorpe, but this was unsuccessful (Northampton Mercury 1854 and 1873). There were, however, a number of other extractive industries in the county.

Stone and slate quarrying
Northamptonshire has rich deposits of many of the important building stones in England. Quarries in the county have been exploited from the Roman period onwards. The large scale extraction of stone from Weldon, Barnack and Helmdon and slate from Collyweston has had a regional and even national importance(Steane, 1968; Parry, 1987). There are also substantial quarries for more local distribution of stone at Kingscliffe, Stanion, Raunds (marble), Watford (marble) and Duston (slate) (Victoria County History, 1906). In the 18th and 19th-centuries 'parish stone pits' were opened up to provide stone for local building purposes. Archaeological work has been undertaken on stone types in the county and their use in individual buildings (Hudson & Sutherland 1990; Steane 1974; Parry 1987) Ongoing work by Sutherland and Hudson has identified quarries from documentary sources, located surviving remains and extracted geological samples; these have been used to identify the sources of stone used in individual buildings in the county (Sutherland pers comm)

The Collyweston slate industry, based in Collyweston, Duddington, Easton-on-the-Hill and Kirby, was of national importance, with slates having been quarried from the Roman period onwards. The peak years for the industry were between 1715 and 1730 with the re-building of Stamford and Oundle. The industry declined during 1850-1870 with competition from Welsh slate (which was made easily available through the railway system), but was revived in the late 19th and early 20th centuries. Collyweston slate was mined underground rather than being subject to open cast quarrying. The slaters did everything on the site including mining the logs, bringing sand and limestone to the surface, dressing the slates, burning the lime, making the laths and fastenings and transporting the slate to individual buildings to be attached to the roof. The 'logs' of Collyweston slate are located between sand and limestone and a large amount of the slaters time was spent excavating sand and providing permanent support for worked out areas; the slate itself is split through frost action. Large number of former quarries are shown on ordnance survey maps indicating that farmers had their own individual slate pits.

Brickworks
Bricks have been produced in Northamptonshire since the Roman period and there have been references to brickworks in the modern sense since the 17th century. The only recorded examples, however, date from the 19th century when there were a large number of brickworks throughout the county. These were located on country house estates, along communication routes (including canals, railway lines and roads) and on the periphery of the towns and villages in the county. By the mid 20th century very few brickworks remained in production; Raunds Manor Farm brickworks was the notable exception as it remained in operation until the late 1970s. A number of buildings and a kiln (believed to be a lime kiln) remain on the site; the kiln is a listed structure. There are other surviving brickwork kilns (at Brixworth, Castle Ashby, Spratton, Great Doddington, Harlestone) (Cadman, pers comm) and a larger number of earthworks created by clay extraction. It is possible that a number of buildings associated with brickworks, such as offices or managers house, may survive.

Ironstone quarrying
The major extractive industry in the county was

the ironstone quarrying industry which began in the 1850s and continued in operation until the 1960s. The development of the industry in Northamptonshire coincided with the recognition of the limitations of the ore deposits in the traditional iron-working regions of Coalbrookedale in Shropshire and the Black Country. The large-scale mechanisation of quarrying commenced with the introduction of the county's first mechanical digger in 1895. The ironstone quarries and mines and their associated railways and machinery had a dramatic impact on the landscape of Northamptonshire during their period of operation. The land has however been re-developed in order to enable re-use and there are few remaining traces of the industry (Trinder 1998). The ironstone industry in the county has been subject to detailed study. Stanley Beaver studied the history and development of ironworking sites and recorded working practices in the 1930s. Geoffrey Starmer undertook a photographic survey of industry in the latter part of the 20th century. Eric Tonks has undertaken a comprehensive survey of the historical development and surviving archaeological remains of the industry and Francis Scopes has chronicled the development of the Corby works in the late 20th century. In the late 1980s and early 1990s remains of the iron ore quarrying industry in the county included disused quarries, bridges, tunnels, disused buildings and derelict cuttings and embankments of the associated railways (Tonks 1988-1992). Sites of particular importance include Irchester Country Park narrow gauge railway and surviving ropeway and tipplers and winding gear at Easton on the Hill.

POWER

The main source of power in the period 1750-1850 was wind or water; with the majority of parishes having a windmill or watermill in close proximity to the main settlement. Many of these structures remained in use throughout the 18th and 19th centuries, but were becoming redundant by the early 20th century. Research is currently being conducted to determine the number, location and survival of watermills and windmills in the county.

The potential sources of power for industry increased dramatically during the course of the 19th century. The steam engine was developed in the 18th century and was in wide-scale use by the 19th century, town gas or coal gas was in use for powering engines from the early 19th century with gas works being established in many settlements in the county between the 1820s and 1870s. Electricity was developed for industrial purposes in the 1880s and electricity works appear to have concentrated in the larger industrial settlements in the county with works at Northampton, Kettering, Wellingborough and Rushden.

PUBLIC UTILITIES

Little is known about the provision of water and sewage facilities in the period immediately following 1750. No extensive documentary or archaeological work has been conducted on the subject. Provision was local and tended to be based on natural sources such as wells, streams and ponds; village pumps were also developed. There are documentary references to health problems caused by the misuse of these water sources. In the early 19th century 'Improvement Acts' were enacted in some settlements in the county including Northampton, Oundle and Brackley; these acts were a first attempt to improve sanitary conditions in the county. Archaeological investigation including detailed topographical survey and excavation may be able to determine to what extent the provisions of these acts were carried out.

There was a large-scale expansion of the provision of public utilities from the early 19th century with the majority of towns and villages gaining provision for gas, water and sewage; the later development of electricity was concentrated in large urban areas. The detail of the establishment of these utilities can be traced through trade directories of the period and the surviving records of the utility companies. Archaeological recording was undertaken at the 19th-century gas works in Kings Cliffe prior to re-development of the site. The gas works was established in 1860 and closed in 1922; it was a small scale works which produced gas for the village of Kings Cliffe. The buildings associated with the works had been used by a garage in later years and many of the original elements of the complex had been demolished or substantially altered, but it was possible to determine some of the original features and the plan of the site. The original gas works had a retort house, coal house, engineers workshop, tar and coke store, purifying house, lime store, meter house and gas holder (Masters and Prentice 2000)

AGRICULTURE

Dramatic changes were occurring in agriculture as well as in industry in the period following 1750. Northamptonshire was one of the midland counties that retained the medieval system of agriculture until a relatively late date; in 1800 over half the county was still operating the open field system. Parliamentary enclosure took place between 1733 and 1901and accounted for 65% of all enclosure in the county. Enclosure had a dramatic impact on the countryside in Northamptonshire with the creation of small, square fields, numerous hedgerows, straight roads and planned farms. Hedgerows dating from this period are now preserved by the Hedgerows Regulations Act of 1997. Planned or model farms were developed away from nucleated villages in the centre of large areas of land. These farms were built to fulfil the functions required by new agricultural methods and techniques without the constraints of earlier development or restricted plots of land. Typically the farms were symmetrical layouts based on a courtyard with barn, stables, cattle sheds and ancillary buildings on each side of the yard. There are likely to be over fifty relatively complete surviving examples of planned farms in Northamptonshire (Bond, pers comm).

Improvements in farming methods, including scientific systems for cattle breeding and new approaches to crop rotation and drainage systems, were developed in the 18th century and were being widely used by the 1820s and 1830s. New machines for agricultural processing were also developed during this period and remnants of these early

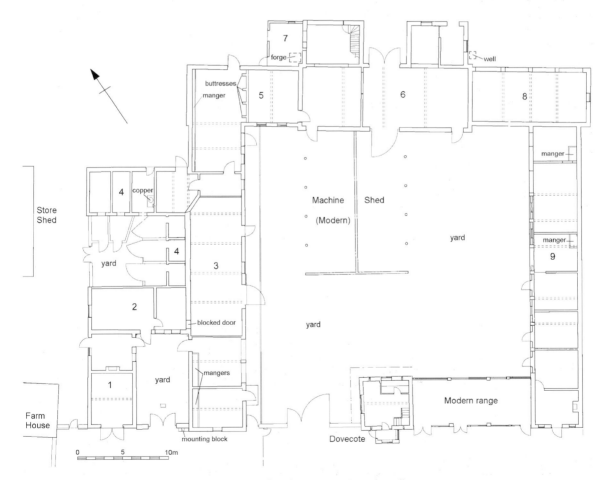

9.4 Plan of Appletree Farm, Aston-le-walls

machines are often found lying disused in farmyards and barns. Increased agricultural mechanisation boosted industrial manufacture and during the 19th century many settlements in Northamptonshire had 'agricultural implement makers' listed amongst their tradesmen. The buildings for these works are often indicated on early Ordnance Survey maps. A combination of archaeological and documentary study of the manufacture and distribution of these machines should provide information about the inter-relationship between towns and the rural environment, the date of production and use of these machines and their effectiveness for agricultural improvements.

SETTLEMENT

The settlement pattern of Northamptonshire in the period 1750-1850 remained relatively consistent from the medieval and post-medieval periods. The population was primarily rural and was based in nucleated villages, although there was some dispersal with farms moving out into the countryside following enclosure. The majority of market towns, which were identified from documentary sources in the mid 18th century, continued in existence as urban centres. The markets at Rockingham, West Haddon and Weldon had, however, gone out of use by the mid 19th century. A number of towns including Towcester, Daventry and Brackley developed an additional role as thoroughfare towns during the coaching era.

From the mid 19th century onwards there was a process of urbanisation with a high proportion of the population shifting from a rural to an urban environment. The large towns of Northampton, Kettering and Wellingborough underwent a substantial growth in the late 19th century, but many of the other traditional market towns such as Daventry, Brackley, Towcester, Oundle and Thrapston did not experience such substantial development. The development of the boot and shoe industry had a major effect on settlement patterns; a number of villages such as Rushden, Raunds, Irthlingborough, Desborough and Earls Barton expanded rapidly due to the domination of this trade in the settlement. Rushden, in particular, developed from an average village into a substantial Victorian town due to the influence of the boot and shoe industry (Fig 9.5). These areas gained large mixed zones, comprising housing, factories, social clubs, chapels and schools, on the edge of the core settlements. The market towns of Higham Ferrers and Rothwell also underwent substantial growth based on boot and shoe production.

There was a massive increase in housing provision in the towns and villages of Northamptonshire in the late 19th century. The majority of houses were built following the establishment of national bye-laws (governing house type and construction, road layout, drainage, sanitation etc) in the 1850s and were therefore of good quality construction. The majority of terraced houses, which were built in Northamptonshire in the 19th century, are still in domestic occupation today. The houses were built by a range of different groups including private entrepreneurs, factory owners, speculative builders, Freehold Land Societies and Co-operative Societies. Freehold Land Societies were established to provide working class people with the opportunity of owning land and ultimately their own homes. Individuals contributed money on a regular basis, once sufficient capital was raised the societies would buy a plot of land and divide it between the members. Individuals were then able to build their own houses, sell the land on or wait until they had sufficient money for the next stage. One particular society in Northampton developed 11 housing estates comprising 67 streets and 3064 houses in this way (Greenhall lecture 2001)

The Extensive Urban Survey funded by English Heritage surveyed 16 industrial towns in Northamptonshire, the character and development of each settlement was analysed allowing comparisons to be made between towns. Key settlements which have not been studied include Northampton, Corby, the canal settlements of Braunston and Stoke Bruerne, the railway settlement of Woodford Halse and the large boot and shoe villages of Earls Barton and Wollaston.

COMMUNICATIONS

Northamptonshire was affected by all of the transport revolutions of the period following 1750; the coaching era, the canal era and the railway era. To a considerable degree Northamptonshire became a thoroughfare county. This is particularly evident in the area between Daventry and Northampton, known as the Watford Gap, where the A5 (road constructed by Thomas Telford on alignment of Roman Road), West Coast Mainline Railway, the Grand Union Canal and M1 all follow the same alignment within a narrow transport corridor.

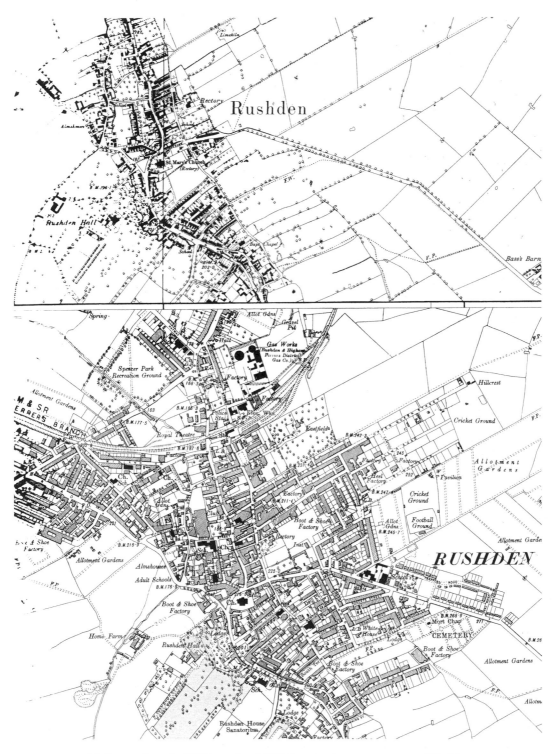

9.5 Extracts from the 1888 (upper) and 1926 (lower) ordnance survey maps of Rushden

Roads

There was a substantial change to the road network in the period following 1750. Enclosure awards established a number of new roads and these were built to standard specifications and widths. Turnpike roads were also developed in the 18th century; 36 turnpike trusts were established by Acts of Parliament for Northamptonshire (and the Soke of Peterborough). The London to Holyhead road was developed in the early 19th century; Thomas Telford directed the engineering work on the route. The road passed through the county on the alignment of Watling Street Roman Road and became a major national communication link which attracted a considerable body of traffic. Many of our modern roads are established on the alignments of the former turnpikes, but no detailed work has been undertaken to determine how many associated structures such as milestone, finger posts, toll houses and inns remain.

There has been some work conducted on turnpike roads in the county, but this has been primarily based on documents (Cossons 1950).

Canals

Water transport was an equally important communication link through the county in the late 18th and early 19th centuries. The River Nene was made navigable following an Act of Parliament in 1756. Work progressed upstream and the river was eventually made navigable to Northampton in 1761. The river made Northamptonshire accessible to the East Coast and was a commercial success; a number of wharves were established in the county. The canalisation of the River Nene also altered communication routes in the county as many former cross-valley tracks and causeways were abandoned. Three canals traverse Northamptonshire; the Oxford Canal constructed between 1769-1793 and straightened 1831-4, Grand

9.6 Aerial photograph of Watford Gap transport corridor showing the successive transport systems. Photo: NCC 1973

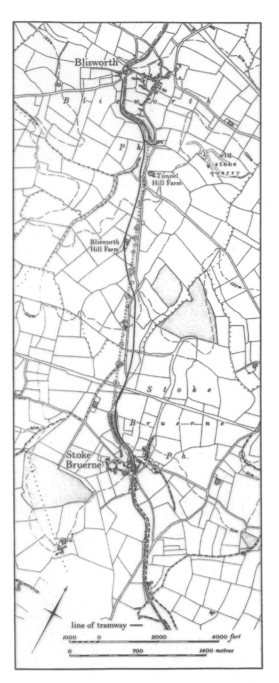

9.7 The line of the Blisworth to Stoke Bruene tramway, surveyed by RCHME

Junction Canal constructed between 1793-1815 with the Northampton Arm completed in 1815 and the Grand Union Canal built between 1810-1841. The early alignment of the Oxford Canal survives in part as an earthwork and the remaining canals are still in use (Blagrove D 1990). In addition to the canals themselves there are a substantial number of surviving locks, tunnels, bridges, pump houses, canal workers cottages, wharves and warehouses in association with the route.

Railway
The first railway in Northamptonshire ran between Stoke Bruerne and Blisworth (colour plate 11). It was established by the Grand Junction Canal Company and was in use between1800 and 1805. The line was used to transport goods between Blisworth and Stoke Bruerne locks during the construction of the Blisworth Tunnel. The line was surveyed by the Royal Commission of Historical Monuments of England in the 1970s and a section of it was excavated in 1969 (RCHME 1981). The remainder of the railway network through Northamptonshire was established from the mid 19th century onwards. The London and Birmingham Railway opened in 1838 and the Midland Railway opened through Kettering and Wellingborough to Bedford and Hitchin in 1857 and to London St Pancras in 1868. There were a substantial number of passenger branch lines established within the county boundary and railway systems were also used extensively for the ironstone quarrying industry (Trinder 1998). The railways had a major impact on industry and settlement in Northamptonshire and are of significance as both transport networks and feats of engineering. A large number of local lines were closed and dismantled during the 1960s, although there are a number of surviving alignments complete with earthworks, embankments, bridges and tunnels; a number of buildings associated with the railway also survive. The London and Birmingham route, the Midland mainline and some sections of the Great Western routes to the south of the county remain in operation. The historical development of the railways in the county has been well documented, but there has been little archaeological work. Recording work was undertaken at Southbridge, Northampton prior to the regeneration of the area. This included an analysis of the commercial, manufacturing, administrative, transhipment, warehousing/storage,

transport regulation and railway infrastructure elements of the site and the detailed recording of the granary, transhipment sheds and railway office buildings (Prentice & Soden 1999).

COMMERCE

In the early phase of the period commercial activity remained centred around the traditional market towns in the county. War Office statistics of 1756 indicate that markets were still in operation at West Haddon, Higham Ferrers, Northampton, Daventry, Kettering, Oundle, Rockingham, Rothwell, Towcester, Wellingborough, Brackley, Weldon and Thrapston. Analysis of carrier networks from trade directories indicates that the majority of journeys within the county were to towns on market days. Market places had been established in the medieval or post-medieval period and were generally in central locations in the towns. Public houses and inns were located in most settlements in the county, but were particularly numerous in market towns and settlements with a large through-trade in the coaching era. The staple retail trades such as butcher, bakers and tailors were found in many villages as well as the market towns. Shop frontages were inserted into existing buildings from the 18th century onwards. The precise nature and function of early retail premises has not been systematically studied.

The mid-19th century saw an expansion in commercial activity; trade directories of the period show the development of a diverse range of retail functions including specialised shops and services such as jewellers, musical instrument dealers, furniture outlets, hat renovators, photographic materials dealers, oil and colour merchants etc. Large purpose-built shops and department stores and architecturally distinctive banks and post offices were erected in the larger towns. Corner shops were constructed in conjunction with terraced houses as part of urban expansion in the late 19th century. Many of the developing Co-operative Societies had an interest in retail and erected large, elaborate commercial premises.

ADMINISTRATIVE AND SOCIAL ORGANISATION

In the period immediately following 1750 the administration of the county was based around the system of hundreds and parishes which had been established in the medieval period. Justice was primarily administered through the hundred system and the parish was involved in a range of issues including provision for the poor and the maintenance of roads. The majority of these administrative functions would not leave material remains that could be examined by archaeological study. The main exceptions were the early workhouses, which were administered by the parish and were forerunners to the workhouses of the post-1834 Poor Law Unions. The total number of such institutions in the county is not known, although there were examples at Kettering, Wellingborough, Rothwell and Oundle (Ballinger 1999).

A wide range of administrative organisations were established during the course of the 19th century. These included Poor Law Unions, borough, rural and urban councils, school boards, burial boards, boards of health and sanitary authorities. A vast range of buildings were erected by these organisations including workhouses, town halls, schools, cemeteries, hospitals, police stations, water and sewage works. There was also a tremendous expansion in the number of social and recreational facilities provided including libraries, parks, art galleries, sports facilities, working men's clubs, theatres, cinemas and non-conformist chapels. These developments were mirrored elsewhere in the country, but in Northamptonshire the provision of these facilities coincided with the primary phase of industrialisation in the county. The administrative, educational, religious and recreational aspects of the development of individual towns was considered as part of the Extensive Urban Survey, but further research is needed on the impact they had on urbanisation. Working class organisations such as working mens clubs, the co-operative movement and the temperance movement also had a considerable influence on the development of Northamptonshire in the 19th century.

The Co-operative Society in Desborough was particularly active with interests in agriculture, industry, retail and housing provision. Industrial production included brick and tile manufacture, ironstone quarrying, coal distribution, boot and shoe production and corset making. The Society was also involved in discussions about the provision of a library, recreation ground and sewage system for the town.

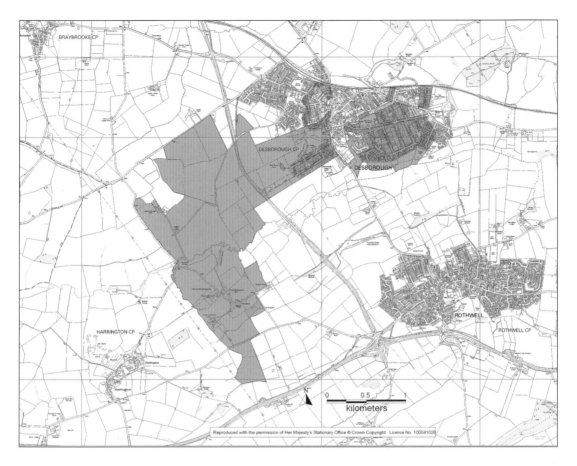

9.8 Map of co-operative society holdings in Desborough

RELIGION

Non-conformity continued to develop and a number of non-conformist chapels were erected in the county in the 18th and early 19th centuries. These were primarily for Baptist, Independent and Methodist denominations, although there were also some Quaker Meeting Houses established. The Royal Commission of Historical Monuments of England conducted a survey of 85 non-conformist chapels in the county in the 1980s, but the survey was primarily architectural and there was little analytical consideration of these structures as a building type (RCHME 1986). The Extensive Urban Survey revealed that there were a large number of non-conformist chapels in each of the settlements throughout the county, with a minimum of three in some of the smaller settlements and over 20 in

the larger settlements of Kettering, Wellingborough and Rushden. A large number of chapel buildings survive, but many have been converted for alternative uses.

There was also a major building programme by the Church of England during the 19th century. New churches were built in many of the larger settlements and new ecclesiastical parishes were established in Northampton, Kettering, Wellingborough and Rushden. A substantial number of medieval churches were also 'refurbished' during this time.

MILITARY

Northamptonshire's geographical location far removed from the coast and the immediate threat of raids and invasion placed it, until the arrival of the Cold War, well behind any notional 'front

9.9 Weedon Depot. Aerial view from the west in September 1983, prior to encroachment of housing down the hillside from the north. In the foreground are the powder magazines set within their walled enclosure. Beyond are a series of wartime Romney and other storage huts, now lost and beyond them the main store buildings located within their own walled enclosure complete with corner bastions. The former barracks and hospital lay to the north under the emerging industrial estate.

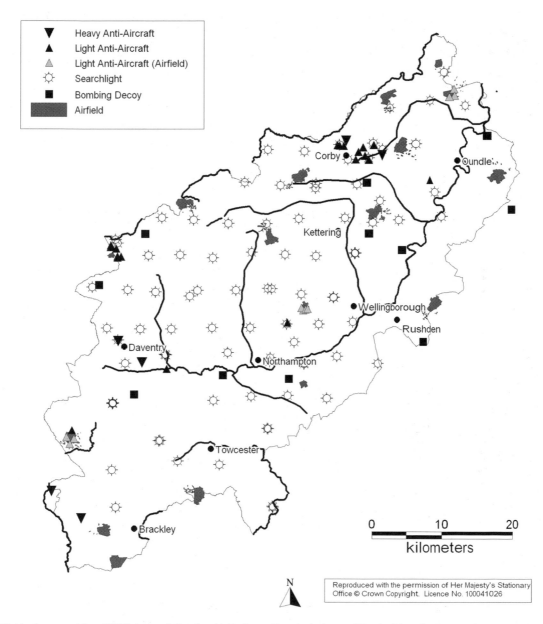

9.10 Northamptonshire – WW2 Active & Passive Air Defences.Even in the heart of England free from any major conurbations defences are widespread. The distribution reflects the extent of sites identified to date through a combination of fieldwork and documentary research. Heavy anti-aircraft guns (active defences) were confined to protecting industrial or communication targets in Banbury, Daventry and Corby. Light anti-aircraft gun provision complemented the latter as well as being focused around select airfields and Rugby. Note the regular distribution of searchlights (passive defences) in areas plotted to date. Compiled by Graham Cadman utilising SMR data, particularly research by Adrian Armishaw.

line'. There are no fortifications or battlefields for the industrial period in Northamptonshire and for the early part of the period there are just two major monuments: Gibraltar Barracks in Northampton and the Royal Ordnance Depot at Weedon Bec. The demands of the Napoleonic Wars and the increase in radicalism at home led to an acceptance of the need for barracks late in the 18th century. Gibraltar Barracks, erected in 1797 for cavalry and subsequently modified and expanded for infantry, was amongst the first wave of permanent barracks built by the new Barracks Board in England (Douet 1998). Only two ranges with some ancillary remains still stand. Weedon Depot was built by Board of Ordnance in the early 19th century, incorporating massive storehouses and magazines. The site is of national importance with its individual structures listed: it has been subject to a recording by Royal Commission of Historical Monuments of England. In addition there is the striking, listed Militia Store in Northampton and at least five 19th-century military encampments identified through metal detecting. The latter are a type of site so far little researched or published (Derby pers comm).

The increasing technological and industrial sophistication of 20th century conflict is evidenced in increased local war production. There were munitions factories from WW1 at Warkworth (Cocroft 2000) now represented by extensive earthworks, and in both world wars at the Abbey Works in Northampton (Northamptonshire Archaeology 1999). Borough Hill, Daventry was a focus for development of radar and the operation of aircraft navigation systems (Gibson 1982). The works at Corby played an important role in the manufacturing of 'PLUTO' (Pipeline under the ocean) and the Mulberry harbours used in the invasion of Europe.

WW2, and the age of 'total war' engulfing entire populations, witnessed a considerable intensification in military activity with consequent impact on the Northamptonshire landscape. The nature and scale of this varied greatly; many of the sites are very prone to decay and loss, being built at a time of emergency with no thought of permanence. Northamptonshire lay behind the static anti-invasion defences established in 1940 and thus lacks evidence for fixed stoplines or associated defences though. Northampton and Kettering were designated as anti-tank islands with all round defences. There was a considerable RAF and US airforce presence in the county, with associated bombing ranges and decoy sites, along with a wide range of training, storage and Civil Defence activities. Considerable scope exists for further locally based investigations, such as recently undertaken on Northampton's anti-invasion defences (Hollowell 1998-9). Key surviving sites include select airfield defences, Weedon Depot, and the two Cold War Thor missile sites at Polebrook and Harrington.

CONCLUSION

The landscape and topography of Northamptonshire has changed dramatically since 1750. Several phases of communication routes have traversed the county, market towns have expanded and villages developed into urban centres, the open fields of the medieval and post medieval period have been divided by enclosure and industries have developed, left their mark and declined. The challenge for the 21st century is to ensure that the sites, monuments, buildings and landscapes of the past two centuries are understood, and where appropriate conserved, before physical evidence for the period is lost in the next phase of change and development in the county.

10
Archaeology in the future

MARTIN TINGLE

21st- CENTURY ARCHAEOLOGY

At the beginning of the twentieth century, archaeology was a new discipline that had only recently developed from the antiquarianism of previous centuries, but transformed by scientific methods and the theoretic frameworks of the social sciences. It was practised by a small group of amateurs drawn from the middle and upper classes amongst whom there were both the talented and innovative as well as an array of incompetents and frauds. A century later archaeology has become a mainstream academic discipline taught in most of the 'old' universities and increasing appearing in some of the 'new'. It is also a multi-million pound sector of the construction industry. It was estimated in 1999 that the number of professional archaeologists, made up of those employed in commercial archaeology, local government planning agencies, national heritage bodies, and museums, numbered over 3000 (Aitchison 1999). In addition to all this, media coverage, especially from television programmes has made archaeology a branch of popular entertainment attracting audiences of millions. It is debatable how

10.1 Time Team filming at the Prebendal Manor House at Nassington in May 2003.

far these programmes actually reflect the true nature of the discipline however it is undeniable that they have raised its public profile

PPG16

The single most important event in the growth of archaeology over recent years was the governments' introduction in 1990 of Planning Policy Guidance Note 16. This instructed local authorities to consider the impact of development on archaeological remains before issuing planning permission. Crucially, it ensured that the cost of investigating the archaeology of any site became the responsibility of the developer rather than the local government. As a result of this, the old county archaeology units were divided into 'curators' and 'contractors'. The curators remained within the county planning departments maintaining a database of all the known archaeological finds within the county (the Sites and Monuments Record) and advising on the level of archaeological intervention that should be applied to each planning application. The 'contractors' who were initially the County Council field archaeologists, became notionally independent bodies bidding to take on the work that had been stipulated by the curators. For a short period the contractors continued to work only within their old county boundaries but this quickly broke down as the more commercially minded units began to bid for contacts in neighbouring areas. In addition senior staff began to leave the county units to set up small independent organisations as did some of the larger university archaeology departments. In a recent review of professional archaeological activity within Northamptonshire during 2003, it was revealed that at least nine separate archaeological contractors had been working within the county (Horne 2003).

The impact of these changes on the archaeology of Northamptonshire has been an increase in the number of rescue excavations in the county carried out by a greater variety of organisations. Since Northamptonshire is situated at the junction of the M1 and M6 and linked to the A1 by the A14, it is unsurprising that recent large scale developments within the county have been connected to transportation and retailing. At sites such as the Daventry International Rail Freight Terminal (DIRFT) and the Retail Parks at Brackmills and Couteenhall on the edge of Northampton, large scale excavations have taken place in advance of development.

The DIRFT site initially covered an area of 73 hectares next to the A5 at Crick. Geophysical surveys indicated three areas of intensive settlement and initially two of these were subject to pre-emptive excavation between August and December of 1994 by Northamptonshire Archaeology (the former county council archaeological unit). This produced evidence of Roman and Anglo-Saxon occupation as well as two Iron Age settlements that were unusual both for their density and the complexity of their formation (see Chapter 4, this volume). A second season of excavations took place at the site between August of 1997 and September 1998, but this time carried out by the Birmingham University Field Archaeology Unit. This produced yet another extensive and long lived Iron Age settlement on either side of a broad palaeochannel. A final excavation, carried out by the Swindon based Foundations Archaeology in 1999 on the site of a proposed hotel, revealed still more Iron Age settlement remains

While it is true that, during the last twenty years, more archaeological work has taken place within the county than at any period previously, there are real problems associated with the expansion of commercial archaeology. Competitive tendering by archaeological contractors can lead to large sites such as DIRFT being divided between a number of organisations, which are under no obligation to co-operate in the final publication of the site. Although most contractors are conscientious in their publication of site reports, commercial pressures could force them to produce reports as 'in house' documentation that will never reach a wider audience. It also begs the question of what would happen to partially completed sites if an archaeological contractor were to become insolvent.

PROJECTED THREATS TO THE ARCHAEOLOGICAL RECORD

Over the last 25 years, the threats to the archaeology of Northamptonshire have remained the same, however the responses to them have changed. Mineral extraction, road building and urban expansion have continued devour the landscape but in recent times, only after some sort of archaeological investigation of the threatened area has taken place. However, strategies to mitigate against the unrecorded loss of archaeological remains are based on our current knowledge of the archaeological record and this has

10.2 The Daventry International Rail Freight Terminal under construction.
Reproduced by permission of the Historic Environment Team. © Northamptonshire County Council

10.3 The earthwork remains at Lilbourne before their destruction in 1993.
Reproduced by permission of the Historic Environment Team. © Northamptonshire County Council

sometimes proved insufficient. Twice in the last five years Roman villas have unexpectedly come to light during construction work in Northamptonshire In 1999 the construction of a roadway across a housing development at Wootton cut through a Roman bath complex while the construction of a composting facility at Stanion in 2002 revealed the entire wing of a villa. However on both occasions, negotiations between the developer and the Historic Environment Team at Northamptonshire County Council resulted in suspension of the development while rescue excavations and recording work took place

Agriculture remains the largest single area in which there is little scope to either restrain or record the destruction of the archaeological record. Although the agricultural erosion of archaeological remains has been a feature of the landscape for thousands of years, the destruction has accelerated with widespread post-war mechanisation. Most of this takes the form of the gradual erosion of subsoil features and thus has no obvious visual impact however a particular problem that affects Northamptonshire and other neighbouring Midland counties is the destruction of medieval earthworks.

It has been estimated that by 1992, 85% of the ridge and furrow that had existed in 1940 was destroyed mostly by ploughing (see D. Hall this volume). Perhaps the most striking single example of this took place at Lilbourne as recently as 1993. When the M1 and then the M5 had been constructed the junction of the two motorways narrowly missed the earthwork remains of a castle mound, associated with house platforms and hollow ways, next to an isolated church and surrounded by ridge and furrow. While the church and the castle mound were legally protected, the surrounding earthworks were not and consequently these were all completely destroyed when the site was ploughed for the first time since the medieval period. Throughout the county, some preservation and recording of the threatened earthworks has been achieved through government sponsored conservation schemes, but these have are limited in their extent and resources

FUTURE RESEARCH AGENDAS FOR NORTHAMPTONSHIRE

In the latter months of 1999, English Heritage began a process of consultation that lead to the production of a series of county based discussion documents, which sought to establish an agenda for the future of archaeological research in various English regions. Within this process, a series of papers were written that documented the current state of archaeology in Northamptonshire and its likely future. It was from the first section of these papers that the preceding chapters of this volume were derived and from the second section that these concluding statements are drawn. The original documents can be viewed at: www.le.ac.uk/ar/east-midlands-research-framework.htm

THE PALAEOLITHIC
(Greg Phillips and Sandy Kidd)

It is hard to deny that the number of Palaeolithic finds from the county is minute when one considers that enormous timespan that is covered by the period even allowing for the fact that for much of this period, the English Midlands would have been on the edge or beyond the limit of human habitation. It is possible that there could be unrecognised examples in archive collections and there is also the possibility of new finds such as the recent discovery of an *in situ* knapping site, just over the county boundary in Leicestershire. Such discoveries may be facilitated simply by re-visiting the locations of the few accurately provenanced lower Palaeolithic finds to establish whether they truly represent individual finds or were part of larger activity areas. The extent of gravel quarrying in the Nene valley around Northampton should in theory enhance the potential of locating primary context palaeo-environmental and archaeological sites.

THE MESOLITHIC
(Greg Phillips)

Within the river valleys a high priority should be given to the to the investigation of gravel islands and alluvial fans. This may involve the utilisation of specific field survey methodologies that are targeted specifically at the discovery of the smaller single use sites. Further analysis is required of existing lithic assemblages, starting with the attempts to refine their dating on typological grounds. Included in this assessment would be an examination of assemblages such as those recovered by Hall and Martin, particularly to identify sites where late Mesolithic and Earliest Neolithic material is present on the same site. Given the likely scale at which Mesolithic communities may have interacted with the landscape, it would be of obvious advantage to establish links with archaeological groups in neighbouring counties.

THE NEOLITHIC AND BRONZE AGE
(Andy Chapman)

Although Northamptonshire may lack a range of upstanding prehistoric field monuments, the county has in recent years been subject to several high quality landscape surveys and excavations. This has included the Raunds Area Project, and the publication of the results will form a benchmark for such studies at a national level. Unfortunately, the inevitable limitations of the current system of contract tendering and developer funding mean we are unlikely to see research within a development project on a comparable scale again. However, this makes it more important that we are flexible enough to exploit the inevitable chance opportunities that will arise within fieldwork carried out primarily on sites of later periods. Within the present system, known major sites of Neolithic date will have a high priority for preservation, but there may be opportunities to explore the environs of such sites, such as in potential development of the area around the causewayed enclosure at Dallington, Northampton. Within the

Bronze Age there are numerous recorded ring ditches of ploughed out round barrows. Many of these will not warrant protection and development may provide opportunities to examine some examples, as with a round barrow adjacent to a new link road to the Brackmills industrial estate in Northampton, where radiocarbon dates have been obtained for both the round barrow and a satellite cremation.

The nature and chronology of the transition between the Mesolithic and Neolithic is far from clear even if it is simply viewed as the extent to which agriculture supplemented or substituted for hunting and gathering. One way of elucidating this may be through more detailed examination of sites that appear to have both later Mesolithic and early Neolithic elements in their assemblages, but it may be that the quality of survival is generally too poor to provide significant advances in understanding within the county.

The excavation evidence from the county has inevitably been biased towards sites on the gravel terraces of the Nene valley, and any opportunities to excavate Neolithic and Bronze Age sites on the higher claylands that cover so much of the county must be fully exploited. The recent discovery of a causewayed enclosure and associated monuments at Husbands Bosworth, Leicestershire near the Northamptonshire border, highlights the potential that exists (Clay 2002).

Further studies of palaeo-environmental evidence for the introduction and development of agriculture should be made together with the increased use of scientific dating techniques. The broad range of survey data that is available for Northamptonshire, particularly from the Raunds Area Project, should also make it possible to examine the way in which different landscape zones were exploited at different times.

THE IRON AGE
(Sandy Kidd)

In order to advance the study of the Iron Age in Northamptonshire, a number of interrelated issues need to be addressed. Firstly to clarify terminology, for instance by establishing a common classificatory/terminological system for IA ceramics based on David Knight's definitions and guidelines (Knight, 1998 and forthcoming). Also to review the potential for scientific dating and to issue guidelines for proper implementation through PPG16.

In the study of settlement and landscape it would be a priority to improve the understanding of how the Iron Age landscapes developed and functioned and the restrictions imposed by the natural environment. Continued aerial survey and morphological analysis, aimed at the integration of excavation, survey and environmental data could achieve this. It would be necessary to recognise the scale of study required to investigate landscape change and ensure the integrated analysis and publication of projects undertaken through PPG16 (e.g. in the Upper Nene valley and at Crick) and major backlog projects (eg Stanwick villa). There is scope for further environmental data for landscape change, especially woodland clearance on the claylands as well as the application of new techniques such as multi-element analysis to enhance understanding of landscape function.

In order to improve understanding of the organisation of social and economic relationships, the following topics should be considered. The application of lipid and stable isotope analyses to improve understanding of the relative importance of pastoral and arable production. Further research into the social and economic role of Northamptonshire's hillforts, including a comprehensive modern restudy of Hunsbury hillfort and its museum archive. Further research into the social and economic significance of distinct settlement types e.g. agglomerated settlements, neighbourhood groups. Sub-regional identity and diversity also need further study. Are Rockingham Forest or northwest Northants socially and/or economically distinct from the better understood Upper Nene valley/Ise valley? Topics that would be appropriate for detailed research would include Northamptonshire's iron industry and pit alignments

THE ROMAN PERIOD
(Myk Flitcroft & Jeremy Taylor)

Northamptonshire generally has a wealth of information on the Roman period although there are still numerous areas in which our knowledge of the period could be extended, as well as completely new areas of research. Recent trends in Romano-British archaeology have tended to emphasis aspects of the interaction between native populations and the incoming power of Roman imperialism

Initially, it would help to establish a better understanding of later Iron Age society in this area given its position on the likely boundary of three tribal groups. A better understanding of the period during and immediately after the conquest would elucidate the nature of the military occupation that led to the establishment of *Civitas* centres out-side the county. The likely re-organisation of the countryside, the development of local centres and even the construction of the road network are all areas that require attention

Specific recommendations for future work might include a study of settlement morphology and land use in particular landscapes such as those of Raunds, Crick, Wollaston and Courteenhall. Other areas with potential for landscape study may be identified by re-evaluating existing survey information (eg Hall & Martin; Foster). There is a marked shortage of botanical and faunal reports from Roman sites in Northamptonshire indicating that palaeo-environmental analysis needs to be prioritised in future project briefs.

There is still great potential in the study of industrial production, particularly regarding the upper and lower Nene Valley potteries and Iron production. For the former, fabric analysis and the study of kiln sites would both increase the understanding of the link between settlement and supply as well as looking at the relationship between the pottery and tile industries. Future research on Iron production should refine the basic information we already possess and concentrate on areas such as Laxton/ Rockingham Forest and/or the Higham Ferrers/ Bedfordshire borders where significant blocks of landscape may still survive to provide contextual study of the industry.

In order to increase the understanding of the way in which regional identities were expressed during this period it may be appropriate to consider factors such as regional variation in settlement architecture or even portable artefacts. Similarly, the evidence from local religious practices, such as structured deposition, human burial, especially in boundary contexts and even the religious associations of architecture may be fruitful areas for future study. As a more immediate and practical outcome for the Roman archaeology of Northamptonshire, the publication of important excavations at small town of Ashton is an urgent priority.

THE ANGLO-SAXON
(Tony Brown & Glenn Foard)

The nature of the Anglo-Saxon conquest of Northamptonshire and the restructuring of the post Roman

economy has yet to be addressed. In consequence, excavation of sites spanning the fifth century is a high priority. In contrast to the ditch systems of the Iron Age and Roman periods, there is no known system of early/middle Saxon land division. Does this imply that Roman fields continued to be used when Roman settlements had been abandoned. There should also be a more wide ranging study of settlement change to examine the apparent retraction of occupation from the boulder claylands.

Since Northamptonshire was cut in half by the creation of the Danelaw, the county provides a suitable setting for a comparative study to examine what effect the political division had the development of settlement. Similarly a study of the 'great re-planning' could examine the nucleation of villages and their relationship to the creation of common fields. A major objective should also be to isolate any features in the open field and village plan forms that derive from an earlier landscape and thus provided the basic framework around which re-planning took place.

The growth of urban areas and the development of markets as well as *burhs* such as Northampton and Towcester requires further study. It would also be desirable to establish the relative importance within regional and national trade networks, of goods originating from Northamptonshire.

THE MEDIEVAL
(Glenn Foard)

Factors such as sparse documentation for the period before the 13th century creates numerous areas which could be illuminated by future research. With the exception of pottery production, there is a lack of knowledge of medieval industry in both urban and rural contexts. Very few pre-15th century buildings are known other than churches and a small number of manor houses. The identification of any surviving buildings of a lower status, such as a small hall house that was recently identified at Gretton, would be an obvious priority.

Northamptonshire and adjacent areas of Leicestershire and Warwickshire represent one of the best preserved areas of medieval field systems. However, a comparison of field systems mapped in the early 1990's with an aerial survey made in 1999 revealed considerable destruction had taken place. This suggests an urgent need for detailed earthwork surveying of threatened areas as well as fieldwalking survey of recently ploughed out field systems to examine the nature and extent of any manuring scatters that were present.

Recent work on smoke blackened thatch roofing has revealed a hitherto unsuspected potential for the preservation of plant remains. A survey of the more than 500 straw thatched buildings in the county is needed to identify and protect this rare resource.

Finally, the morphology of settlement remains a priority both at currently occupied and deserted earthwork sites. Although most of the latter have already been surveyed by the Royal Commission for Historic Monuments, considerable additional detail could be added to their plans

THE POST MEDIEVAL
(David Hall)

The post-medieval period has an enormous wealth of documentary evidence relating to all its physical and social aspects. In the past, the known existence of written records has encouraged an unwarranted neglect of later archaeological remains, by medievalists, on the premise that 'everything was known'. For all the selected topics, except field systems, the extent and importance of the archaeological resource is not fully known because of lack of a full assessment of the historical record.

For the countryside, good examples of hedges and of ridge and furrow, have been identified. Forest earthworks need protection, and the areas of medieval woods require mapping on the SMR so that informed advice can be provided about tree-planting schemes. Parks and gardens need both historical and ground survey work, and comparative assessment with neighbouring counties.

Urban settlements need study to ascertain why and how they developed in terms of commerce and industry. The significance of inns, alehouses and stabling requires further work.. The early industries of cloth and leather still have several unknowns about their respective decline and growth. Building materials and buildings require considerable input to make the most of the important information that they can reveal.

The recent research assessment exercise sought to identify areas where specific historical work is required urgently, and to ensure that suitable landscapes and monuments are preserved to enable future archaeological and historical researches to be fruitful. Local groups need to be to encouraged to undertake specific tasks that are essential to progress the research frameworks currently being

devised. For instance, many topics are suitable for a mature degree or post-graduate study, or for publication in county archaeological and historical journals. In all cases there should be some clearly defined (academic) end-product for the authors, so they do not feel they are doing unpaid work for Local Government (even though they are). There are many suitable topics, and, above all, many types of building survey are required. In some cases a particular need is clear enough to be presented as a short-term project worthy of an application for funding from English Heritage or other bodies. In the absence of supporting historical studies, it will be impossible to be aware of all the many categories of physical remains likely to survive, and they will not be adequately dealt with before they disappear. If action is not taken, the post-medieval period will be not be properly recorded or preserved because of failure to generate interest because it is 'too recent'.

INDUSTRIAL ARCHAEOLOGY
(Jenny Ballinger)

The study of the industrial period lags far behind that of other periods and a considerable amount of work is required to ensure that industrial and modern sites and monuments are given due weight alongside earlier archaeology. However since 2000 the profile of the archaeology of industrialisation has been raised in the county and a substantial amount of work undertaken.

Northamptonshire Industrial Archaeology Group (NIAG) continue their sterling work on behalf of industrial archaeology in the county and local volunteers continue recording of modern military archaeology. The Emergency Recording Team of English Heritage (formerly Royal Commission of Historical Monuments of England) have undertaken a survey of all surviving buildings (including factories, workshops, warehouses and leather preparation premises) relating to the boot and shoe industry and a representative sample of these buildings have been added to the statutory list. A similar survey of all watermill sites in the county has also been undertaken by Geoffrey Starmer of Northamptonshire Industrial Archaeology Group. English Heritage have complete studies of the Cold War monuments including making scheduling recommendations in Northamptonshire. Former industrial and modern military sites are routinely assessed through the planning process using supplementary planning guidance 15 (Planning and the Historic Environment) and PPG 16 (Planning and Archaeology) and a substantial number of buildings have been recorded prior to demolition, conversion or redevelopment. Where possible active conservation of sites is encouraged through use of Defra's agri-environment schemes. To date there has been only one excavation specifically targeted at the industrial period – on the line of the former Stoke Bruerne to Blisworth plateway. *Northamptonshire's Modern and Industrial Heritage: A Management Strategy 2001-2006* has been produced and although not formerly adopted and only partially implemented due to resource issues this document lays down a framework for the future development and study of the industrial period in Northamptonshire. In a wider context Diane Sutherland has produced *Northamptonshire Stone*, an authoritative work on the geology and building stone of the county.

There is, however, a considerable amount of work yet to be done, particularly on the larger research questions. Why did the county not experience large-scale industrialisation until after 1850? Were the factors behind industrialisation/urbanisation in Northamptonshire similar or different to those in counties that had experienced industrialisation at an earlier date? Did industrialisation / urbanisation improve or worsen the living conditions of the population of Northamptonshire. What was the full extent and impact of military activity up to and including the Cold War?

There are a wide range of individual research topics which would beneficially aid an understanding of the industrial period in Northamptonshire. These include the link between craft industry and larger scale manufacturing with emphasis on the type of accommodation used for domestic industry; the relationship between urbanisation / communications revolution within the county with an emphasis on the production and distribution of bricks; power sources for factories and other industrial complexes; the relationship between development of planned farms, enclosure, land ownership and new 'scientific' methods of farming; better understanding of the role and extent of field buildings in the landscape; continuity and change in settlement patterns in the county and the impact of the Co-operative Movement on the social, economic and physical development of settlements.

ONGOING ARCHAEOLOGY IN NORTHAMPTONSHIRE

While most of the archaeological activity that is carried out in the county is generated by building developments, mineral extraction and transport projects, an element of purely academic research is still present. These range from multi-disciplinary studies initiated from university departments to the work of local societies and individual fieldworkers.

The villa at Piddington was originally discovered in 1781 by limestone quarriers but then was virtually forgotten until 1979. Since then it has been the subject of one of the longest running programmes of excavations in British archaeology. The Upper Nene Archaeological Society has raised funds to convert a local chapel into a museum and will continue with fieldwork at the site for the foreseeable future. As well as Piddington, important excavations have taken place at Easton Maudit, where a villa, apparently with round towers at each end, was revealed and at Rushton, the Ise Valley Archaeological Society are continuing to excavate an important roman site. In the upper Nene valley the Whitehall Farm project is a re-examination of the villa at Nether Heyford linked to a Community Landscape & Archaeology Survey Project (CLASP)

At a migration period site at Polebrook, excavations and geophysical survey are being conducted by a team from the Middle Nene Archaeological Society, the Nene Valley Archaeological Trust and the University of Brunei. This has produced evidence for a series of rectangular buildings within a regular and well planned settlement.

In the spring of 2000 a two year pilot project began to prepare for a long-term multi-disciplinary study of the Medieval landscape in the Whittlewood area. The project, which will look at 11 parishes in Northamptonshire and Buckinghamshire, has been established by the Medieval Settlement Research Group to investigate the origin and survival of contrasting patterns nucleated and dispersed settlements in the area. It is intended to look at the influence of Romano-British land use on later settlement as well as the chronology of medieval settlement formation and the significance of environment, demography and lordship settlement patterns. There will also be a consideration of the functioning of villages in the 13th and 14th centuries, which will include the varied experience of contraction after 1350. The methodology will combine documentary and place

10.4 The excavation of a migration period settlement at Polebrook

10.5 Dennis Jackson at the Hunsbury Hillfort during geophysical survey of the interior.

name evidence with fieldwalking, earthwork survey, environmental sampling, geophysics and eventually, small-scale excavation (Jones 2000). The progress of many of these various projects can be accessed through the website of the Northamptonshire Archaeological Society (www.northants-archaeology.org.uk).

In 2004, Dennis Jackson began a study within the Hunsbury hillfort, both to assess the nature and extent of surviving archaeological and to examine the options for their long-term preservation and management.. This began with a geophysical survey of the area around the east entrance, which revealed the location of the quarry edge within the hillfort. This was confirmed by subsequent trial trenching which demonstrated that far more of the hillfort interior had survived than had previously been imagined.

In addition, the Northamptonshire Gardens Trust have an ongoing programme of historic parks and gardens surveys while the Northamptonshire Industrial Archaeology Group have a continue to study the countys' rapidly disappearing industrial legacy. Military archaeology was recently promoted by a national survey of the 'Defences of Britain' which have a regional expression in groups such as the Sywell Aviation Museum and the Carpetbagger Aviation Museum at Harrington. A national scheme for the identification and recording of individual finds, the local Portable Antiquities Scheme, has lead to the appointment of a Finds Liaison Officer for Northamptonshire. This post has been particularly important in encouraging metal detectorists to provide information about their finds·which can be incorporated within the county sites and monuments record. Individual metal detectorists and groups

Fig Higham Caption: In sub zero temperatures during December 2002, two young visitors experimenting with Roman writing tablets were amongst the 400 who attended an Oxford Archaeology open day in Higham Ferrers

such as MARS (Midlands Archaeological Research Society) have been invaluable in rescue excavations and research projects such as work on the Naseby battlefield and the Grafton Regis Civil War siege.

The tradition of individual fieldworkers continues to be represented by the likes of David Hall who is completing his long term Northamptonshire Survey, parish by parish. Similarly, Gill Johnston and Burl Bellamy are currently engaged in research on Fineshade, castle, abbey and its landscape and Mark Richardson and Mark Patenhall continue to record worked flint from the quarries and fields around Wollaston and Irchester.

CONCLUSION

Archaeology in Northamptonshire has been transformed in the last 30 years. The county, and indeed most of central England, was once dismissed as an area devoid of significant archaeological remains that predated the early medieval period. Today we know this to be untrue. In terms of finds alone, Northamptonshire boasts the only known upper Palaeolithic Lyngby Axe, the only known Iron Age lead torc, the only demonstrable Roman vineyard, two of the five known Roman baptismal fonts with Chi-Rho monograms and one of only four Anglo-Saxon helmets yet found. It has one of the most completely excavated Roman villas in the country at Piddington and at Raunds, the largest and most comprehensive integrated excavation and landscape survey ever carried out in Britain. Despite the destruction of the last 50 years it still retains some of the country's best surviving medieval earthworks of field systems and villages.

In 1974 John Steane wrote *The Northamptonshire Landscape* as part of a series edited by WG Hoskins entitled *The Making of the English Landscape*. It was then the latest attempt in a tradition that dated back to John Bridges, to summarise and explain the historic environment of Northamptonshire. Thirty years later this volume has attempted to continue the process, in the hope that if people understand their archaeological heritage, they will appreciate its value and ensure its continued preservation and study for the archaeologists of the future.

Bibliography

Adams, B. and Jackson, D. 1988-89. The Anglo-Saxon Cemetery at Wakerley, Northamptonshire. Excavations by Mr D Jackson, 1968-9, *NorthamptonshireArchaeology*, 22, 69-183.

Aitchison, A. 1999. *Profiling the Profession. A Survey of Archaeological Jobs in the UK*. CBA, English Heritage and IFA Report.

Allcroft, A. H. 1908. *Earthwork of England*. Macmillan, London.

Allison, K. J. Beresford, M. W. and Hurst, J. G., 1966. *The Deserted Villages of Northamptonshire*.

Arnold, M. 1991. John Bridges 1666-1724 *Northamptonshire Archaeology* 23, 2-3.

Atkins, R. and Steadman, S. 2001. *Land off Mallard Close, Earls Barton, Northamptonshire. Post-excavation assessment and updated project design* Northamptonshire Archaeology report.

Audouy, M. 1991. The Priory Church of St Mary, Canons Ashby, *Northamptonshire Archaeology*, 23, 70-78.

Audouy, M., Dix, B., and Parsons, D. 1995. The Tower of All Saints Church, Earls Barton, Northamptonshire: its construction and context, *Archaeological Journal*, 152, 73-94.

Avery, M. Sutton, J. E. and Banks, J. W. 1967. Rainsborough, Northants, England: Excavations1961-5, *Proceedings of the Prehistoric Society*, 33, 207-306.

Baile, J. 2002. The Prebendel Manor Research Project, Nassington. *Northamptonshire Archaeology*, 30, 116-118.

Baker, G. 1822-1836. *The History and Antiquities of the County of Northampton*, London, 2 vols.

Baker, R. S. 1880. On the discovery of Anglo-Saxon remains at Desborough, Northamptonshire, *Archaeologia*, 45, 466-71.

Baker, Rev. R. S. 1891. Hunsbury or Danes Camp in *Associated Architectural Societies Reports and Papers*, 21, 53-74.

Bamford, H. M. 1985. *Briar Hill. Excavation 1974-1978*. Northampton Development Corporation Archaeological Monograph No.3.

Bellamy, B. 1994. Anglo-Saxon Dispersed sites and woodland at Geddington in the Rockingham Forest, Northamptonshire, *Landscape History*, 16, 31-37.

Bellamy, B. Jackson, D., and Johnston, G. 2000-01. Early Iron smelting in the Rockingham Forest Area: a survey of the evidence, *Northamptonshire Archaeology*, 29, 103-28.

Blair, J 1996. Palaces or Minsters? Northampton and Cheddar reconsidered, *Anglo-Saxon Studies*, 13, 97-121.

Blinkhorn, P. 1996. *Policy Report on Saxon and Medieval Ceramics in Northamptonshire*, unpublished report for Northamptonshire Heritage.

Boddington, A. 1996. *Raunds Furnells. The Anglo-Saxon Church and Churchyard*. English Heritage Archaeological Report 7, London.

Bowden, M. 1991. *Pitt Rivers. The Life and Archaeological Work of Lieutenant-General Augustus Henry Fox Lane Pitt Rivers, DCL, FRS, FSA*. Cambridge University Press. Cambridge.

Bridges, J. (ed Whalley) 1791. *The History and Antiquities of Northamptonshire* (from data collected c.1720).

Brown, A.E. 1972. Roman pottery kilns at Harrold, Bedfordshire 1970. *Milton Keynes Journal of Archaeology and History* 1, 12-50.

Brown, A. E. 1974. Higham Ferrers Castle or Otherwise, *Northamptonshire Past and Present*, 6, 79-84.

Brown, A. E. 1991. *Early Daventry: an Essay in Early Landscape Planning*, University of Leicester Department of Adult Education and Daventry District Council

Brown, A. E. 1991. Field survey at Grafton Regis: a village plan explained, *Landscape History* 11, 73-7.

Brown, A. E. and Alexander, J. A. 1982. Excavations at Towcester 1954 – the Grammar School site. *Northamptonshire Archaeology* 17, 24-59.

Brown A. E. and Foard, G. 1998. The Saxon landscape: a Regional Perspective, in *The Archaeology of Landscape* (eds Paul Everson and Tom Williamson), Manchester University Press, 667-94.

Brown A. E. Gelling M., and Orr, C. 1978. The details of the Anglo-Saxon landscape: Badby revisited,. *Northamptonshire Past and Present*, 8(2), 87-95.

Brown, A. E. and Taylor, C. C. 1975. Four Deserted Settlements in Northamptonshire, *Northamptonshire Past and Present*, 6, 178-198.

Brown, A. E, and Woodfield, C. S. 1983. Excavations at Towcester Northamptonshire: the Alchester Road suburb. *Northamptonshire Archaeology* 18, 43-140.

Brown, A. E. 1998/9. Dick Hollowell (1916-1998), Field Archaeologist. *Northamptonshire Archaeology* 28, 1- 4.

Brown, A. E. and Foard, G. 1994. *The Making of a County History. John Bridges' Northamptonshire*. University of Leicester.

Brown, A. G. 1999. Characterising prehistoric lowland environments using local pollen assemblages. *Quaternary Proceedings No. 7*, 585-594.

Brown, A.G. and Meadows, I. .M. 1996-97. Environmental Analysis of a Neolithic/Early Bronze Age Palaeochannel of the River Nene at Turnell's Mill Lane, Wellingborough, Northamptonshire, *Northamptonshire Archaeology*, 27, 185-191.

Buteux, S. (ed) 2001. *Grange Park, Courteenhall, Northamptonshire. Archaeological Investigations 1999. Post-excavation assessment and research design*. Birmingham University Field Archaeology Unit.

Buteux, S. and Jones, L. 2000. *Archaeological evaluation excavation at Pineham Barn, Upton, Northamptonshire*. BUFAU.

Cadman, G. E. 1983. Raunds 1977-1983: an Excavation summary, *Medieval Archaeology*, 27, 107-122.

Cadman, G. 1989. Guilsborough enclosure archaeological evaluation, July 1989, unpublished Northamptonshire Archaeology Unit report.

Cadman, G. 1995. *Harlestone Heath and Dallington Heath. Report on Archaeological earthworks survey*. Unpublished Northamptonshire Heritage Report.

Castleden, R. 1976. The floodplain gravels of the River Nene. *Mercian Geologist Vol. 6*, 3-47.

Chapman, A. 1995. Crick, *South Midlands Archaeology*, 25, 37-39.

Chapman, A. 1996-97. The excavation of Neolithic and Medieval Mounds at Tansor Crossroads, Northamptonshire, 1995, *Northamptonshire Archaeol*, 27, 3-50.

Chapman, A. 1998. Brackmills, Northampton. An early Iron Age torc, *Current Archaeology*, 159, 92-95.

Chapman, A. 1998-9. Excavation of the town defences at Green Street, Northampton, 1995-6. *Northamptonshire Archaeology* 28, 25-60.

Chapman, A. 1999. *Neolithic and Bronze Age Northamptonshire*, East Midlands Archaeological Resource Assessment.

Chapman, A. 2000-01. Excavation of an Iron Age settlement and a Middle Saxon cemetery at Great Houghton, Northampton, 1996 *Northamptonshire Archaeology*, 29, 1-41.

Chapman, A. forthcoming. *Excavations at West Cotton, Raunds.*

Chapman, A. and Jackson, D. 1992. Wollaston Bypass, Northamptonshire, Salvage Excavations 1984, *Northamptonshire Archaeology*, 24, 67-75.

Condron, F. 1997. Iron production in Leicestershire, Rutland and Northamptonshire in Antiquity. *Transactions of the Leicestershire Archaeological and Historical Society* 71, 1-20.

Cook, J. and Jacobi, R. 1994. A Reindeer antler or 'Lyngby' axe from Northamptonshire and its context in the British Late Glacial. *Proceedings of the Prehistoric Society* 60, 75-84.

Cooper, N. 1999. *East Midlands Archaeological Research Frameworks; Resource assessment and Research Agenda.* Unpublished University of Leicester Archaeological Services project design.

Cramp, R. Everson, P. and Hall, D. 1977. Brixworth Archaeological Research Committee: Excavations at Brixworth, 1971and 1972, *Journal of the British Archaeological Association*, 130, 52-132.

Crawford, O. G. S. 1953. *Archaeology in the Field.* Phoenix Press, London.

Cunliffe, B. W. 1991. *Iron Age communities in Britain* (3rd edition), Routledge, London.

Curteis, M. 1996a. An Analysis of the circulation patterns of Iron Age coins from Northamptonshire, *Britannia*, Vol XXVII, 17-42.

Curteis, M. 1996b. *Evenley, Northamptonshire. Assessment of the Significance of Material Recovered by Metal Detecting*, unpublished report.

Curteis, M. 1997. Iron Age Coinage, *The Field Archaeologist*, 28, 21-22.

Curteis, M., Jackson, D. and Markham, P. 1998-99. Titchmarsh late Iron Age and Roman settlement, *Northamptonshire Archaeology*, 28, 164-175.

Davison, B. K. 1977 Excavations at Sulgrave, Northamptonshire, 1960-76 *Archaeological Journal*, 134, 105-14.

Dix, B., 1986-7. The Raunds Area Project: second interim report. *Northamptonshire Archaeology* 21, 3-30.

Dix, B., 2001. Raunds Area Project. In *Medieval Archaeology. An Encyclopedia.* P.J. Crabtree (Ed) Garland Publishing, New York and London, 278-279.

Dix, B. and Taylor, S, 1988. Excavations at Bannaventa (Whilton Lodge, Northants) 1970-71. *Britannia* 19, 299-330.

Dix, B. and Jackson, D. 1989. Some late Iron Age defended enclosures in Northamptonshire in Gibson, A. (ed) *Midlands Prehistory: Some recent and current researches into the prehistory of central England*, BAR British Series 204, 158-179.

Dix, B. Masters, P. and Webster, M. 1991. *Archaeological Evaluation at Irchester, Northants.* Unpublished Northamptonshire Archaeology Unit report.

Dix, B. and Masters P. 1992. *Geophysical survey at Irchester Roman town, Northamptonshire 1992.* Unpublished Northamptonshire Archaeology Unit report.

Dix, B. Masters, P. and Webster, M. 1994. *Further archaeological investigation at Irchester Roman Town, Northants.* Unpublished Northamptonshire Archaeology Unit report.

Dobson, S. *Northamptonshire watermills* (Sheffield).

Driver, J. T. 1997. 'The Career of Richard Buckland, Knight of the shire for Northamptonshire', *Northamptonshire Past and Present* 9, 309-323.

Dryden, H., 1882. Hunsbury or Danes Camp, and the discoveries there. *Associated Architectural Societies Reports and Papers*, 198-203.

Dryden, H. E. L. 1885. Hunsbury or Danes Camp, and the discoveries there, *Associated Architectural Societies Reports and Papers*, 18, 53-61.

Dyer, A. 1978. Northampton in 1524, *Northamptonshire Past and Present*, 6, 73-80.

English Heritage 1997. English Heritage Archaeology Division Research Agenda (Draft).

Enright, D. and Thomas, A. forthcoming. Excavation of an Iron Age settlement at Wilby Way, Great Doddington.

Evans, J. G. 1975. *The Environment of Early Man in the British Isles.* Elek Books,London.

Flitcroft, M. and Bond A., 2000. Fieldwork Reports Received by Northamptonshire Heritage. Northamptonshire Heritage Document and Internet publication, www.northants-archaeology.org.uk

Fell, C. I. 1936. The Hunsbury hillfort, Northants: a new survey of the material, *Archaeological Journal*, 93, 57-100.

Foard, G. 1985. The administrative organisation of Northamptonshire in the Saxon Period, *Anglo-Saxon Studies in Archaeology and History*, 4, 185-222.

Foard, G. 1991. The Medieval pottery industry of Rockingham Forest, Northamptonshire, *Medieval Ceramics*, 15, 13-20

Foard, G. 1994. The Civil War defences of Northampton, *Northamptonshire Past and Present* 9, 4-44.

Foard, G. 1995. *Naseby: The Decisive Campaign.*

Foard, G. 1995. The early topography of Northampton and its suburbs, *Northamptonshire Archaeology*, 26, 109-122.

Foard, G. forthcoming. Settlement, industry and agriculture in Rockingham Forest, Northamptonshire, *Medieval Archaeology.*

Foard, G. forthcoming. *Northamptonshire Towns*, Northamptonshire Record Society.

Foard, G. Ballinger J.. and Taylor, J., 2001. *The Northamptonshire Extensive Urban Survey*, unpublished report for Northamptonshire Heritage.

Foard , G. Hall, D. and Britnell, T. 2004. Unpublished report in the Northamptonshire SMR, Northampton.

Foard, G. and Pearson, T., 1985. The Raunds Area Project: first interim report. *Northamptonshire Archaeology* 21, 3-22.

Ford, S. 1994. The Excavation of a Saxon settlement and a Mesolithic flint scatter at Northampton Road, Brixworth, Northamptonshire, 1994. *Thames Valley Archaeological Service Excavation Report.*

Ford, S. 1995. The Excavation of a Saxon settlement and a Mesolithic flint scatter at Northampton Road, Brixworth, Northamptonshire. *Northamptonshire Archaeology Vol.* 26, 79-108.

Foster, P. J. 1988. Changes in the landscape: An archaeological study of the clay uplands in the Brigstock area of Northamptonshire, unpublished BA dissertation, University of Sheffield.

Foster, P. 1998-9. Late Iron Age/Early Roman Northamptonshire: A study in the use of ceramic analysis to investigate social, economic and landscape changes. *Northamptonshire Archaeology* 28, 129-135.

Foster, P. Johnston, G. and Baile, J. 1989. The Prebendal Manor House at Nassington, Northamptonshire, *Archaeological Journal,* 146, 555-59.

Foundations Archaeology 2000. *Latimer Park, Burton Latimer, Northamptonshire Archaeological Excavation.* Unpublished Excavation Report.

Fox, C. 1933. *The personality of Britain: Its influence on inhabitant and invader in prehistoric and early historic times.* National Museum of Wales, Cardiff.

Franklin, M. J. 1984. The Identification of Minsters in the Midlands, *Anglo-Norman Studies* 7, 69-88.

Friendship-Taylor, R. M. 1974. The excavation of the Belgic and Romano-British settlement at Quinton, Northants, 1971-2. *Journal of the Northampton Museum and Art Gallery* 11, 3-59.

Friendship-Taylor, R. M. 1979. The excavations of the Belgic and Romano-British settlement at Quinton, Northamptonshire, Site B, 1973-7. *Journal of the Northampton Museum and Art Gallery* 13, 2-176.

Friendship-Taylor, R. M. and Friendship-Taylor, D. E. 1989. Iron Age and Roman Piddington: An Interim report on the excavation of a Late Iron Age settlement and Romano-British villa in Northamptonshire, Upper Nene Archaeological Society Report.

Friendship-Taylor, R. M. and Friendship-Taylor, D. E. 1997. From round house to villa. Upper Nene Archaeological Society.

Friendship-Taylor, R. M. 1998. *Aspects of late La Tene Pottery of the Nene and Welland Valleys of Northamptonshire: with particular reference to channel-rim jars.* unpublished M.Phil thesis, Nottingham University.

Friendship-Taylor, R. M. 1999. Piddington. *South Midlands Archaeology* 29.

Friendship-Taylor, R. M. 2000 *Aspects of late La tene pottery of the Nene and Welland valley of Northamptonshire: with particular reference to channel-rim jars.* BAR British Series 280.

Fulford, M. G. and Huddleston, K 1991. *The current state of Romano-British pottery studies.* English Heritage Occ. Paper 1.

George, T. 1887. Notes on Pre-Historic Man in Northamptonshire. *Journal of the Northamptonshire Natural History Society.* 4, 333-342.

George, T. J. 1917. Hunsbury with a description of the relics found, Northampton (reprinted from *Journal of the Northamptonshire Natural History Society and Field Club*, 18-19).

Gibson, A. M. and McCormick, A. 1985. Excavations at Grendon Quarry, Northamptonshire, Part 1: Neolithic and Bronze Age sites excavated in 1974-5, *Northamptonshire Archaeol*, 20, 23-66.

Giggins, B. 1999. *Northampton Castle*, MA dissertation, University of Leicester.

Giggins, B. Foard, G. and Hall, D. in preparation. Catesby, *Northamptonshire Past and Present.*

Goodfellow, P. 1980. The bridges of Northampton, *Northamptonshire Archaeology*, 15, 138-155.

Goodfellow, P. 1987. Medieval markets in Northamptonshire, *Northamptonshire Past and Present*, 7, 305-323.

Greenall, R. 2000. *A History of Northamptonshire*, Phillimore, Chichester.

Greenfield, E., 1963. The Romano-British shrines at Brigstock, Northants. *Antiquaries Journal* 43, 228-63.

Haigh, P. A., 1997. *Where both hosts fought : The rebellions of 1469-1470 and the Battles of Edgcote and Lose-Cote-Field*, 32-57.

Hall, D. 1974. 'Paulerspury Survey 1973', *Milton Keynes Journal of Archaeology and History,* 3, 67-71.

Hall, D. 1985. Survey Work In Eastern England. In (Eds.) S. Macready and F. H. Thompson *Archaeological Field Survey In Britain and Abroad.* Society of Antiquaries Occasional Paper VI . 25-44.

Hall, D. 1993. *The open fields of Northamptonshire; the case for preservation* (Northamptonshire County Council).

Hall, D. 1995. *The open fields of Northamptonshire,* Northamptonshire Record Society, Vol 38.

Hall, D. 1997. Enclosure in Northamptonshire, *Northamptonshire Past and Present* 9, 350-367.

Hall, D. 1997. *The Heathlands of Northamptonshire*, unpublished report for Northamptonshire County Council and English Nature.

Hall, D. 2001. *Turning the plough : Midland open fields: landscape character and proposals for management.*

Hall, D. N. and Nickerson, N. 1967. Excavations at Irchester, 1962-3 in *Archaeological Journal*, 124, 65-99.

Hall, D. and Harding, R. E., 1985. *Rushden, a Duchy of Lancaster Village* (Rushden).

Hall, D. and Hutchings, J. 1972. The distribution of archaeological sites between the Nene and Ouse valleys, *Bedfordshire Archaeol J*, 7, 1-16.

Hall, D. N. and Coles, J. 1994. Fenland survey: An essay in landscape and persistence, English Heritage Archaeological Report 1.

Hatley, V. A. 1973. *Northamptonshire Militia Lists 1777,* Northamptonshire Record Society, vol. 25.

Hawkes, J and Hawkes, C. 1943. *Prehistoric Britain.* Pelican Books, Harmondsworth.

Healy, F, and Harding, J, forthcoming *Raunds Area Project: The Neolithic and Bronze Age landscapes of West Cotton, Stanwick and Irthlingborough, Northamptonshire*, English Heritage Monog.

Heward, J. and Taylor, T. 1996. *The Country Houses of Northamptonshire*, RCHM.

Hill, J. D. 1995. Ritual and Rubbish in the Iron Age of Wessex, BAR British Series 242.

Hill, J. .D. 1997. Changes in everyday things in the later Iron Age and early Roman periods, *The Archaeologist*, 28, 20-21.

Hindle, B. P. H. 1993. *Roads , Tracks and their interpretation.* Batsford, London.

Horne, B. 2003. *South Midlands Archaeology 3,.37-56.*

Howe, M. D. and Perrin, J. R. 1980. *Roman pottery from the Nene Valley: a Guide.* Peterborough Museums.

Hudson, J. D. and Sutherland D. S. 1990. The geological description and identification of building stones: Examples from Northamptonshire' *Quarrying and Building in England AD 43-1525.*

Hughes, G. 1998. The excavation of an Iron Age settlement at Covert Farm (DIRFT East), Crick, Northamptonshire. Post-excavation assessment and updated research design, unpublished BUFAU report.

Hull, G. 1998. The excavation of a late Bronze Age ringwork and pits and late Iron Age pits on land off Hunitingdon Road, Thrapston, Northamptonshire, unpublished report, Thames Valley Archaeological Services.

Hunter, R. and Mynard, D. 1977. Excavations at Thorplands near Northampton, 1970 and 1974. *Northamptonshire Archaeology* 12, 97-154.

Humble, J. 1994. Evaluation of the Cotton henge, Raunds, *Northamptonshire Archaeol,* 25, 177-179.

Ingle, C. 1993-4. The quernstones from Hunsbury Hillfort, Northamptonshire, *Northamptonshire Archaeology*, 25, 21-34.

Jackson, D. A. 1974. Two new pit alignments and a hoard of currency bars from Northamptonshire, *Northamptonshire Archaeology*, 9, 13-45.

Jackson, D. A. 1975. An Iron Age Site at Twywell, Northamptonshire, *Northamptonshire Archaeology*, 10, 31-93.

Jackson, D. A. 1976. Two Iron Age sites north of Kettering, Northamptonshire, *Northamptonshire Archaeology*, 11, 71-88.

Jackson, D. A. 1976. The Excavation of Neolithic and Bronze Age sites at Aldwincle Northamptonshire, 1969-71. *Northamptonshire Archaeology Vol.* 11, 12-70.

Jackson D. A. 1977. Further excavations at Aldwincle Northamptonshire, 1969-71. *Northamptonshire Archaeology Vol.* 12, 9-54.

Jackson, D. A. 1977b. Petrology of Iron Age pottery from Weekley, *Northamptonshire Archaeology*, 12, 183-184.

Jackson, D. A. 1981. Archaeology at an ironstone quarry in the Harringworth-Wakerley area 1968-79, *Northamptonshire Archaeology*, 16, 14-33.

Jackson, D. A. 1982. Great Oakley and other Iron Age sites in the Corby area, *Northamptonshire Archaeology*, 17, 3-23.

Jackson, D. A. 1983. The excavation of an Iron Age site at Brigstock, Northants 1979-81. *Northamptonshire Archaeology* 18, 7-33.

Jackson, D. A. 1984. The excavation of a Bronze Age barrow at Earls Barton, Northamptonshire. *Northamptonshire Archaeol,* 19, 3-30.

Jackson, D. A. 1990. An iron age enclosure at Wootton Hill Farm, Northampton. *Northamptonshire Archaeology* 22, 3-21.

Jackson, D. A. 1990. *An Archaeological Evaluation at Brixworth, Northamptonshire*. Unpublished Excavation Report.

Jackson, D. A. 1993/4. Excavations of the hillfort defences at Hunsbury, Northampton, in 1952 and 1988. *Northamptonshire Archaeology* 25, 5-20.

Jackson, D. A. 1993-94. Iron Age and Anglo-Saxon settlement and activity around the Hunsbury Hill-fort, Northampton, *Northamptonshire Archaeology,* 25, 35-46.

Jackson, D. A. 1993-4b. The Iron Age Hillfort at Borough Hill, Daventry, excavations in 1983, *Northamptonshire Archaeology*, 25, 63-68.

Jackson, D. A. 1995 Archaeology at Grendon Quarry, Northamptonshire. Part 2: Other prehistoric, Iron Age and later sites excavated in 1974-75 and further observations between 1976-80, *Northamptonshire Archaeology*, 26, 3-32.

Jackson, D. A. 1996-97. Further evaluation at Borough Hill, Daventry, Northants, *Northamptonshire Archaeology*, 27, 143-164.

Jackson, D. A. 1998/9. Dennis Jackson: An archaeological bibliography. *Northamptonshire Archaeology* 28, 152.

Jackson, D. A, Harding, D.W, and Myres, J. N. L . 1969. The Iron Age and Anglo-Saxon Site at Upton, Northants, *Antiquaries Journal,* 49(1), 202-21.

Jackson, D. A. and Ambrose, T. M. 1976. A Roman timber bridge at Aldwincle Northamptonshire. *Britannia* 7, 39-72.

Jackson, D. A. and Ambrose, T. M. 1978. Excavations at Wakerly, Northants, 1972-75, *Britannia*, IX, 115-288.

Jackson, D. A. and Knight, D. 1985. An Early Iron Age and Beaker site near Gretton, Northamptonshire, *Northamptonshire Archaeology*, 20, 67-86.

Jackson, D. A. and Dix, B. 1986-7. Late Iron Age and Roman settlement at Weekley, Northants, *Northamptonshire Archaeology*, 21, 41-94.

Jackson, D. A, and Dix, B. 1988 Late Iron Age and Roman settlement at Weekley, Northants. *Northamptonshire Archaeology* 21, 41-93.

Jackson, D. A. and Foard, G 1993-4 Anglo-Saxon Occupation at Yardley Hastings, Northants, *Northamptonshire Archaeology,* 25, 93-98

Jackson, D. A. and Tylecote, R.F. 1988 Two new Romano-British Iron working sites in Northamptonshire. A new type of furnace? *Britannia* 19, 275-98.

Jacobi, R. M. 1978a. Population and landscape in Mesolithic Lowland Britain. In *The Effect Of Man On The Landscape : The Lowland Zone* Ed. S Limbrey and J G Evans, 75-85. CBA Research Report 21, London.

Jacobi, R. M. 1978b. The Mesolithic of Sussex, in P L Drewett (ed) *Archaeology in Sussex* to AD 1500, 15-22, CBA Research Report 29, London.

Johnston, D. E. 1969. Romano-British pottery kilns near Northampton. *Antiquaries Journal* 39, 75-97.

Johnson, G. forthcoming. Report on excavations of pottery kilns at Glapthorn.

Jones, E. T., Laughton, J., Clark, P., 2000. *Northampton in the Late Middle Ages.*

Jones, R. 2000. The Whittlewood Project. Internet Publication www. bham.ac.uk/whittlewood/outline.htm

Keevill, G. D. 1992. Life on the edge: archaeology and alluvium at Redlands Farm, Stanwick, Northamptonshire, in S. Needham and M. Macklin (eds.) *Alluvial Archaeology in Britain: Proceedings of a Conference Sponsored by the RMC Group.* Oxbow, 25-32.

Keevill, G. D. and Booth, P. 1997. Settlement, sequence and structure: Romano-British roundhouses at Redlands Farm, Stanwick (Northants), and Alchester (Oxon), in R. M. and D. E. Frienship-Taylor (eds.) *From Round House to Villa: The proceedings of a Conference held in 993 to celebrate the Upper Nene Archaeological Society's 30th Anniversary.* Upper Nene Archaeological Society.

Keevill, G. D. and Williams, R. J. 1995. The excavation of a Roman road and a medieval causeway at Ditchford pit, Wellingborough, Northamptonshire. *Northamptonshire Archaeology* 25, 47-77.

Klingelhoffer, E. 1984. Rockingham Castle in 1250, *Northamptonshire Past and Present*, 7, 16 n35.

Knight, D. 1984. Late Bronze Age and Iron Age settlement in the Nene and Great Ouse Basins, BAR British Series 130, Oxford.

Knight, D. 1986-7. An Iron Age hillfort at Castle Yard, Farthingstone, Northamptonshire, *Northamptonshire Archaeology*, 21, 31-40.

Knight D. 2002. A regional ceramic sequence: Pottery of the first millennium BC between the Humber and the Nene in Hill, J.D. and Woodward, A.E (eds), *Prehistoric Britain: the Ceramic Basis*, Oxbow Monograph.

Knocker, G. M. 1965. Excavations in Colleyweston Great Wood, Northamptonshire. *Archaeological Journal* 122, 52-72.

Laughton, J., forthcoming. Catesby, *Northamptonshire Past and Present.*

Law, E. F. 1880. Ruins of the Old Castle, *Northampton. Associated Architectural Societies Reports and Papers*, 198-203.

Lee, F. 1954. A new theory of the origins and growth of Northampton, *Archaeological Journal*, 110, 164-74.

Lewis, C., Mitchell-Fox, P. and Dyer, C., 1997. *Village, Hamlet and Field.*

Letts, J. 1999. Smoke blackened thatch. University of Reading/ English Heritage.

Macklin, M. G. 1999. Holocene river environments in Prehistoric Britain'. Human interaction and impact. *Quaternary Proceedings* No. 7, . 521-530.

Mackreth, D. F. 1996. *Orton Hall Farm: a Roman and early Anglo-Saxon farmstead*, East Anglian Archaeology 76.

Margary, I. D. 1955. *Roman roads in Britain.*

Marney, P. T. 1989. *Roman and Belgic pottery from excavations in Milton Keynes 1972-82.* Aylesbury: Milton Keynes Archaeology Unit.

Martin, J. 1978. *Cartularies and Registers of Peterborough Abbey.*

Martin, J. 1980. *The Court and Account Rolls of Peterborough Abbey: A Handlist.*

Martin. P. and Hall, D. 1980. Brixworth. Northamptonshire: New evidence for early prehistoric settlement and agriculture. *Bedfordshire Archaeological Journal Vol.* 14, 5-14.

Masters, P. 1997. *Archaeological Evaluation at the proposed Chester Farm heritage park, Northants.* Unpublished Northamptonshire Archaeology Unit report.

Meadows, I. 1993a. Three Roman sites in Northamptonshire: excavations by E Greenfield at Bozeat, Higham Ferrers and Great Oakley between 1961 and 1966. *Northamptonshire Archaeology* 24, 77-94.

Meadows, I. 1993b. Ecton: Anglian Water pipeline. *South Midlands Archaeology* 23, 47-8.

Meadows, I. 1995. Wollaston, *South Midlands Archaeology*, 25, 41-45.

Meadows, I. 1996. Wollaston. *Current Archaeology* 150, 212-15.

Meadows, I. 1996/7. The Pioneer Helmet. *Northamptonshire Archaeology* 27, 192-3.

Meaney, A. 1964. *A Gazetteer of early Anglo-Saxon burial sites*, London, 186-97

Moore, W. R. G. 1998. The development of archaeology in Northamptonshire. Internet Publication (First appeared in print, March 1979-March 1981, *Northamptonshire History News*).

Moore, W. R. G. and Williams, J. H. 1975. A later Neolithic site at Ecton, Northampton. *Northamptonshire Archaeology* 10 , 3-30.

Moore-Colyer, R. 1997. 'Land and people in Northamptonshire: the case of Great Oakley c.1700-1850', *Ag. Hist. Rev.*, 45(2), 149-64.

Moore-Colyer, R. 1999. 'The small landholder in Northamptonshire: Corby c.1700-1850' *Northamptonshire Past and Present*, 52, 57-68.

Mordant, D. and Mordant, C. 1992. Noyen-Sur-Seine: A Mesolithic waterside settlement. In B. Coles (Ed) *The Wetland Revolution In Prehistory*, 55-64, Wetland Archaeological Research Project Occasional Paper 6, Exeter.

Morton, J. 1712. *The Natural History of Northamptonshire.*

Mudd, A. 1995. Late Saxon ditches at Brookfield, Nutcote, Naseby, *Northamptonshire Archaeology*, 26, 149-152.

Myres, J. N. L. 1977. *A Corpus of Anglo-Saxon Pottery,* 2 vols, Cambridge University Press.

Northamptonshire Archaeology, 1999. *An Archaeological Evaluation at Pitsford, Northamptonshire.* Unpublished Northamptonshire Archaeology report.

Neal, D. S 1989. The Stanwick Villa, Northants: An Interim Report on the excavations of 1984-88, *Britannia*, XX, 149-168.

Neeson, J. M. 1993. *Commoners: Common Right, Enclosure and Social Change in England, 1700-1820.*

Ovenden-Wilson, S. M. 1997. Grange Park, Northamptonshire, unpublished Geophysical Surveys of Bradford Report.

Page, F. M., 1936, *Wellingborough Manorial Accounts, 1258-1323.*

Parker, G. 1981. 'The Hermitage of Grafton Regis', *Northamptonshire Past and Present*, 7, 247-252.

Parry, E. G. 1987. 'Helmdon Stone', *Northamptonshire Past and Present* VII (4), 158-70.

Parry, S. 1994. Rounds Area Survey, in *Looking at the Land. Archaeological Landscapes in Eastern England* (eds M Parker-Pearson and T Schadla-Hall), Leicestershire Museums, Arts and Record Service, 36-42.

Parry, S. forthcoming. *Raunds Area Survey.*

Pearce, J. 1999. The dispersed dead: preliminary observations on burial and settlement space in rural Roman Britain, in P Baker, C Forcey, S Jundi and R Witcher (eds) *TRAC98*, 151-62.

Pettit, P. 1968. *The Royal Forests of Northamptonshire 1558-1714.*

Piggott, S. 1949. *British Prehistory.* Oxford University Press, Oxford.

Piggott, S. 1989. *Ancient Britons and the Antiquarian Imagination.* Thames and Hudson, London.

Prehistoric Society 1999. *Research Frameworks For The Palaeolithic And Mesolithic Of Britain And Ireland : A Report By The Working Party For The Palaeolithic And Mesolithic Day Meeting And The Council Of The Prehistoric Society.* Prehistoric Society, Salisbury.

Pryor, F. 1974. *Excavations at Fengate, Peterborough, England. The First Report.* Royal Ontario Museum Archaeological Monograph 3. Toronto.

Pryor, F. 1998. *Farmers in Prehistoric Britain*, Tempus, Stroud.

Pryor, F. 2002. *Seahenge: a quest for life and death in Bronze Age Britain*, Harper Collins.

Quinnell, H. 1992. The villa and temple at Cosgrove, Northamptonshire. *Northamptonshire Archaeology* 23, 4-66.

Randall, A. L. 1970. 'The Kettering worsted industry in the eighteenth century' *Northamptonshire Past and Present* 4 (5), 312-20.

Randall, A. L.,1971-2. 'The Kettering worsted industry in the eighteenth century 2' *Northamptonshire Past and Present* 5 (6), 349-56.

RCHME. 1975, 1979, 1981, 1982. An Inventory of the Archaeological Sites in the County of Northamptonshire, 4 vols.

RCHME. 1960. *A Matter of Time: An archaeological survey of the river gravels of England*, Royal Commission on Historical Monuments (England).

RCHME. 1975. *An Inventory of the Historical Monuments in the County of Northampton Volume 1: Archaeological Sites in North East Northamptonshire.* HMSO.

RCHME. 1980. *Northamptonshire: An Archaeological Atlas.*

RCHME. 1981. *An Inventory of the Historical Monuments in the County of Northampton*, vol III, HMSO, London.

RCHME. 1982. *An Inventory Of The Historical Monuments In The County Of Northampton*, Vol. 4. HMSO, London.

RCHME. 1985. *An Inventory of Archaeological Sites and Churches in Northampton*, Royal Commission on Historical Monuments, HMSO, London.

RCHME. 1986. Non-conformist Chapels and Meeting Houses; Northamptonshire and Oxfordshire HMSO, London.

RCHME. 1996. The Country Houses of Northamptonshire, HMSO, London.

Richmond, H. 1986. Outlines of church development in North-amptonshire, in Butler, L A S, and Morris, R. K. (eds.), The Anglo-Saxon Church, CBA Research Report, 60.

Roberts, B. K. and Wrathmell, S. 2000. An Atlas of Rural Settlement in England, English Heritage, London.

Robinson, M. 1994. Overview of the Saxon and Medieval Environmental Archaeology of the West Cotton Area, unpublished report for English Heritage for the Raunds Area Project.

Robinson, M. forthcoming. Environmental archaeology of the Raunds area excavations in Parry, forthcoming.

Saville, A. 1977. Two Mesolithic implement types. North-amptonshire Archaeology, Vol. 12 (1977), 3-8.

Saville, A. 1981a. Mesolithic industries in central England: An exploratory investigation using microlith typology. *Archaeological Journal* Vol. 138 (1981), 49-71.

Saville, A. 1981b. Honey Hill, Elkington: A Northamptonshire Mesolithic site. *Northamptonshire Archaeology, Vol. 16* (1981), 1-13.

Schrufer-Kolb, I. 1999. Roman Iron production in the East Midlands, England, in Young, S. M. M, Pollard, A. M. Budd, P. Ixer, R. A. (eds.) *Metals in Antiquity*, 227-233. BAR Int. Ser. 792. Oxford.

Seabourne, M. V. J. 1966. *'Cob Cottages in Norhamptonshire'*, Northamptonshire Past and Present, *3, 215.*

Sharp, S. 1882. Description of the antiquities found on the site of the Castle at Northampton. *Associated Architectural Societies Reports and Papers*, 243-51.

Shaw, M 1993-94. The Discovery of Saxon sites below fieldwalking scatters: Settlement evidence at Brixworth and Upton, Northants, *Northamptonshire Archaeology*, 25, 77-92.

Shaw, M. 1997. 'Recent work in Medieval Northampton', *Northamptonshire Archaeology* 27, 101-41.

Shaw, M. Webster, M. and O'Hara, P. 1990. A r c h a e o l o g i c a l evaluation at King's Heath, Northampton, unpublished Northamptonshire Archaeology Unit Report.

Smith, D. J. Hird, L. and Dix, B., 1988-9. The Roman Villa at Great Weldon, Northamptonshire. *Northamptonshire Arch-aeology* 22, 23-68.

Smurthwaite, D. 1995. *Northampton 1460*, unpublished report for English Heritage.

Smurthwaite, D. 1995. *Edgecote 1469*, unpublished report for English Heritage.

Soden, I 1996-7. Saxon and Medieval Settlement remains at St John's Square, Daventry, Northamptonshire, July 1994-February 1995, *Northamptonshire Archaeology*, 27,51-99.

Spandl, C. 1996. Higham Ferrers, Land near Kings Meadow Lane, *South Midlands Archaeology*, 26, 43.

Sparks, B. W. and Lambert, C. A. 1961. The post glacial deposits at Apethorpe, Northamptonshire. *Proceedings Of The Malacological Society.*

Steane, J. M. and Bryant, G. F. Excavations at the deserted Medieval settlement at Lyveden, *Journal of the Northampton Museum and Art Gallery*, 2, 1967; 5, 1969; 9, 1971; 12, 1975.

Steane, J. M. 1967. Building materials used in Northampton-shire and the area around, *Northamptonshire Past and Present*, 4, 71-80.

Steane, J. M. 1970. The Medieval fishponds of Northamp-tonshire, *Northamptonshire Past and Present*, 4, 299-310.

Steane, J. M. 1973a. The Forests of Northamptonshire in the early middle ages, *Northamptonshire Past and Present*, 5, 7-17.

Steane, J. M. 1973b. The Medieval parks of Northamptonshire, *Northamptonshire Past and Present*, 5, 211-233.

Steane, J. M. 1974. *The Northamptonshire Landscape.*

Sutherland, D and Parsons, D 1984. The petrological con-tribution to the survey of All Saint's Church, Brixworth, Northamptonshire: an Interim Study, *Journal of the British Archaeological Association,* 137, 47-64.

Tate, W. E. 1967. *The English Village Community.*

Taylor, S. and Dix, B. 1985. Iron Age and Roman settlement at Ashley, Northants. *Northamptonshire Archaeology* 20, 87-112.

Taylor, C.C. and Fowler, P.J., 1980. *Northamptonshire. An Archaeological Atlas.* RCHME. London

Thomas, A. 1998. Grange Park, Courteenhall, Northampton. archaeological evaluation, unpublished Cotswold Archaeo-logical Trust Report.

Till, Eric, 1997. 'Fact and conjecture – the building of Burghley House 1555-1587', *Northamptonshire Past and Present*, 9, 232-32.

Tingle, M. forthcoming. The past is a foreign country: Darwinism, colonialism and the perceptions of prehistoric Britain. *Landscapes.*

Todd, M. 1987. *The South-West to A.D. 1000*. Longman. London.

Turland, R. E. 1977. Towcester, Wood Burcote. *Northamp-tonshire Archaeology* 12, 218-23.

Upex, S. 2001. The Roman villa at Cotterstock, Northampton-shire. *Britannia* 32, 57-93.

Van der Veen, M. and O'Connor, T. 1998. The expansion of agricultural production in Late Iron Age and Roman Britain, in J Bayley (ed.) *Science in Archaeology*. English Heritage, 127-44.

Victoria County History ,Volume 2 (1906, reprint 1970).

Waddington, C. 2000. Recent research on the Mesolithic of the Millfield Basin, Northumberland. In R Young (ed.), *Mesolithic Lifeways: Current Research from Britain and Ireland.* Leicester Archaeological Monograph 7.

Walker, G. 1992. Towcester Retail Development, Northampton-shire: Report on the results of an archaeological evaluation. Cotswolds Archaeological Trust Report.

Williams, J. H. 1974. *Two Iron Age Sites in Northampton*, Northampton Development Corporation Monographs No.1.

Williams, J. H. 1976. Excavations on a *Roman site at Overstone near Northampton. Northamptonshire Archaeology* 11, 100-33.

Williams, F. 1979. Excavations on Marefair, Northampton, 1977, *Northamptonshire Archaeology*,14, 38-79.

Williams, J. H. 1979. *St Peter's Street Northampton. Excavations 1973-1976,* Northampton Development Corporation.

Williams, J. H. 1982 *Saxon and Medieval Northampton*, North-ampton Development Corporation.

Williams, J. H. and McCarthy, M. R. 1974. A double ditched enclosure at Blackthorn, in J. H. Williams (ed.) *Two Iron Age Sites in Northampton.* Northampton Development Corporation, 44-66.

Williams, J. H and Shaw, M. 1981. Excavations In Chalk Lane, Northampton, 1975-1978. *Northamptonshire Archaeology,* 16, 87-136.

Williams, J. H. Shaw, M. and Denham, V. 1985. *Middle Saxon Palaces at Northampton,* Northampton Development Corporation, Archaeological Monograph 4.

Windell, D, 1989. A late neolithic ritual focus at West Cotton, Northamptonshire, in A M Gibson (ed) *Midlands Prehistory. Some Recent and Current Researches into the Prehistory of Central England,* British Archaeol Reperts British Series, 204, 85-94.

Windell, D. 1981. Great Doddington Iron Age enclosure, *Northamptonshire Archaeology,* 16, 65-72.

Windell, D. 1982. *Excavations at Clay Lane 1980: An Iron Age and Roman Rural Settlement.* Northamptonshire Archaeology Unit Level III Report.

Windell, D. 1983. Clay Lane 1980: interim report, *Northamptonshire Archaeology,* 18, 33-42.

Windell, D. 1984. Irchester Roman Town: excavations 1981-2. *Northamptonshire Archaeology* 19, 31-52.

Windell, D. Chapman, A. and Woodiwiss, J. 1990. *From Barrows to Bypass.Excavations at West Cotton, Raunds, Northamptonshire, 1985-1989,* Northamptonshire Archaeology Unit and English Heritage.

Woods, P. J. 1970. Excavations at Brixworth, Northamptonshire, 1965-70. The Roman Villa Part 1 – the Roman coarse pottery and decorated samian ware. *Journal of the Northampton Museum and Art Gallery* 4.

Woodfield, C. T. P. 1980. The Egg Rings: a defended enclosure in Salcey Forest, *Northamptonshire Archaeology,* 15, 156-158.

Woodfield, C. T. P. 1981. The larger Medieval houses of Northamptonshire, *Northamptonshire Archaeology,* 16, 153-196.

Woodfield, C. T. P. 1992. The defences of Towcester, Northamptonshire, *Northamptonshire Archaeology,* 24, 13-66.

Wymer, J. J. 1977. *Gazetteer Of Mesolithic Sites In England And Wales.* CBA Research Report No. 20.

Index